READINGS ON EQUAL EDUCATION
(Formerly *Educating the Disadvantaged*)

READINGS ON EQUAL EDUCATION

Volume 24

ENHANCING INSTITUTIONAL AND STATE INITIATIVES TO INCREASE STUDENT SUCCESS

STUDIES OF THE INDIANA PROJECT ON ACADEMIC SUCCESS

Volume Editors
Don Hossler
Jacob P. K. Gross
Mary Ziskin

Series Editor
Edward P. St. John

Managing Editor
Phyllis Kreger Stillman

AMS PRESS, INC.
NEW YORK

READINGS ON EQUAL EDUCATION
VOLUME 24
Enhancing Institutional and State Initiatives to Increase Student Success
Studies of the Indiana Project on Academic Success

Copyright © 2009 by AMS Press, Inc.
All rights reserved

ISSN 0270-1448

Set ISBN-10: 0-404-10100-3
Set ISBN-13: 978-0-404-10100-8

Volume 24: ISBN-10: 0-404-10124-0
Volume 24: ISBN-13: 978-0-404-10124-4
Library of Congress Catalog Card Number 77-83137

All AMS Books are printed on acid-free paper that meets the guidelines for performance and durability of the Committee on Production Guidelines for Book Longevity of the Council on Library Resources.

AMS PRESS, INC.
BROOKLYN NAVY YARD
63 FLUSHING AVENUE – UNIT #221
BROOKLYN, NY 11205-1073, USA
www.amspressinc.com

Manufactured in the United States of America

VOLUME 24   **CONTENTS**

CONTRIBUTORS' NOTES

RODERICK S. BROWN is director of remediation and basic skill development at Ivy Tech Community College of Indiana. He previously held the position of department chair of liberal arts and academic services at Ivy Tech's Richmond campus, where he also served as associate professor of English. Mr. Brown holds master's degrees in English and college student personnel administration from Indiana University and a B.A. in psychology from the University of Notre Dame. His student affairs experience includes six years on the counseling faculty at William Rainey Harper College.

AFET DADASHOVA is a research associate for the Project on Academic Success and a Ph.D. student in the education policy studies program with a minor in sociology at Indiana University. She holds a master's degree in the social and philosophical foundations of education. Afet is currently involved in projects on transfer among college students and mobile working students. She is also interested in research methods in education.

NATE J. DAUN-BARNETT is the director of university relations and policy research on the Presidents Council, State Universities of Michigan. His research focuses on college access and the transition from high school to college. In particular, he has examined state high school graduation requirements, the role of precollege outreach programs, remedial education, state policies to improve academic preparation and financial access to college, transfer articulation, and Web-based strategies to improve college access. He is a doctoral candidate in higher education administration, with a focus on public policy, at the University of Michigan–Ann Arbor.

AMY S. FISHER is a graduate student at the Center for the Study of Higher and Postsecondary Education at the University of Michigan. Her academic interests include privatization of public higher education, financial aid policy and its relationship to access and persistence, and the formation of academic capital in high school students. She holds an Ed.M. and an M.A. from Teachers College, Columbia University, and a B.A. from Brandeis University.

JACOB P. K. GROSS is a doctoral candidate in educational leadership and policy studies and is the associate director for research at the Project on Academic Success at Indiana University. His general research interests relate to the ways education policies reproduce or challenge social inequality. He focuses on academic success for underrepresented students in U.S. postsecondary education. Specific areas of interest include financial aid, racial and gender equity policies, postsecondary financing, and how institutional contexts affect student success.

EBELIA HERNANDEZ is a doctoral student in higher education and student affairs at Indiana University. She holds an M.S. in counseling, with a specialty in college counseling and student affairs from California State University, Northridge. Her research interests center on the development of Latino college students—how college experiences, gender, and level of political engagement influence their ethnic identity and their cognitive and interpersonal development.

DON HOSSLER, director of the Project on Academic Success at Indiana University, is a professor of educational leadership and policy studies at Indiana University, where he has served as vice chancellor for enrollment services for IU Bloomington, associate vice president for enrollment services for the seven campuses of the IU system, executive associate dean for the IU School of Education, and chair of educational leadership and policy studies. His areas of specialization include college choice, student financial aid policy, enrollment management, and higher education finance.

JOHN V. MOORE III is a research associate for the Project on Academic Success and a doctoral student in higher education and inquiry methodology at Indiana University. He previously worked for the National Survey of Student Engagement and the Beginning College Survey of Student Engagement. His research interests include identity development, working students, and the philosophical underpinnings of methodologies.

MELANIE A. RAGO is director of policy and development for Campus Philly, a nonprofit organization supporting economic growth through the enrollment, engagement, and employment of college students in the Philadelphia tri-state region. She is also a doctoral student in higher education and student affairs at Indiana University, where previously she was a research associate for the Project on Academic Success. Her research interests include working students and the impact of college students on a region's community and economy.

PAULINE J. REYNOLDS is an assistant professor of higher education at the University of Redlands. Her research interests include higher education in society, student retention, women in higher education, and social justice issues. Several of her ongoing projects explore through the qualitative analysis of film the portrayal of higher education in popular culture.

LESLIE J. ROBINSON is director of the Academic Support Center, a collaborative program that provides academic assistance to students at Indiana University Bloomington. Her research interests focus on the role of gender in student success and in higher education. She received her Ph.D. in higher education and her M.A. in English from Indiana University and her B.A. in English from Emory University.

EDWARD P. ST. JOHN is Algo D. Henderson Collegiate Professor of Higher Education at the University of Michigan's Center for the Study of Higher and Postsecondary Education. His research focuses on the effects of public on equal opportunity and moral reasoning in professional practice. His recent books include *Education and the Public Interest: Education Reform, Public Finance, and Access to Higher Education* and *Action, Reflection, and Social Justice: Integrating Moral Reasoning into Professional Development*.

KRYSTAL L. WILLIAMS is a doctoral student in higher education with a concentration in public policy at the Center for the Study of Higher and Postsecondary Education at the University of Michigan. She holds an M.S. in pure mathematics from Clark Atlanta University. Her research focuses on financial aid policy and college access for underrepresented groups.

MARY ZISKIN, Ph.D., senior associate director of the Project on Academic Success at Indiana University, conducts research on college student persistence and academic success. A graduate of the University of Michigan, her research interests also include the racial stratification of educational opportunity, discourses surrounding academic merit, and critical research methodologies. She teaches qualitative methods and survey research at the Indiana University School of Education.

ACKNOWLEDGMENTS

The authors wish express thanks to several individuals and organizations for their support and contributions to this volume. First, we want to thank Dr. Edward P. St. John and Dr. Charlie Nelms for their invaluable contributions to the work represented in this volume in the *Readings on Equal Education* series. Dr. Nelms's vision and leadership during his tenure as Vice President of Academic Support and Diversity at Indiana University secured the funding for the Indiana Project on Academic Success (IPAS), and his support for the project was critical to its success. Dr. St. John, founding director of IPAS, was the guiding force for the research efforts described here. Employing his model of action inquiry and reflecting his commitment to equity and student success, this volume is a direct product of Ed's intellect and his passion for the work of IPAS. The authors benefited greatly from the enthusiasm and support he provided while he was IPAS director and professor at Indiana University and from his continuing support and encouragement after he joined the faculty at the University of Michigan. All of the chapters in this book and the positive changes at several IPAS campuses documented here could not have been realized without Ed's vision and energy.

We also want to thank the Lumina Foundation for Education and the Indiana Commission for Higher Education (ICHE). Funding from the Lumina Foundation and ongoing support and advice from Sam Cargille, David Cournoyer, and Jill Kramer helped make the IPAS effort possible. In addition, the partnership that was forged with ICHE, and in particular Stan Jones, Jeff Stanley, and Jennifer Seabaugh, which enabled us to use student data from students enrolled in public institutions in the State of Indiana, was an essential element of the work undertaken by IPAS policy analysts. The relationship that we have forged is unique among state policy makers and policy researchers at Indiana University. We continue to appreciate their assistance and their trust.

Finally, we wish to thank Ms. Sarah Martin, whose editing of this volume went beyond simply improving the quality of the manuscript to include substantive improvements in the clarity of the thinking expressed in our writing. She has worked with IPAS since its inception and has helped make this project successful.

INTRODUCTION

Enhancing Institutional and State Initiatives to Increase Student Success: Studies of the Indiana Project on Academic Success

Don Hossler, Mary Ziskin, and Jacob P. K. Gross

This volume of Readings on Equal Education draws on research and program evaluation activities produced under the auspices of the Indiana Project on Academic Success (IPAS). Funded by the Lumina Foundation for Education, IPAS research has focused in particular on campus-based efforts to enhance student success and institutional improvement. From the project's inception under the leadership of Edward P. St. John in 2003, the work of IPAS has centered on three goals: (1) using action research to identify potential institutional interventions to enhance student success, (2) evaluating targeted interventions to enhance student success, and (3) using a state student information database to inform campus-based and state postsecondary educational decision making. In this volume, we present, consider, and reflect on what we have learned from the action research projects undertaken as part of IPAS. In addition, we examine the impact of participating in IPAS on the institutions and, in some cases, on the individuals who were involved.

We have organized this volume around broad themes that shed light on the three primary goals of the IPAS project. The three sections of chapters show the work of IPAS from three corresponding angles. First, we examine patterns in students' educational pathways from the viewpoint of state and national data sets. These chapters (Chapters 1–3) consider a variety of factors—student financial aid, student transfer, working students, and student engagement—that play into student pathways. Turning to more locally situated inquiry, the second section (Chapters 4–6) explores the evaluation of programs aimed at supporting student academic success. A set of three studies—examining math tutoring, supplemental instruction, and orientation programs—focuses on persistence and major choice as outcomes

xiii

related both to pathways and student success. In the third section (Chapters 7–8), contributors take a reflective look at the IPAS process itself, presenting results from interviews with participants at IPAS institutions and exploring factors that influenced successful institutional engagement in the action research process. Together, the chapters in this volume show how a collaborative action research project can connect the dots from macrolevel patterns to immediate implications through program evaluation to the reflective practice of action research.

In many cases, what is unique about the studies described in this volume is the use of the Indiana student unit record database, compiled and developed at the Indiana University Project on Academic Success to undertake campus-based studies of programs to enhance student success and analyses of state policy trends. The use of student unit record (SUR) databases for such purposes is relatively new. The recent attention given to SUR systems by the Spellings Commission and the National Center for Education Statistics is indicative of the growing interest among researchers and policy makers in using unit record data to illuminate recurring questions in the field. From the early 1990s onward, a small but growing cadre of scholars, including Ed St. John and Steve DesJardins, has advocated the use in research of extant data from SUR systems, arguing that such systems enable researchers to model more accurately the complexities of student pathways to academic success. Furthermore, researchers and policy makers have long acknowledged the inadequacy of single-institution data systems in tracking increasingly mobile students across multiple institutions over prolonged periods of time. The four-year portrait of a student attending one institution no longer reflects the reality of postsecondary education. State and even regional SUR databases are seen as potential solutions in the current milieu of accountability and complexity. The work of St. John and colleagues on financial aid, college choice, and persistence (St. John, Chung, Musoba, Simmons, & Mendez, 2004; St. John, Gross, Musoba, & Chung, 2006) has begun to demonstrate the utility of SUR systems in furthering our understandings of academic success in postsecondary education. The studies reported in this volume extend this line of inquiry by connecting statewide patterns with institutional-level outcomes and implications.

Another unique feature of the work assembled in this volume is the centrality of the collaborative partnerships through which campus-based administrators and IPAS researchers designed, implemented, and evaluated programs. While the chapters focus on the efficacy of campus-based interventions, ultimately they are also about efforts to bring about change on participating campuses, with early chapters describing in many cases the roles of senior and middle managers in their support for or resistance to the collaborative efforts. Among these explorations we highlight the efforts of a collaborative research project focusing on working students that emerged in the northwestern corner of Indiana. The Northwest Collaborative on Working Students illustrates the positive, serendipitous outcomes that can emerge from funded projects. Engaging the issue of collaboration at a still more explicit level, the final chapters provide an external review of the IPAS process and insiders' views of the campuses involved with IPAS.

We urge readers to pay close attention to the complexities that accompany efforts to use action research to bring about organizational change. Moreover, we encourage them to consider how the ways in which institutions organize themselves influence their ability to create targeted interventions to enhance student success.

References

St. John, E. P., Chung, C. G., Musoba, G. D., Simmons, A. B., & Mendez, J. P. (2004). *Expanding college access: The impact of state finance strategies.* Indianapolis, IN: Lumina Foundation for Education.

St. John, E. P., Gross, J. P. K., Musoba, G. D., & Chung, A. S. (2006). Postsecondary encouragement and academic success: Degree attainment by Indiana's Twenty-First Century Scholars. In E. P. St. John (Ed.), *Readings on equal education: Vol. 21. Public policy and equal educational opportunity: School reforms, postsecondary encouragement, and state policies on postsecondary education* (pp. 257–291). New York: AMS Press, Inc.

Section I

Examining Patterns in Students'

Educational Pathways

CHAPTER 1

LATINO STUDENTS' RECEIPT OF FINANCIAL AID: PATTERNS, PROBLEMS, AND POSSIBILITIES

Jacob P. K. Gross

Despite 50 years of postsecondary policies designed to increase access for historically underrepresented groups, the much-debated education gap between Latinos[1] and Whites continues to widen. This gap—perhaps better described as a *gulf*—at the high school and postsecondary levels represents "the greatest disparity in educational outcomes between the nation's largest minority group and the White majority" (Suro & Fry, 2005, p. 174). Those who increasingly form the bedrock of the United States are those who suffer the greatest educational inequality. This lamentable yet persistent picture warrants further consideration.

The annual status report on minorities in U.S. higher education reported that from 2000 to 2002 just 61.5 percent of Latinos graduated from the nation's high schools compared to 87.1 percent of Whites (Harvey & Anderson, 2005). Findings from the National Education Longitudinal Study (NELS:88/2000) show that of the Latinos in the 1988 eighth-grade cohort who graduated from high school with a diploma or GED, 82 percent had enrolled by 2000 in a postsecondary institution—a percentage equal to that of Whites and second only to Asians. After high school, however, a tremendous gap emerges in postsecondary completion rates. In the same 1988 cohort, just 23 percent of Latinos compared to 47 percent of Whites had obtained a bachelor's degree by 2000 (Hudson, Shieh, & Cohen, 2003).

In Indiana, among the cohort of first-time, first-year students who enrolled in the state's public four-year institutions in 2000 (the primary focus of this chapter), 45 percent of Latinos compared to 56 percent of Whites persisted through their fourth year of school. The persistence gap is even wider when we look at progress from the first to second year among students who enrolled in community colleges during that same year. Of that group of students, just 39 percent of Latinos compared to 63 percent of Whites reenrolled the following year.

---

[1]As used here, the term Latino includes both males and females.

3

Unfortunately, recent evidence suggests this gap is likely to continue widening nationally for the foreseeable future. In traditional Latino settlement states, such as Arizona, California, Illinois, New Mexico, and New York, most Latinos who go to college begin at a two-year community college and never transfer to a four-year institution to finish their baccalaureate degree. In these states, the gap in degree completion continues to widen because most enrollment growth has occurred at two-year institutions. Students who begin at a two-year institution are not likely to transfer to a four-year institution and are less likely to earn a baccalaureate degree than their peers who begin at four-year schools (Fry, 2005a).

Olivas (1985) has argued that students who attend community colleges tend to have less access to forms of support, such as financial aid, that are instrumental in overcoming systemic barriers to academic success. To combat Latino students' "cooling out" in community colleges and missing out on opportunities for support for further education, policy makers need a better understanding of the interplay between student aid and educational attainment to craft aid policies and programs that promote equity—with the goal of overcoming the disparity in completion rates. In every step along the postsecondary enrollment pathway—from the decision to enroll to the choice of college to the calculation about whether to persist—financial aid may figure into the likelihood of student success. Trends in higher education policy that are possibly affecting academic outcomes differently for students along racial/ethnic lines include (a) increasing student enrollment in two-year colleges as a cost-efficient alternative to four-year schools, (b) simplifying the aid application process, (c) the shifting of individuals' financing of education from grants to loans, and (d) the growing use of merit criteria in awarding institutional aid. Simplifying the aid application process, for example, may have the effect of increasing the number of Latino applicants, who are overrepresented among low-income students, and making college more affordable for them through more grant awards.

The more we know about the interplay of aid and educational attainment for Latino students, the better we can estimate the effects of policy changes on these students and shape policies that promote educational success as well as access. In short, understanding the patterns of aid use among Latinos and identifying and acknowledging problems with aid policies opens the door to identifying and promoting possible solutions.

Financial Aid, Latino Students, and Academic Success

Although it is only one of several important elements of student academic success, financial aid is especially important for Latino students, who come disproportionately from lower-income families with parents who did not attend college. Financial aid alone may not remove barriers to success for students from low-income families (Stinebrickner & Stinebrickner, 2003), yet studies have shown that it can have an equalizing effect across racial and ethnic groups (Lichtenstein, 2002; Nora, 1990; St. John, Paulsen, & Carter, 2005) not only by removing financial barriers to access, but also by encouraging preparation and enabling students to focus more fully on academic concerns, although the effects of aid likely vary among different underrepresented racial groups (Heller, 1997). Moreover, as St. John, Paulsen, Starkey (1996), and others (Cabrera, Nora, & Castañeda, 1993; Nora, 1990) suggest, financial aid has direct effects (e.g., enabling low-income students to attend school) and indirect effects (e.g., enabling students to focus on academics without worrying about tuition bills).

Indiana: The State Context

Although not a traditional settlement state for Latinos, Indiana provides a useful context for understanding the postsecondary pathways of Latino students in that it is among those states that have seen the greatest growth in their Latino population over the past 15 years. Although Indiana has fewer Latinos (around 273,000) than some other states, the rate of growth in the Latino population in the state has been higher than in any of Indiana's midwestern neighbors except Illinois. Indeed, most of Indiana's population growth over the past few years is attributable to the increase in Latinos. As in new settlement states in the South, the arrival of Mexicans and Mexican Americans has fueled most of this growth (Fry, 2005b), which has concentrated in the northwest of the state near Chicago and in Indianapolis—the city with the fifth highest Latino growth rate from 2000 to 2004 of any metropolitan area in the country (Clark & Heet, 2006).

Although the growth rate in Indiana of Latino school-age children has outpaced that of Whites, there are considerable gaps in educational outcomes between Latinos and Whites in the state. Data from the 2000 census show that nearly half of all Mexicans in Indiana did not complete high school, for example, while all other racial and ethnic groups in the state were nearly twice as likely to have completed a postsecondary degree. Clark and Heet (2006) assert, "The single most important policy issue confronting Indiana vis-à-vis the growing Mexican population is in the realm of education. Mexican educational attainment suffers woefully compared to non-Mexican attainment" (p. 33).

With more and more Latino children entering Indiana's educational system and given the existing gap in educational outcomes, it is increasingly important to understand how public policy affects educational opportunity. It is projected that by 2020 Latino students will comprise 22 percent of the total U.S. undergraduate population and 8 percent of the Indiana undergraduate population (Santiago & Brown, 2004). If access to postsecondary education is disproportionately limited by affordability for this growing group of students—as an expanding body of research on financial aid and affordability suggests—more and more students will be left out.

Data and Research Methods

This study used longitudinal student-level data to explore trends in financial aid receipt. Much of the prior research on aid receipt among Latino students has relied on cross-sectional data. For example, a recent study by Excelencia in Education used the National Postsecondary Student Aid Study for 2003-04 (NPSAS:04) to explore patterns of aid application among Latino students in the aggregate, comparing these patterns with those of students in 1995 (Santiago & Cunningham, 2005). Although such work contributes to our general understanding of how Latinos use financial aid, analysis based on cross-sectional data cannot capture temporal changes in the use of aid and may obscure aid gaps that open as a student traverses educational pathways.

The effort to have a more complete understanding of how Latinos use financial aid was guided by these research questions:

1) How do Latino students compare to their White peers with respect to educational pathways in Indiana (i.e., enrollment intensity, institutional type, and housing)?
2) What are the patterns of aid receipt among Latino students?
3) How do Latino students compare to their White peers in their receipt and use of financial aid over time?
4) What are the differential effects of financial aid—both need and merit—on Latino students' persistence from their first to second year of college and how does this compare to that of their White peers when controlling for other factors known to affect persistence?

Population and Analytic Approach

First-time, first-year students enrolled in Indiana public postsecondary institutions, particularly four-year colleges and universities, were the focus of this study. To provide a baseline for comparison and context, enrollment patterns and characteristics for first-time, first-year students in both two-year and four-year sectors from 2000–2004 are described. Because intensity of enrollment (full-time or part-time), type of institution attended (four-year or two-year), and residence (on-campus or off-campus) are all factors that affect the cost of attendance, it is important to describe the ways enrollment patterns for Latinos compare to those of their White peers. For purposes of comparing longitudinal receipt and use of financial aid the author follows the cohort of students who enrolled in four-year public institutions in fall 2000 and persisted (that is, remained enrolled for any amount of credit continuously) to 2004 (Latinos, n=364; Whites, n=14,146). The intention of this descriptive analysis of aid packages for persisters is to begin to chart patterns in how continuously enrolled students rely on financial aid as well as to determine whether there are differences in these patterns along racial and ethnic lines (as we would expect).

Although this descriptive analytic approach helps fill out the picture of aid packaging for persisters, it does not permit drawing strong conclusions about the efficacy of aid in encouraging persistence. For that purpose, a multivariate analysis of the effects of aid on first-to-second-year persistence was conducted, focusing on the 2001 cohort of students (Latinos, n=279; Whites, n=14,198) enrolled in three doctorate-granting, public institutions. These institutions were selected primarily because they had the resources to award substantial amounts of institutional gift aid and also had sufficient variation in amounts of aid awarded to test the effects of institutional aid on student success. To gain a better sense of the relationships between persistence and financial aid for Latinos and Whites, the author used logistic regression to control for student background, academic preparation, and some college experiences. Of particular interest in these models is the effect of institutional and merit aid on the likelihood of a Latino or White student reenrolling the following year.

Data and Method

Data for this study come from the Indiana Commission for Higher Education's (ICHE) student information system (SIS). By law, every public postsecondary institution is required to report student information annually from the institution's transactional data systems. These data include student background (e.g., race/ethnicity and gender), academic preparation (e.g., high school degree type; SAT scores, if taken; and high school rank), college enrollment (e.g., full-time or part-time and choice of major), and financial aid information (e.g., type and amount of aid received from institutional, state, and federal sources). For this study, annual data files were merged and student cases were matched using unique identifiers to create a longitudinal database.

Although every student who has enrolled in higher education in Indiana is represented in the database, in some cases data for particular variables are missing. For example, not all institutions require students to take the SAT or to report SAT scores. In most cases, narrowing the population (i.e., focusing on first-time, first-year students at four-year institutions) enables the interpretation of the missing data. Regarding financial aid, missing data means the student did not apply for financial aid. Some research (e.g., King, 2006; St. John, 1992) has suggested that students with missing aid data are those who did not need aid or did not qualify for it. However, it is likely that some low-income students who qualified for aid did not apply for it.

To develop a comparative baseline of aid packaging and enrollment patterns, analyses relied on descriptive statistics, percentages, and averages. For enrollment characteristics and patterns from 2000–2001 to 2003–2004, the author reports four academic-year averages. As mentioned above, multivariate analysis employed logistic regression, controlling for student background, academic preparation, and college experiences.

Care must be taken in interpreting findings from these analyses for several reasons. Although descriptive analysis enables us to gain a clearer sense of underlying patterns of aid use, thereby helping to sharpen research questions and models, we cannot reasonably make causal or inferential claims about the relationships between aid and academic success. Furthermore, measures of merit aid used in the multivariate analysis are likely proxies for other factors (such as academic preparation or wealth) thought to affect persistence. Although the use of logistic regression allows us to control statistically for a variety of factors, the results cannot shed light on the causal relationships between aid and persistence. Rather, these findings are largely descriptive in nature and serve as a point of departure for framing questions for further research.

Finally, when looking at the longitudinal receipt of aid for the 2000 cohort of Latinos it is important to note that the aid amounts are aggregated across all types of four-year institutions—regional (i.e., campuses that are part of a multicampus university system), state (i.e., public institutions that are not part of a multicampus university system), and urban (i.e., institutions that are located in an urban area and that are not regional or state institutions). However, as we might expect there are fairly significant differences in the amounts of aid received by Latinos attending research institutions compared to those attending regional campuses. For example, Latinos at research universities received an average of just under $5,500 during their first year of enrollment, whereas Latinos at regional campuses received an average of just under $2,000. Table 1.1 shows the average aid amounts of first-year Latinos enrolled in each of the four-year institution sectors in 2000–2001. Although future analysis will benefit from controlling for the types of four-year institutions in which students enrolled, for purposes of this analysis data are aggregated to give an overall picture of the longitudinal receipt of aid.

Table 1.1. Average Aid Amounts for Latino Students in 2000–2001 by Type of Aid and by Institutional Sector

	Institutional Gift Aid	Work-Study	Federal Grants	State Grants	Loans	Total
State	$ 1,093.70	$ 247.55	$ 599.99	$ 888.76	$ 1,924.84	$ 4,754.84
Regional	$ 40.17	$ 37.58	$ 621.53	$ 468.25	$ 748.26	$ 1,915.79
Urban	$ 78.93	$ -	$ 400.70	$ 251.11	$ 756.67	$ 1,487.41
Research	$ 1,372.41	$ 116.25	$ 705.69	$ 825.61	$ 2,449.79	$ 5,469.75

Findings

Analyzing enrollment intensity, institutional type, and housing provides a general picture of the educational pathways taken by Latino students in Indiana. By comparing their pathways to those of White students we gain a sense of similarities and differences in educational access and success along racial/ethnic lines.

Across the two-year and four-year sectors from 2000–2001 to 2003–2004, Latinos tended to enroll in regional four-year institutions in greater proportion than their White peers, were less likely to attend full time, and were more likely to live off campus. Averaged across four years, the proportion of Indiana's Latino college students enrolled in regional four-year institutions was 33 percent, followed by two-year colleges at 31 percent, and research universities at 22 percent of Latino students. By comparison, 18 percent of Whites enrolled in regional universities, 30 percent in two-year colleges, and 29 percent in research universities (Figure 1.1).

A smaller proportion of Latino students than of White students enrolled full time and lived on campus, although the differences were relatively small because the majority of both Latino and White college students in Indiana enrolled full time and lived off campus. On average, from 2000–2001 to 2003–2004, 71 percent of Latinos versus 75 percent of Whites enrolled full time in the fall semester. Just over three-fourths (76%) of Latinos lived off campus compared to slightly more than two-thirds (67%) of Whites.

Family income plays a central role in determining eligibility for financial aid. Moreover, income is directly related to ability to pay as well as to the socioeconomic position of a student. A portrait of longitudinal use of aid among Latinos must include a description of reported income. As we might expect given the racial/ethnic structure of economic mobility and social class, even among college-going students the families of Latinos tended to have lower incomes than the families of Whites. While 16 percent of White students reported family incomes below $30,000, around 24 percent of Latinos reported their families were in this income category (Figure 1.2). The greatest proportion of Latino students enrolled in public institutions in Indiana came from families with incomes less than $30,000. In contrast, among White students with reported family incomes the greatest proportion (23%) came from families earning more than $70,000 annually. Even more intriguing are the similar percentages of Latinos and Whites with missing income data. On average, from 2000–2001 to 2003–2004, 37 percent of Latinos and 39 percent of Whites had missing income data, indicating that nearly equal proportions of Latinos and Whites did not apply for financial aid—as income data were available for all students who applied for aid. This suggests that despite greater levels of financial need, Latino students may be paying for school by means other than financial aid.

Figure 1.1. **Comparison of White and Latino Student Enrollments in 2000–2001 by Institutional Sector**

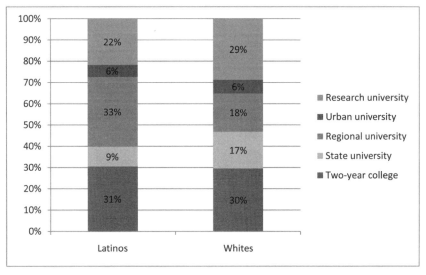

Figure 1.2. **Family Incomes Reported by Latino and White Students, 2000–2003 Averages**

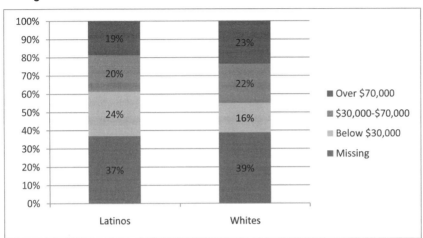

Given the differences in family income between Latinos and Whites, we would assume differences in receipt of aid between these groups. Consistent with this assumption, more Latino students than White students relied on federal and state grant aid, whereas slightly more Whites than Latinos received institutional aid. Among first-time, first-year students who enrolled in four-year public institutions and received financial aid, the greatest proportion of Latinos received federal grant aid (36%), followed by recipients of loans (35%), state grant aid (26%), and institutional aid (18%) (Figure 1.3). In comparison, more Whites relied on loans (36%), followed by federal grant aid (22%), institutional aid (20%), other aid packages (20%), and state grant aid (18%). Thus, clear differences and some similarities (e.g., Latinos and Whites relied on loans in similar proportion) existed in the initial receipt of aid during the first year of school for the 2000 cohort enrolled in four-year institutions.

Among those students who persisted from 2000–2001 to 2003–2004, we also found differences between Latinos and Whites in amounts of aid received. The median amount of federal grant aid received by the 2000 Latino cohort was $1,650 compared to $1,912 for Whites. However, during their second year of school, the median amount increased to $2,644 for Latinos compared to $2,200 for Whites (Figure 1.4). Aid received by both Latinos and Whites increased throughout their four years of school, with Latinos receiving a greater median amount in years two through four. Latinos received a greater amount of state

Figure 1.3. Latino and White Students' Receipt of Aid by Type of Aid, 2000 Cohort

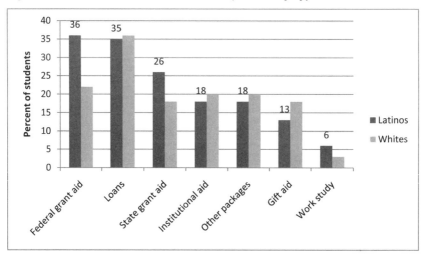

grant aid than their White peers, including during their first year of school. In 2000, Latinos received $794 more per recipient in state grant aid than Whites, although this gap decreased to just under $500 by year four.

A different picture emerges when comparing receipts of institutional gift aid. Although Latinos received more institutional aid in 2000 compared to Whites ($2,012 and $1,860 per recipient respectively), the median amount fluctuated year-to-year more for Latinos than for White students (Figure 5). The median amount of institutional aid for Whites fluctuated by less than $200 throughout the four years. In contrast, institutional aid appeared to be more volatile for Latinos year-to-year, fluctuating more than $500 over the four years from a high of $2,012 in year one to a low of $1,500 in year two.

Although similar proportions of Latinos and Whites received loans, White students tended to receive greater loan amounts than Latinos as they moved from year one to year four. In year one, the median loan amount received by Latinos and Whites was $2,625. Differences emerged in year two, with White students receiving $500 more per recipient in loans ($3,500 compared to $3,000 for Latinos). In years three and four, White students received $5,500 per recipient in loans. From year two to three, the median loan amount Latinos received increased from $3,000 to $3,500. The most dramatic change in loans

Figure 1.4. Median Federal Grant Awards to Latino and White Students in the 2000 Cohort, 2000–2003

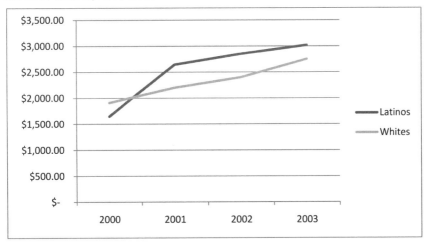

Figure 1.5. Median State Grant Awards to Latino and White Students in the 2000 Cohort, 2000–2003

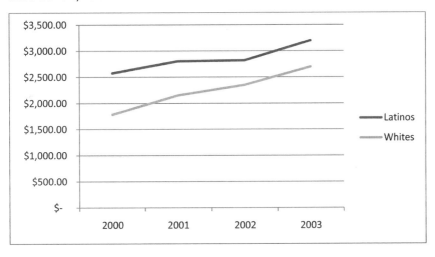

was between years three and four, when the median loan amount received by Latinos increased by $2,000, to $5,500, equal to the amount received by Whites.

To get a sense of the specific contributions of financial aid to persistence, an exploratory study was conducted on the effects of aid on the likelihood of students enrolled in three doctorate-granting public institutions controlling for academic preparation, student background, and college enrollment characteristics. The author was particularly interested in the effects of institutional gift aid and merit aid. For the purposes of this study, merit aid is defined as aid awarded by the institution to students who did not qualify for need-based aid. Assessing the effects of merit aid is particularly challenging because institutions do not often report specific forms of merit aid to governmental agencies (as is the case in Indiana). Moreover, receipt of merit aid may serve as a proxy for other characteristics that are highly correlated with the likelihood of persistence.

Overall, White students received merit aid at slightly higher rates (49.2%) than their Latino peers (45.5%). Students whose families earned over $70,000 received merit aid at higher rates (73.9%) than students from families earning $30,000–$70,000 (40.6%) and students whose families earned less than $30,000 (19.6%). A $1,000 increase in institutional gift aid was associated with about a four-percent increase in the likelihood of a student persisting, controlling for all else. By comparison, receipt of merit aid was associated with just over a twelve-percent increase in the likelihood of persistence, holding all else constant.

Separate models for Latinos and Whites illustrate the differential effects of aid across racial and ethnic groups. Latinos from families who earned less than $30,000 per year were less likely to persist than Latinos whose families earned $30,000–$70,000. A $1,000 increase in grants (federal and state) increased the likelihood of Latino students' year-to-year persistence by over 30 percent, but had no apparent effect on the persistence of White students. Institutional and merit aid played a significant role in the likelihood of White but not Latino students' persisting (Table 1.2).

Discussion

The findings from this study indicate that postsecondary enrollment patterns of Latinos in Indiana are similar to those of Latinos nationwide. Compared to the average undergraduate, Latino students nationally are more likely to be first-generation college attendees, to be enrolled part time, to live with their parents, to have relatively lower family incomes, and to attend institutions that have comparatively low tuition and fees. A study by Santiago and Cunningham (2005) found that 76 percent of Latinos were enrolled at institutions with tuition and fees of less than $5,000 per year.

***Table 1.2.* Comparison of Factors Affecting Persistence from 2001–2002 to 2002–2003 of First-Year, First-Time Latino and White Students**

Variables	Latinos		Whites	
	Sig.	Odds	Sig.	Odds
Institutional Aid		0.93	**	1.04
Grant Aid (Noninstitutional)	*	1.33		1.03
Loans		1.01		1.01
Other		1.13		1.00
Work-Study+		0.83		0.81
Merit Aid+		1.73	*	1.15
Need-Based Aid+		2.43		1.12
Unmet Need		1.01	**	1.02
Men Compared to Women and Missing	*	1.96	**	1.17
Compared to Middle-Income Students				
High-income (>$70,000)		1.16	**	0.85
Lowest income (<$30,000)	*	0.27	**	0.74
Income not reported and missing		3.07	****	0.73
Compared to Students in Top-Quartile of HS Class				
Second quartile			**	1.13
Third quartile			**	1.23
Lowest quartile				1.40
Missing				0.91
College GPA	****	2.79	****	2.14
Living On Campus Compared to Off Campus		1.00	****	1.28
21st Century Scholars Compared to Non-Scholars		0.22		1.25
% correctly predicted		70.1		66.4
Nagelkerke		0.197		0.081
N		279		14,198

Note. Aid and cost amounts in units of $1,00
****p<0.001, ***p<0.01, **p<0.05, *p<0.10
+Dichotomous variable denoting receipt of specified aid type

Interestingly, in contrast to the enrollment patterns in other states, the majority of Latino students in Indiana enrolled in four-year regional institutions rather than two-year colleges. This is likely an artifact of the unique development of Indiana's postsecondary structures. Historically, Indiana had no community college system. In fact, it was not until 2004 that a community college was officially constituted in the state, when Ivy Tech Community College of Indiana was formed from the Ivy Tech Vocational College system. Traditionally, the state's regional campuses served many of the same functions as a two-year college system. These structural differences raise interesting questions about the relationships between educational opportunity and educational structures (D. Hossler, personal communication, June 21, 2007).

With the community college system continuing to develop across the state, it will be important over the next few years to observe whether Latino enrollments shift to the two-year sector as this would have implications for Latino students' opportunities and outcomes. Olivas (1985) points out that students who enroll in four-year colleges often have greater access to federal financial aid. In this context, shifts in enrollment from four-year to two-year institutions may be particularly problematic for Latinos if a pattern already exists, as suggested by some evidence from this analysis, that Latinos are less likely than Whites to apply for financial aid. Among Latino students nationally, 78 percent applied for aid in 2003–2004 (Santiago & Cunningham, 2005) compared to only 63 percent of Latinos in Indiana.

Federal and state grant aid, along with loans, were the sources of support Latinos relied on most. Although a smaller proportion of Latinos had state grants than had federal grants, the state grants came with a larger dollar amount, particularly during the first year of school. Consistent with Santiago and Cunningham's (2005) findings, in this analysis the amount of federal grant aid received by Latinos in their first year of school was lower than that of Whites. However, the median amount of federal grant aid was greater for Latinos than Whites in the second through fourth years of college, suggesting that federal grant aid may play an increasingly important role in financing Latino students' education as they progress through school. Latinos students' enrollment patterns—living at home, attending less costly institutions, and enrolling part time—may in part be cost control strategies. Although a greater proportion of Latinos in the 2000 cohort relied on federal grants, they received less federal grant aid during their first year of school than Whites.

The use of state grants appears to have had the greatest increase between the third and fourth years of enrollment. A higher proportion of Latinos in Indiana received state grant aid (26%) compared to national figures (16%) (Santiago & Cunningham, 2005). The multivariate analysis of year-to-year persistence among students at three doctorate-granting institutions provides further evidence that federal and state grants have had a particularly strong effect on Latino students' persistence. Although patterns of reliance on federal and state grant aid likely differ in other states, these findings underscore the need to consider aid receipt in a longitudinal fashion whenever possible.

Loans were another important source of aid for Latino students attending four-year institutions. Nearly equal proportions of Latinos and Whites relied on loans to finance their education. Similar to national figures (Santiago & Cunningham, 2005), about one-third of Latinos received loans in their first year of school, and the median loan amount ($2,625) was greater than the federal grant amount ($1,650). While the amount of money borrowed among Latinos and Whites who persisted from 2000–2001 to 2003–2004 was the same, Latinos increased their reliance on loans more gradually than Whites until their fourth year, when Latinos and Whites borrowed in nearly equal amounts.

This may suggest that Latinos initially find ways other than loans to pay for school. Data from NPSAS:04 (National Center for Education Statistics, 2005) of enrollments in public four-year institutions across Indiana, for example, indicate that more Latinos than Whites had to work to pay for school. While just over 14 percent of Latinos said they could afford school without working, 20 percent of Whites reported they did not need to work. On average, Latinos reported working just over one hour more per week than their White peers.

Finally, Latinos and Whites relied on institutional aid in similar proportions, although the amount of institutional aid Latinos received appeared to fluctuate more from year to year, suggesting that for Latinos institutional aid is a less reliable support than other forms of aid—a conclusion reinforced by findings from the multivariate analysis. Institutional aid appeared to have no effect on the likelihood of Latino students persisting from their first to second year of school. In contrast, receipt of merit aid—which flowed primarily to upper-income and White students—was associated with a significant increase in students' likelihood of persisting, although as measured here merit aid was probably a proxy for other variables positively associated with persistence. Results further suggest that coming from a higher-income family—regardless of race or ethnicity—contributes to a greater likelihood of persisting.

Implications for Future Research

A largely exploratory endeavor, this study raises a number of questions for future research about the academic pathways of Latino students, the role financial aid plays in their academic success, and the potential for education policy to promote educational equity. It appears that college-going Latino students in Indiana do not apply for aid in proportion to their financial need. As King (2006) has suggested, students who have the greatest financial need may be less likely than their higher-income peers to apply for aid, in part because of a lack of familiarity with the lengthy and often complicated process. Future research should explore whether Latino students are less likely than their peers in other racial/ethnic groups to apply for all forms of financial aid. In addition, it is important to learn whether higher-income Latino students apply for aid at greater rates than their lower-income peers and whether there are generational differences; for example, if second- or third-generation Latino students are more likely to apply for aid, controlling for income.

Failing to consider, understand, and ultimately address the factors that influence whether and how Latino students rely on aid would render ineffective even the most progressive and generous aid policies. For example, Indiana's relatively successful Twenty-First Century Scholars grant program can have no effect on closing the completion gap between Whites and Latinos (in fact, it could contribute to a widening of the gap) if low-income Latinos are less likely to apply to the program. Sound research on how aid policies are "appropriated" at the local level can inform the design and implementation of new or revised aid policies with understandings that can help disentangle the interactions of race, class, historical contexts, and other sociocultural structures (Sutton & Levinson, 2001).

One of the most striking findings emerging from this study is the stark difference in first-to-second year persistence rates for Latino students at two-year compared to four-year institutions. Among all first-time, first-year Latinos who began in 2000 at a community college, only 39 percent enrolled the following year at any two-year or four-year public institution, compared to 63 percent of White students. Latinos at four-year institutions fared relatively better, with 71 percent persisting compared to 76 percent of Whites. Future research should explore in greater depth what factors contribute to dramatically low year-to-year persistence rates for Latino students at two-year institutions. Why do Latino students persist at higher rates at four-year institutions than at community colleges? One possible explanation is that Latino students who attend two-year colleges have less access to financial aid, as discussed above—although the costs of attending a two-year institution are relatively lower so aid may not be needed. Latinos may also have less access to other forms of support, such as mentoring from faculty and staff. Another possible explanation is that students who decide to enroll in two-year schools have different educational aspirations and goal commitments than students who decide to enroll in four-year schools. Moreover, differences in support for and commitment to students may exist between two-year and four-year institutions that affect students' decisions whether to stay enrolled or to leave higher education altogether. Fry (2004), for example, has suggested that more selective institutions offer Latinos more support and financial aid than less selective or two-year institutions do.

Finally, some research has suggested that some Latinos may enroll in two-year rather than four-year institutions to stay close to home, to fulfill family commitments, and to earn money for school (Santiago, 2007). All of these factors in addition to financial aid are important to consider and explore in order to make sense of why Latinos at two-year institutions depart at nearly twice the rate of their four-year peers.

As state policy makers consider ways to increase two-year college enrollments, they should be especially alert to possible structural inequalities between two-year and four-year institutions. Like a number of other states, Indiana is increasingly looking to its community college system for lower-cost, more efficient education for workforce development (ICHE, 2007). However, given the place of community colleges in the disparities found in this study, policy makers may want to proceed with caution until more is known about barriers to academic success for Latinos.

Evidence from a national study of Latino students' academic pathways (Fry, 2005a) throws additional light on these disparities. Fry found that between 1996 and 2001 Latino postsecondary enrollments grew at both two-year and four-year schools, while growth in White enrollments was concentrated in four-year schools. On average, enrollment in a two-year college was associated with a significantly lower chance of baccalaureate degree completion. Fry concluded that these enrollment patterns, in part, contribute to the widening gap between Latinos and Whites in educational attainment at the postsecondary level. Taken as a whole, these findings point toward the need for more research in this area. Until we can improve educational outcomes for all students in community colleges, policies that encourage Latinos to enroll in two-year rather than four-year institutions may not be as economically efficient as they appear and may even include the high cost of non-completion.

Another area of research emerging from this study focuses on the strategies of Latino students to make postsecondary education more accessible by reducing costs—for example, by enrolling in less expensive institutions, by enrolling less intensively, and by living off campus. As discussed above, findings from the National Postsecondary Student Aid Study suggest that to pay for school Latino students may rely on earnings from work more than their White counterparts do. Additional research is needed to gain a better understanding of the trade-offs between incurring debt and engaging in other efforts to control costs and the effects of these strategies on persistence.

Finally, the differential patterns of aid use over time, along with the relatively greater efficacy with respect to persistence of some forms of aid over others, raise a host of questions about the interrelationship of aid and educational attainment. For example, recall that Latino students who enrolled in four-year institutions initially relied less on loans than their White peers. However, during their fourth year of school, the median loan amount for Latinos increased $2,000 to nearly the same amount as for their White peers. Does the smaller initial loan amount reflect a greater aversion to indebtedness and risk during the first years of college? Does the increase in the median loan amount beginning in the fourth year of college indicate students' increased certainty of successful completion? These questions raise the possibility that the causal effects of loans and other forms of aid may shift across the duration of enrollment. Receipt of loans may initially have a causal effect on enrollment decisions and choice of college, as prior research suggests (e.g., Dowd, 2006). However, as a student develops a college-going identity (Tierney, Corwin, & Colyar, 2005) through year after year of success, perhaps the causal relationship becomes more reciprocal. In other words, persistence may lead to taking out loans.

Closing the postsecondary completion gulf between Latinos and Whites is an ethical imperative as well as a social, economic, and democratic requirement. To find practical solutions to the dominant patterns and problems that have created and widened this gulf, researchers, policy makers, educators, students, and communities need to work together. As Suro and Fry (2005) note, the United States is in the midst of a demographic shift as significant as the mass migrations around the turn of the 20th century or the baby boom following World War II. Latinos, both foreign and domestic born, are at the center of this wave. Concurrently, and for a variety of reasons, access to postsecondary education is eroding for Latinos. The confluence of these currents has the potential to speed the erosion of the equity ground gained during the civil rights era, creating a de facto state of segregation where economic mobility and full participation in democracy follow racial and ethnic lines.

Financial access to postsecondary education, a necessary but not sufficient component of educational equity, will not alone bridge the education gulf between Whites and Latinos—the minority group becoming the majority. Nonetheless, ensuring that college-qualified Latinos are able to attend postsecondary education regardless of their financial wherewithal is arguably an easier first step than overcoming persistent issues such as institutional racism and the cross-generational persistence of poverty. As part of the long-term effort to overcome these and other barriers, we must continue to find ways to make college affordable for all.

References

Cabrera, A. F., Nora, A., & Castañeda, M. B. (1993). College persistence: Structural equations modeling test of an integrated model of student retention. *The Journal of Higher Education, 64*(2), 123–139.

Clark, J., & Heet, J. (2006). *Connecting Mexico and the Hoosier heartland: Policy briefing.* Indianapolis, IN: Sagamore Institute for Policy Research.

Dowd, A. (2006). *A research agenda for the study of the effects of borrowing and the prospects of indebtedness on students' college-going choices.* Boston, MA: University of Massachusetts, New England Resource Center for Higher Education.

Fry, R. (2004). *Latino youth finishing college: The role of selective pathways.* Washington, DC: Pew Hispanic Center.

Fry, R. (2005a). *Recent changes in the entry of Hispanic and White youth into college.* Washington, DC: Pew Hispanic Center.

Fry, R. (2005b). *A statistical portrait of Hispanics at mid-decade.* Washington, DC: Pew Hispanic Center.

Harvey, W. B., & Anderson, E. L. (2005). *Minorities in higher education: Twenty-first annual status report.* Washington, DC: American Council on Education.

Heller, D. E. (1997). Student price response in higher education: An update to Leslie and Brinkman. *The Journal of Higher Education, 68*(6), 624–659.

Hudson, L., Shieh, Y. Y., & Cohen, B. (2003). *Racial/ethnic differences in the path to a postsecondary credential.* Washington, DC: Institute of Education Sciences, National Center for Education Statistics.

Indiana Commission for Higher Education (ICHE). (2007). *Reaching higher: Strategic directions for higher education in Indiana.* Indianapolis, IN: Author.

King, J. E. (2006). *Missed opportunities revisited: New information on students who do not apply for financial aid.* Washington, DC: American Council on Education.

Lichtenstein, M. (2002). *The role of financial aid in Hispanic first-time freshman persistence.* Paper presented at the 42nd Annual Forum for the Association for Institutional Research, Toronto, ON, Canada.

National Center for Education Statistics, U.S. Department of Education. (2005). *2003–04 National Postsecondary Student Aid Study (NPSAS:04).* Washington, DC: Author.

Nora, A. (1990). Campus-based aid programs as determinants of retention among Hispanic community college students. *Journal of Higher Education, 61*(1), 312–331.

Olivas, M. A. (1985). Financial aid packaging policies: Access and ideology. *The Journal of Higher Education, 56*(4), 462–475.

St. John, E. P. (1992). Workable models for institutional research on the impact of student financial aid. *Journal of Student Financial Aid, 22*(3), 13–26.

St. John, E. P., Paulsen, M. B., & Carter, D. F. (2005). Diversity, college costs, and postsecondary opportunity: An examination of the financial nexus between college choice and persistence for African Americans and Whites. *Journal of Higher Education, 76*(5), 545–569.

St. John, E. P., Paulsen, M. B., & Starkey, J. B. (1996). The nexus between college choice and persistence. *Research in Higher Education, 37*(2), 175–220.

Santiago, D., & Brown, S. (2004). *Federal policy and Latinos in higher education*. Washington, DC: Pew Hispanic Center.

Santiago, D. (2007). *Choosing Hispanic-serving institutions: A closer look at Latino students' college choices*. Washington, DC: Excelencia in Education.

Santiago, D., & Cunningham, A. (2005). *How Latinos pay for college: Patterns of financial aid in 2003–04*. Washington, DC: Excelencia in Education.

Stinebrickner, R., & Stinebrickner, T. R. (2003). Understanding educational outcomes of students from low-income families: Evidence from a liberal arts college with a full-tuition subsidy. *The Journal of Human Resources, 38*(3), 591–617.

Suro, R., & Fry, R. (2005). Leaving the newcomers behind. In R. H. Hersh & J. Merrow (Eds.), *Declining by degrees: Higher education at risk* (pp. 169–183). New York: Palgrave MacMillan.

Sutton, M., & Levinson, B. A. (2001). *Policy as practice: Toward a comparative sociocultural analysis of educational policy* (Vol. 1). Westport, CT: Ablex Publishing.

Tierney, W. G., Corwin, Z. B., & Colyar, J. E. (2005). *Preparing for college: Nine elements of effective outreach*. Albany, NY: State University of New York Press.

CHAPTER 2

TRACKING THE NEW MOBILITY IN COLLEGE ENROLLMENT PATTERNS: COMPARING LATERAL-TRANSFER, REVERSE-TRANSFER, AND NONPERSISTING STUDENTS

Don Hossler, Jacob P. K. Gross, and Afet Dadashova

Student mobility within postsecondary education is gaining increasing attention among policy makers, campus practitioners, and scholars—and with good reason. Nationwide, about 25 percent of first-time, degree-seeking students who begin at four-year institutions and 43 percent of students who begin at two-year institutions transfer at least once (Wellman, 2002). Adelman (1999) estimates that the multi-institutional attendance rate for students exceeds 60 percent (compared to 40% and 54% in the 1970s and 1980s respectively), with up to 40 percent of students crossing state lines. Yet, despite apparent growth in students' mobility—or transfer—in attending postsecondary institutions, relatively little is known about the variety and complexity of these movements: from a two-year to a four-year school (traditional transfer), from a four-year to a four-year school or from a two-year to a two-year school (lateral transfer), from a two-year to a four-year to a two-year school ("swirling"), and from a four-year to a two-year school (reverse transfer)—as well as myriad other permutations (Wawrzynski & Sedlacek, 2003).

Most research on student transfer has focused on students who transfer in a traditional fashion from a two-year college to a four-year institution, and less attention has been given to reverse- and lateral-transfer students. Our study focuses on lateral and reverse transfer, but rather than simply describe these patterns of movement, we explore the characteristics that contribute to lateral or reverse transfer compared with continuing at the same institution or departing higher education altogether. Our inquiry contributes to recent work on student transfer (Townsend, 2000; Townsend & Dever, 1999; Winter, Harris, & Ziegler, 2001; Yang, 2006) while also extending the long line of persistence research (e.g., Bean, 1985; Pascarella & Terenzini, 1980; Tinto, 1975) that seeks to understand and differentiate forms of and reasons for student departure from higher education.

Contexts: Shifts in Enrollment Patterns

Higher education institutions have been encountering the phenomenon of student transfer at least since the early 1900s, when transfer agreements between two-year colleges and four-year institutions were first created (Townsend, 2001). The early two-year college, often referred to as junior college, was viewed as an extension of high school—offering some collegiate activities but emphasizing vocational training (Kintzer, 1996). Indeed, one of the enduring complexities of the transferability of higher education has been determining how to academically evaluate courses taken at institutions with a more vocational, or applied, focus.

In the 1960s many states became involved in recommending and developing transfer agreements. The Master Plan for Higher Education in California (1968–1978), for example, established a system and recommended procedures for intersegmental transfer, i.e., transfer within a multicampus system (Kintzer, 1996). During this same period, volunteer efforts toward intersegmental transfer developed in Illinois, Michigan, and Washington, while Florida, Georgia, Illinois, and Texas developed state intersegmental transfer plans. States' involvement in articulation and transfer agreements expanded during the 1980s, and the 1990s saw even more changes in universities that would affect articulation and transfer. Kintzer describes these changes as "efforts to improve access to higher education for disadvantaged populations, employer-sponsored education, proprietary school training, and training for military, which was provided externally by colleges and universities" (p. 9).

More recently, growing postsecondary enrollments nationwide are generating greater interest among institutional, state, and federal policy makers in the transferability of credits across the two-year and four-year public and private sectors of higher education. State education agencies are not only encouraging or mandating articulation and transfer agreements but also are promoting transfer between the two-year and four-year sectors (Anderson et al., 2006; Ignash, 2000). The magnitude and depth of transfer agreements at the state and national levels can seem overwhelming at first glance. One researcher identifies several developments as possible causes for this activity:

> There are a number of trends that are probably affecting the size and nature of pools of potential transfer students, including improved high school preparation for four-year college admission; questions about the propriety of affirmative action and other outreach programs to assist students who have been historically underrepresented in higher education; higher university admission standards;

higher university costs, together with uncertainty about the availability of student financial aid; and increasing emphasis on vocational and technical education at high schools and community colleges levels including school to career programs (Knoell, 1996, p. 55).

Because the number of students beginning their postsecondary education at a community college has been increasing (Dougherty & Kienzl, 2006), perhaps out of sheer necessity administrators at four-year institutions with large numbers of transfer students are addressing questions about the transferability of credits and the academic preparation of incoming transfers.

A national report (Wellman, 2002)—projecting that by 2010 community college enrollments will have grown by 26 percent in Florida, 21 percent in California, 20 percent in North Carolina, and 12 percent in Texas—points to several factors in this increase: (a) the growing number of high school graduates entering community colleges; (b) the rising proportion of traditionally underrepresented groups beginning their college careers at community colleges; (c) higher admission requirements at four-year colleges; and (d) the preference of public policy makers that more students start at community colleges because of lower costs and less impact on state budgets.

Not all transfer students move to four-year institutions after starting their postsecondary education at two-year colleges, however. Some transfer students, known as lateral transfers, go from one four-year (or two-year) institution to another. Other students, reverse transfers, start at a four-year campus and transfer to a two-year campus. Still others, intercampus transfers (ICTs), move from one campus of a multicampus institution to another campus at the same institution. In an additional variation, often called swirling (de los Santos & Wright, 1989; Townsend, 2001), students attend multiple institutions or move back and forth among several institutions over several semesters (Kearney, Townsend, & Kearney, 1995).

Federal policy makers have also become more interested in this topic. In recent years, for a variety of reasons, many higher education organizations have been urging Congress in its next reauthorization of the Higher Education Act to include recommendations facilitating the transfer of credit between institutions. Proprietary schools, for example, have been strongly advocating that two-year and four-year sector institutions at least evaluate their courses for consideration for transfers into associate and baccalaureate degree programs (Hurley, 2005).

Transfer and Educational Equity

Going beyond the concerns of public policy makers, research on transfer has the potential—as well as the obligation—to help discern to what extent mobility and attainment are contingent on sociocultural structures (race, class, and gender, for example) as well as student behaviors. For example, some researchers have drawn attention to the disparity in educational outcomes, including earning a degree from a four-year college, between students who start out in community colleges and students who begin at four-year institutions (Ayers, 2005; Clark, 1960; Dougherty, 1992). Others have highlighted the ways mobility and attainment differ along racial and ethnic lines (Fry, 2005; Kocher & Pascarella, 1990; Santiago, 2007; Swail, Cabrera, & Lee, 2004; Turner, 1992; Wassmer, Moore, & Shulock, 2004; Wawrzynski & Sedlacek, 2003).

Adelman (1999, 2006) has suggested that not all forms of student movement are equal, noting that some movement (movement he calls "purposeful") may contribute to degree attainment, whereas other forms of movement may be negatively related to degree completion. Adelman's work focused on graduation, however, not on mobility. Therefore, it provides only a limited picture of the ways student background, academic preparation, financial aid, and college experiences interact to affect mobility and, ultimately, attainment. Wassmer et al. (2004) found in their analysis of transfer rates in California that the two-year institutions with higher percentages of Latinos or African Americans had lower transfer rates than the colleges with higher percentages of Asian American students. Even after accounting for such factors as academic preparation and socioeconomic status, racial and ethnic disparities remained. Kocher and Pascarella (1990) concluded that transfer from one four-year institution to another had significant negative effects on educational attainment for all four subgroups they studied: African American and White men and women. The negative impact was twice as large for African American men as for White men, however, and three times as large for African American women as for White women. Most of the studies reviewed in Castañeda's (2002) examination of the literature on transfer by geographic location found that students from rural areas have transfer rates and attainment levels lower than those of their suburban or urban peers. A richer understanding of the transfer patterns of undergraduates could provide a more detailed picture of the role of education policy in the status attainment process and the degree of social stratification evident in the types of students who persist at their native institutions, who transfer, and who fail to persist in their degree programs.

Challenges in the Study of Student Transfer

Among the many problems associated with studying the enrollment patterns of transfer students is the lack of robust student information databases at many community colleges (Delaney, 1995). Most four-year institutions also lack the ability to track individual students as they move from one institution to another (American Association, 2006). Overall, 40 states maintain student unit record data systems, but even states with a student database often lack sufficient staff to study the enrollment patterns of transfer students. Among the states that do report transfer patterns, just eight include transfers from four-year institutions; most states focus on two-year to four-year transfer (Ewell & Boeke, 2007). Welsh and Kjorlien (2001) found that 43 states "have some form of information system that (a) includes specific data elements pertaining to transfer students and (b) is maintained on a continuous basis" (p. 319). Based on their interviews with the officials of the state higher education agencies, however, the authors concluded that the impact of the collected data on transfer students or its usage by the higher education policy community was very limited: "[s]lightly less than one-half of state higher education agencies were able to report any evidence of impact of the data on transfer students" (p. 329). Their study emphasizes the importance of aligning student information systems with the policies intended to support the transfer function of the institutions.

With both institutional and state policy makers lacking the information they need on the enrollment patterns of transfer students, especially students who transfer from four-year institutions, research on the movement of transfer students is all the more important. In this context, it is not surprising that federal and state policy makers have started to call for more research on how students move through our decentralized systems of postsecondary education.

Research Questions

In this chapter we examine the enrollment patterns of students who began at four-year public institutions across Indiana and transferred to any other public institution—two-year or four-year. Using a statewide unit record database, we examined factors that contribute to propensity to transfer compared to continuing at the same institution or to not persisting. In particular, we were interested in determining if the student characteristics associated with transfer suggested that transferring was a positive decision made by academically successful students looking for a better *student-institution fit* or if the characteristics of transfer students were more like those of students who dropped out.

Earlier studies indicated academic difficulty was one of the major reasons for reverse transfer (Berry as cited in Townsend, 2000; Heinze & Daniels as cited in Townsend, 2000). Yet, single-institution studies conducted later found that most reverse-transfer students had not had prior academic difficulty (Rooth as cited in Townsend, 2000). Kajstura & Keim (1992), who studied reverse-transfer students at community colleges in Illinois, reported several factors in these students' decisions, including proximity of the community college, low tuition, convenient class times, instructional quality, job training opportunities, GPA improvement, and relatives'/friends' advice. In a recent study focusing on a single midwestern state, Winter et al. (2001) found that reverse-transfer students gave more importance to completing an associate's degree, improving basic skills, completing courses for transfer to another institution, and improving GPA.

Our purpose in conducting a series of models was not only to make comparisons between persisters, nonpersisters, and transfer students but also to differentiate lateral- and reverse-transfer students. We also wanted to explore specific questions: In comparisons of students who persisted with those who dropped out and with those who transferred, are the profiles of students who did not persist at the same institution similar to those of students who dropped out? Are students who transfer or drop out more likely to come from low-income backgrounds? Are they more likely to have lower high school and/or college GPAs? Are students who transfer or dropout more likely to have indicators of being at risk, such as enrollment in developmental courses? Do the differences between persisters, transfers, and nonpersisters provide evidence of social inequality and stratification?

Method

Our analysis focused on students who were first-time freshman entrants at four-year public postsecondary institutions (PSIs) in 2004–2005 and were enrolled part time or full time in associate or baccalaureate degree programs (n=29,930). Our selection criteria for the cohort excluded students (n=3,305) who—through dual enrollment in high school or Advanced Placement courses—may have been first-time entrants classified as sophomores enrolled in associate's or baccalaureate degree programs (student level=5 or 7). (Of these 3,305 students who entered at the sophomore level in 2004–2005, just 35 transferred in 2005–2006.) In total, 1,732 students in our cohort transferred to another PSI in 2005–2006. We further disaggregated transfer by the type of destination institution (two-year institution compared to four-year institution).

Limitations

The primary limitations of this study are associated with the database we used. First, the findings would be more robust if it had been possible to track students over a longer period of time. Some of the students identified as dropouts in this study may have been stop-outs who reenrolled in 2006–2007. Had we been able to track this cohort of students in 2006–2007, we would likely have found a more complex and varied pattern of continued enrollment, transfer, and student withdrawal. A more significant limitation is that we were unable to track students who might have transferred to private institutions within Indiana as well as private and public institutions outside of Indiana. Thus, some of the students that identified as nonpersisters may, in fact, have transferred.

Data Sources and Definitions

The secondary data used in this study came from two sources: the Indiana Commission for Higher Education (ICHE) statewide student unit record database and the State Student Assistance Commission of Indiana's (SSACI) Free Application for Federal Student Aid (FAFSA) database. ICHE data are derived from the student information systems (SIS) of all public universities, colleges, and community colleges in Indiana. SIS data—usually collected for enrollment-related transactions—include courses taken, grades received, race/ethnicity, and all other information necessary for institutional business. These data include information on standardized testing, family income, and any financial aid from institutional, state, and federal sources.

SSACI is responsible for overseeing FAFSA for all Indiana citizens as well as for administering a number of state scholarship programs. SSACI's FAFSA data—with information about the institution where a student is enrolled as well as student and family characteristics such as parental education, family income, and students' educational expectations—were used in this study to determine whether a student was enrolled in an independent or proprietary college after leaving a public postsecondary education institution.

Methods and Models

Because the primary outcome of interest was student persistence, a dichotomous variable, the use of logistic regression was appropriate. Using ordinary least squares in this case would violate Gauss-Markov assumptions that the error term was normally distributed and the dependent variable was continuous. Equation 1 provides the general logit model, where P is the probability that the student persisted.

Equation 1. Logit Model

$$\ln\left(\frac{P_i}{1-P_i}\right) = x_i\beta + \varepsilon_i$$

Specific variables included in the model were (a) student characteristic variables ($\beta1$), including gender, race/ethnicity, age, and student/family income level; (b) academic preparation variables ($\beta2$), including high school rank and SAT score; (c) college experience variables ($\beta3$), including college GPA, whether a student lived on campus or off campus, developmental courses, major choice, and participation in the Twenty-First Century Scholars program

Table 2.1. Specific Variables Included in the Logistic Models

Student Characteristics	Gender Race/ethnicity Age Family income*
Academic Preparation	High school rank* Combined SAT score*
College Experience	College GPA Living on campus or off campus Developmental courses Major choice 21st Century Scholar
Financial Aid	Institutional aid Federal grant aid State grant aid Loans Other gift aid Work-study* Dependency status
Academic Momentum	Total year-one credits Total summer credits PSI enrollment gap Earned 20 credits in year one? Earned summer credits?

Note. *Denotes ratio-scale variables included as categorical variables for this analysis.

(a means-tested, early commitment, last-dollar aid program to promote college participation among low-income and first-generation students in Indiana); (d) financial aid variables (β5), including institutional aid, grant aid, loans, private gift aid, work-study participation, and dependency status; and (e) measures of academic momentum (β4), including total credits earned during the first year, total credits earned during the summer, the number of months between high school graduation and college enrollment, and dichotomous variables representing whether a student earned any summer credits and whether the student earned 20 credits in the first year. Table 2.1 lists the specific variables included in the logistic models.

Our research questions focused on propensity to transfer and likelihood of persistence. To compare what factors contribute to student mobility—in terms of continuing at the institution of origin, transferring to a four-year institution, transferring to a two-year institution, or not persisting—we ran a series of logistic models with each of these outcomes and with varying reference groups (see Table 2.2).

Table 2.2. Outcomes of Interest and Reference Groups for Each Logistic Model

Model	Outcome of Interest	Reference Group
1	Transferred to four-year institution *(lateral transfer)*	Continued at native institution
2	Transferred to four-year institution *(lateral transfer)*	Did not persist
3	Transferred to two-year institution *(reverse transfer)*	Continued at native institution
4	Transferred to two-year institution *(reverse transfer)*	Did not persist
5	Continued at native institution	Transferred anywhere

Though outcomes varied in each of the five models, each regression took the general form of Equation 2.

Equation 2. Persistence Model

$$Persistence / Transfer = x_i \beta_1 + x_i \beta_2 + x_i \beta_3 + x_i \beta_4 + x_i \beta_5 + \varepsilon_i$$

In testing the logical models, each category of variables was entered into the regression as a block to determine whether the category itself significantly contributed to the overall explanatory power of the model. Based on chi-square tests of statistical significance, we determined that each block improved our model at the 0.05 level of significance. These findings, considered together with findings from the research cited above, support the use of these logical models to explore what factors contribute to persistence, transfer, and nonpersistence.

Findings and Implications

Descriptive Findings

Of the 29,930 students who began as first-time associate's or baccalaureate degree-seeking students at four-year institutions in 2004, the majority (just over 74%) continued in 2005–2006 at the same institution where they had enrolled in 2004-2005, just over 20 percent did not persist in any public institution, and nearly six percent (or 1,723) transferred to another institution. Most of the students who transferred were lateral transfers (1,136 or about 66%), that is, they went to another four-year institution; the remainder were reverse transfers (587 or about 34%), that is, they transferred from a four-year to a two-year institution. It should be noted that most studies of transfer from four-year institutions search for reasons why students who originally intended to graduate from a baccalaureate institution transferred to a two-year college. In our study, the majority of students who decided to transfer chose another four-year institution. Kocher and Pascarella (1990) found that although transferring from one four-year institution to another is not always bad, such "institutional discontinuities" may have negative consequences for an individual's educational attainment and early career. For this reason we think lateral transfer needs more research, and we hope our analysis will bring further understanding to this important issue.

When we compared lateral-transfer and reverse-transfer students to students who continued at their native institutions we found some differences by income, academic preparation, race/ethnicity, and other selected characteristics. Students with the highest reported incomes were more likely to transfer laterally than to reverse transfer compared to all other groups for which income data were reported. In both lateral and reverse transfers, White students transferred at lower rates than African American and Latino students. However, African Americans and Latinos who transferred were more likely than White students who transferred to transfer to a four-year institution rather than to a two-year institution. Women transferred at higher rates than men to both two-year and four-year institutions. Students aged 21 or younger transferred to two-year and four-year institutions at higher rates than their older peers, who continued at their native institution in greater proportions.

Generally, it appears that students with the highest SAT scores and in the top quartile of their high school class continued at their native institutions at higher rates than students with SAT scores below 1120 or who were in the second or third quartile of their high school class. The proportion of students who reverse transferred increased as the composite SAT score decreased. For example, the percentage of students who transferred to two-year institutions was higher among those with SAT scores below 920 than among those with SAT scores above 920. Similarly, students who took no developmental courses in college or who had an A average during their first year of college were more likely to continue at their native institution than to transfer laterally or to reverse transfer. Students who were undecided about their choice of major were more likely to transfer to a two-year or a four-year school than those who had chosen a major. With respect to receipt of financial aid, few differences were apparent between transferring and continuing at the native institution.

Overall, when comparing students who continued at their native institutions to students who transferred anywhere, we found the highest rates of transfer among women, Indiana residents, African Americans, and dependent students; among students from middle-income families, with SATs below 920, with no declared major, with college GPAs of C or lower, and age 21 or younger; and among students who took developmental math and language courses in college, lived on campus, were in the third quartile of their high school class, received financial aid, and (particularly) received need-based aid.

We next compared students who transferred to two-year or four-year institutions to those with no evidence of continuing enrollment at any public postsecondary institution (classified in this study as dropouts) and found some differences along selected characteristics here as well. Students whose families earned between $30,000 and $70,000 appeared most likely to depart from postsecondary education altogether, or to not persist. The highest income students were more likely to transfer than to not persist. Women were more likely than men to transfer to a two-year or four-year institution than to not persist. African Americans were more likely than other racial and ethnic groups to not persist. Asian American/Pacific Islanders transferred at higher rates than not persisting, compared to other racial and ethnic groups. Students age 22 or older were much more likely to depart public postsecondary education than to transfer in comparison to traditional-age students (age 21 and younger).

Differences in transfer and nonpersistence emerged as well when we looked at the academic characteristics of students. Students with a combined SAT score over 1120 were more likely to transfer to a two-year or a four-year institution than to leave public postsecondary education altogether. Students with the lowest SAT scores left higher education at the highest rates compared to those who transferred. Among students with reported GPAs for their first year of school, students with a C average or lower had the highest rates of nonpersistence of any group, and students with an A average were more likely to transfer than to not persist. Similarly, students who took developmental courses were more likely to depart higher education compared to students who took no such courses, while students who took no developmental courses were more likely to transfer, particularly to four-year institutions, than to not persist. Students in the two lowest quartiles of their high school classes were more likely to depart than to transfer to any type of institution, while students in the top quartile were more likely to transfer, particularly to four-year institutions, than to leave public postsecondary education. Finally, students who received financial aid, particularly need-based aid, were more likely to transfer than to not persist.

Inferential Findings

　　　Controlling for factors known to affect persistence decisions, we looked first at the likelihood of transferring versus continuing at the native institution (*Model 5*). Overall, compared to transferring and controlling for all else, we found a greater likelihood of continuing at the native institution among students among the following groups: men, age 21 to 29, with no reported income, with a higher cumulative college GPA, with a declared major, with more credits completed during the academic year, and with credits earned during the summer. Associated with a greater likelihood of lateral or reverse transfer, *ceteris paribus,* were living on campus, being a resident of Indiana, and earning at least 20 credits during the first year.

　　　Looking closer at factors affecting transfer to a two-year or a four-year institution compared to continuing at the native institution (*Models 1 and 2*), our results confirmed what we found in the preceding model. Men were more likely than women to continue than to transfer, although they appeared to be somewhat more likely to transfer to a four-year institution, controlling for all else. Students age 21 to 29 were less likely to transfer to a four-year institution than to continue at their native institution, and age was not significantly related to likelihood of reverse transfer. Although income was not significantly related to propensity to transfer compared to continuing at one's native institution, high-income students were significantly less likely than their middle-income peers to transfer to a two-year institution, holding all else constant. Students in the second and third quartiles of their high school classes were more likely than students in the top quartile to transfer to a two-year institution than to continue, *ceteris paribus.* High school rank was not significantly related to lateral transfer, however. As cumulative college GPA increased, the likelihood of transferring to a two-year or a four-year institution decreased. Students who lived on campus were more likely to transfer, particularly to four-year institutions, than to continue. Indiana residents were much more likely than nonresidents to transfer compared to continuing.

Academic momentum appeared to be significantly related to likelihood of transfer. An increase in credits earned during the first year was associated with a decreased likelihood of transferring to a two-year institution compared to continuing, though total credits earned was not significantly related to four-year transfer. Earning summer credits was similarly associated with a decreased likelihood of transferring to a two-year institution compared to continuing at the native institution, but this was not significantly related to lateral transfer.

When we looked at factors related to likelihood of transferring compared to not persisting, we found African Americans were more likely than Whites to transfer to a four-year institution than to not persist, holding all else constant. Asian American/Pacific Islanders were more likely than Whites to transfer to a two-year institution than to not persist. Although no significant differences with respect to gender were found, students age 22 and older were less likely than traditional-age students to transfer to a four-year institution than to leave public postsecondary education. Students with low SAT scores were more likely than students with midrange scores to transfer to a two-year institution than to depart. Similarly, students in the second quartile of their high school class were more likely than top quartile students to transfer to a two-year institution than to depart. Indiana residents were much more likely than nonresidents to transfer as opposed to not persisting. An increase in the number of credits earned during the academic year was associated with an increased likelihood of transferring to a four-year but not a two-year institution, compared to departing all together. Crossing the 20-credit threshold during the first year was associated with an increased likelihood of transferring to a two-year but not to a four-year institution compared to not persisting. The amount of time between high school graduation and college enrollment increased the likelihood of transferring to a two-year institution rather than departing postsecondary education. Having declared a major was also associated with a greater likelihood of persisting than of transferring or dropping out. Finally, a somewhat unanticipated finding was the apparently small role across our analyses of financial aid in persistence, transfer, or withdrawal. (For full models and results, see Table 2.3 appended to this chapter).

Implications

This chapter examines the factors that contribute to lateral transfer or reverse transfer from a four-year institution and whether these transfer behaviors are more similar to persisting in or to departing from higher education. Our analyses indicate that students with higher levels of academic performance (as measured by college GPA or class rank) are more likely to remain at their first institution than to transfer or to drop out and are more likely to transfer than to drop out. Students who ranked in the bottom two quartiles of their high school class are more likely to drop out than to persist or to transfer. These patterns with respect to academic performance are consistent with previous research.

One puzzling pattern in our findings reveals that students over age 21 are more likely to transfer than to continue at their native institutions, and yet students in this age group also demonstrate a relatively high propensity to drop out rather than to transfer. We speculate that we have actually captured in these data a complex set of behaviors among different groups of students. Many students age 21 or older in our sample were enrolled in four-year residential institutions. Because they were probably close to completing their degrees, it is unlikely that they would choose to transfer or to withdraw. Other students in this age group were attending commuting institutions, however, and were probably working as well as going to school. The options of these students are more constrained: they can either continue at their current institution or they can drop out. Such students very likely don't have the option of considering an institution in another geographical area. Work or family conflicts and responsibilities may be the factors that force them to drop out or stop out.

Overall, this pattern of results suggests a continuum of student characteristics associated with persisting at the institution of first enrollment, transferring, or dropping out. Generally, students who persist at their native institution or who transfer to another four-year institution are more likely to be White and male, to have stronger academic credentials, to demonstrate no financial need, to live on campus, and to have declared an academic major. At the other end of the continuum, students with weak academic preparation as well as individuals who have not declared a major and students from low- to moderate-income families are the most likely to withdraw. In the middle of the continuum, Latino students, students with average academic records, and students who do not live in residence halls are more likely to transfer to a two-year or a four-year institution. The outliers to these patterns are 21- to 29-year-old students, who demonstrate a mixed pattern of persistence at their native institutions along with a higher probability of dropping out. In addition, African Americans, if they transfer, are more likely to transfer to another four-year college or university, but they are also more likely to withdraw.

With the available data we did not find patterns of persistence, transfer, and student withdrawal evidencing strong social stratification and inequality based on family background. However, our data set does not include information indicating which students were first-generation postsecondary students—information that might have revealed some patterns of social stratification. While we found that students from low- and moderate-income families were more likely to drop out, we did not find that family income and financial aid eligibility had a consistent impact on the enrollment behaviors of students. Separate from family income, race/ethnicity does appear to influence student enrollment patterns, as we consistently found that White students were more likely to remain continuously enrolled and less likely to drop out.

While the addition of future cohorts to this database will enhance the robustness of research on this topic, efforts should also be made to obtain, through the National Student Clearinghouse, the names of students who did not reenroll in public institutions to determine whether they transferred to another private institution within the state of Indiana or to a public or private institution in another state. The use of discriminant analysis might be a fruitful statistical technique to further specify the differences between persisters, transfers, and nonpersisters.

In general, these findings support what many educators may already know from their day-to-day work with their students: Not all forms of transfer are equal with respect to postsecondary success and not all patterns of attendance are traditional. Although it would be a mistake to treat student characteristics—like gender, race/ethnicity, family income, and academic preparation—as sole causal factors in whether a student persists or transfers or departs postsecondary education altogether, we can think of these characteristics as proxies indicative of students' social and academic milieu.

References

Adelman, C. (1999). *Answers in the tool box: Academic intensity, attendance patterns, and bachelor's degree attainment.* Jessup, MD: National Institute on Postsecondary Education, Libraries, and Lifelong Learning.

Adelman, C. (2006). The tool box revisited: Paths to degree completion from high school through college. Washington, DC: U.S. Department of Education.

American Association of State Colleges and Universities. (2006, Fall). Graduation rates and student success: Squaring means and ends. *Perspectives.* Retrieved September 29, 2007, from http://www.aascu.org/pdf/06b_perspectives.pdf.

Anderson, G. M., Sun, J. C., & Alfonso, M. (2006). Effectiveness of statewide articulation agreements on the probability of transfer: A preliminary policy analysis. *The Review of Higher Education, 29*(3), 261–291.

Ayers, D. F. (2005). Neoliberal ideology in community college mission statement: A critical discourse analysis. *The Review of Higher Education, 28*(4), 527–549.

Bean, J. P. (1985). Interaction effects based on class level in an explanatory model of college student dropout syndrome. *American Educational Research Journal, 22*(1), 35–64.

Castañeda, C. (2002). Transfer rates among students from rural, suburban, and urban community colleges: What we know, don't know, and need to know. *Community College Journal of Research and Practice, 26*(5), 439–449.

Clark, B. R. (1960). The "cooling-out" function in higher education. *The American Journal of Sociology, 65*(6), 569–576.

Delaney, M. A. (1995). Reverse registrants in community colleges. (Doctoral dissertation, University of Connecticut, 1995). *Dissertation Abstracts International, 57,* 0561.

de los Santos, A. G., & Wright, I. (1989). Community college and university student transfer. *Educational Record, 79*(3/4), 82–84.

Dougherty, K. J. (1992). Community colleges and baccalaureate attainment. *The Journal of Higher Education, 63*(2), 188–214.

Dougherty, K. J., & Kienzl, G. S. (2006). It's not enough to get through the open door: Inequalities by social background in transfer from community colleges to four-year colleges. *Teachers College Record, 108*(3) 452–487. Retrieved September 29, 2007, from http://www.tcrecord.org/content.asp?contentid=12332.

Ewell, P. T., & Boeke, M. (2007). *Critical connections: Linking states' unit record systems to track student progress* (New Agenda Series). Indianapolis, IN: Lumina Foundation for Education.

Fry, R. (2005). Recent changes in the entry of Hispanic and White youth into college. Washington, DC: Pew Hispanic Center.

Hurley, P. (2005, fall). Navigating the Higher Education Act: What it means to California Community Colleges. *I Journal: Insight Into Student Services*, No. 11. Retrieved Sept. 29, 2007, from http://www.ijournal.us/issue_11/ij_11_02_articleframe_Hurley.html.

Ignash, J. M., & Townsend, B. K. (2000). Evaluating state-level articulation agreements according to good practice. *Community College Review, 28*(3), 1–21.

Kajstura, A., & Keim, M. (1992). Reverse transfer students in Illinois community colleges. *Community College Review, 20*(2), 39–44.

Kearney, G. W., Townsend, B. K., & Kearney, T. J. (1995). Multiple-transfer students in a public urban university: Background characteristics and interinstitutional movements, *Research in Higher Education, 36*(3), 323–344.

Kintzer, F. C. (1996). A historical and futuristic perspective of articulation and transfer in the United States. In T. Rifkin (Ed.), *Transfer and articulation: Improving policies to meet new needs* (New Directions for Community Colleges, Vol. 24, No. 4, Winter, pp. 3–13). San Francisco: Jossey-Bass.

Knoell, D. M. (1996). Moving toward collaboration in transfer and articulation. In T. Rifkin (Ed.), *Transfer and articulation: Improving policies to meet new needs* (New Directions for Community Colleges, Vol. 24, No. 4, Winter, pp. 55–64). San Franscisco: Jossey-Bass.

Kocher, E., & Pascarella, E. (1990). The impact of 4-year college transfer on the early status attainment of Black-American and White-American students. *Journal of College Student Development, 31*(2), 169–175.

Pascarella, E. T., & Terenzini, P. T. (1980). Predicting freshman persistence and voluntary dropout decisions from a theoretical model. *The Journal of Higher Education, 51*(1), 60–75.

Santiago, D. A. (2007). Choosing Hispanic-serving institutions: A closer look at Latino students' college choices. Washington, DC: Excelencia in Education.

Swail, W. S., Cabrera, A. F., & Lee, C. (2004). *Latino youth and the pathway to college.* Washington, DC: Pew Hispanic Center.

Tinto, V. (1975). Dropout from higher education: A theoretical synthesis of recent research. *Review of Educational Research, 45*(1), 89–125.

Townsend, B. K. (2000). Rationales of community colleges for enrolling reverse transfer students: A second chance for whom? *Community College Journal of Research and Practice, 24*(4), 301–311.

Townsend, B. K. (2001). Blurring the lines: Transforming terminal education to transfer education. In D. D. Bragg (Ed.), *The new vocationalism in community colleges* (New Directions for Community Colleges, Special Issue, Vol. 2001, No. 115, pp. 63–71). San Francisco: Jossey-Bass.

Townsend, B. K., & Dever, J. T. (1999). What do we know about reverse transfer students? In B. K. Townsend (Ed.), *Understanding the impact of reverse transfer students* (New Directions for Community Colleges, Vol. 106, Summer, pp. 5–14). San Francisco: Jossey-Bass.

Turner, C. S. V. (1992). It takes two to transfer: Relational networks and educational outcomes. *Community College Review, 19*(4), 27–33.

Wassmer, R., Moore C., & Shulock, N. (2004). Effect of racial/ethnic composition on transfer rates in community colleges: Implications for policy and practice. *Research in Higher Education, 45*(6), 651–672.

Wawrzynski, M. R., & Sedlacek, W. E. (2003). Race and gender differences in the transfer student experience. *Journal of College Student Development, 44*(4), 489–501.

Wellman, J. V. (2002, August). *State policy and community college–baccalaureate transfer* (National Center Report No. 02–6). Washington, DC: National Center for Public Policy and Higher Education, Institute for Higher Education Policy.

Welsh, J. F., & Kjorlien, C. (2001). State support for interinstitutional transfer and articulation: The impact of databases and information systems. *Community College Journal of Research and Practice, 25*(4), 313–332.

Winter, P. A., Harris, M. R., & Ziegler, C. H. (2001). Community college reverse transfer students: A multivariate analysis. *Community College Journal of Research and Practice, 25*(4), 271–282.

Yang, P. (2006). UCLA Community College Review: Reverse transfer and multiple missions of community colleges. *Community College Review, 33*(3/4), 55–70.

Table 2.3. 2004 Cohort First-Time First-Year Students Who Began at Four-Year Institutions

	Model 1: Four-Year Transfer vs. Continuing		Model 2: Four-Year Transfer vs. Nonpersist		Model 3: Two-Year Transfer vs. Continuing		Model 4: Two-Year Transfer vs. Nonpersist		Model 5: Continuing vs. Transfer Anywhere	
	Sig.	Exp(B)	Sig.	Exp(B)	Sig.	Exp(B)	Sig.	Exp(B)	Sig.	Exp(B)
Men Compared to Women	**	0.85		1.02	**	.0.80		0.93	****	1.23
Compared to Whites										
Race Unknown, Native American, Other		0.81	*	0.57	**	0.33	**	0.25	**	1.66
Asian/Pacific American		1.01		1.28	**	1.88	**	2.44		0.78
African American	**	1.14	**	1.43	*	0.71		0.86		1.08
Hispanic		1.02		0.80		0.64		0.61		1.13
Compared to Students under 21										
Age 21–24	**	0.27	****	0.23		0.67		0.50	**	2.70
Age 25–29	**	0.15	*	0.23		1.30		1.52	**	2.69
Age 30 and over	*	0.20	*	0.17		1.08		1.12		2.88
Compared to Middle Income ($30,000–$70,000)										
Below $30,000		0.96		0.83		0.81		0.82		1.12
Over $70,000		0.97		1.20	**	0.74		0.88		1.12
Not Reported and Missing		0.94		0.00	**	0.74		0.00	*	1.17

Table 2.3 *(continued)*. 2004 Cohort First-Time First-Year Students Who Began at Four-Year Institutions

	Model 1: Four-Year Transfer vs. Continuing		Model 2: Four-Year Transfer vs. Nonpersist		Model 3: Two-Year Transfer vs. Continuing		Model 4: Two-Year Transfer vs. Nonpersist		Model 5: Continuing vs. Transfer Anywhere	
	Sig.	Exp(B)	Sig.	Exp(B)	Sig.	Exp(B)	Sig.	Exp(B)	Sig.	Exp(B)
Compared to Midrange Combined SAT Scores										
Low SAT (<=918)		0.96		1.05		1.18	*	1.26		0.98
High SAT (>=1114)		0.94		0.89		0.99		1.02		1.01
Compared to Students in Top HS Quartile										
Second Quartile		1.02		1.10	**	1.28	*	1.26		0.96
Third Quartile		1.00		1.00	**	1.47		1.27		0.89
Lowest Quartile		0.90		1.01		1.24	*	1.41		1.00
Cumulative College GPA	****	0.85	****	2.04	****	0.32		0.94	****	1.70
Twenty-First Century Scholar	*	0.74	**	0.55		1.08		0.92		1.10
Compared to Students who Took No Developmental Courses										
Developmental Math		0.87	**	0.65		1.18		0.93		1.00
Developmental Language		0.79		1.09		0.65		0.76		1.39
Both Math and Language		0.86		0.71		1.08		0.88		1.04

Table 2.3 (continued). 2004 Cohort First-Time First-Year Students Who Began at Four-Year Institutions

	Model 1: Four-Year Transfer vs. Continuing		Model 2: Four-Year Transfer vs. Nonpersist		Model 3: Two-Year Transfer vs. Continuing		Model 4: Two-Year Transfer vs. Nonpersist		Model 5: Continuing vs. Transfer Anywhere	
	Sig.	Exp(B)	Sig.	Exp(B)	Sig.	Exp(B)	Sig.	Exp(B)	Sig.	Exp(B)
Students with Declared Majors		0.92		1.08	**	0.76	**	0.81	**	1.16
Students Who Lived on Campus	****	1.50	****	1.70	**	1.33	****	1.48	****	0.71
Federal Grants		0.99		0.97		1.02		1.01		0.99
State Grants		0.98		1.04		1.02		1.05		1.02
Institutional Aid		0.97		1.00		1.00		1.01		1.02
Other Gift Aid		0.98		1.05		1.01		1.05		1.01
Loans		1.00		1.00		1.01		1.02		1.00
Work-Study		1.21	**	2.83		1.01		1.49		0.88
Participated in Work-Study		0.91		0.61		0.92		0.97		1.10
Compared to Dependent Students										
Dependency Status Indeterminate						1.00				
Self-Supporting		1.05		0.85		1.00		1.03		0.92
Indiana Residents	****	7.74	****	19.29	****	2.22	****	4.25	****	0.20

Table 2.3 (continued). 2004 Cohort First-Time First-Year Students Who Began at Four-Year Institutions

	Model 1: Four-Year Transfer vs. Continuing		Model 2: Four-Year Transfer vs. Nonpersist		Model 3: Two-Year Transfer vs. Continuing		Model 4: Two-Year Transfer vs. Nonpersist		Model 5: Continuing vs. Transfer Anywhere	
	Sig.	Exp(B)	Sig.	Exp(B)	Sig.	Exp(B)	Sig.	Exp(B)	Sig.	Exp B)
Total Credits Earned, First Year		1.00	****	1.10	****	0.94		1.02	**	1.02
Earned 20 Credits, First Year		1.16	**	1.39	****	7.66	****	3.32	****	0.51
Total Summer Credits	**	0.97	*	0.72		1.05		0.99		0.98
Earned Summer Credits	*	0.63		2.61	**	0.47		0.68	**	1.94
Months From HS Grad to PSI Enrollment		1.00		1.00		0.99	*	0.99		1.00
N=		21,799		6,539		22,617		6,008		22,351
% Correctly Predicted		72.94		74.23		81.04		65.58		68.05
Nagelkerke		0.07		0.46		0.20		0.20		0.10
Cox and Snell		0.02		0.27		0.04		0.09		0.04

Note. ****p<0.001, ***p<0.01, *p<0.10.

CHAPTER 3

PATTERNS IN MOTIVATION AND ENGAGEMENT AMONG WORKING STUDENTS

John V. Moore III and Melanie A. Rago

Colleges have been assisting students who need financial support since at least the turn of the 20th century, when many newer colleges tried to boost enrollment by creating work-study programs for lower income students (Lucas, 1994; Rudolph, 1977). Although these programs were not particularly successful in recruiting students, their existence shows an early acknowledgement by universities that not all students have the finances to attend college and that students may, at times, need to balance their studies with forms of employment that allow them to get a college education. In recent years, more and more students have been working while attending college. Stern and Nakata (1991) found the number of college students working had increased from 29 percent in 1959 to 43 percent in 1986. More recently, King (2003) noted that 80 percent of college students were working in 1999–2000—an 8 percent increase from the previous decade. Cuccaro-Alamin and Choy (1998) found that 72 percent of students were both working and attending college. Although many researchers have examined the effects of working while in college, the outcomes of these projects have been varied and contradictory. This study, by examining the effects of employment on working students' engagement with their university, addresses the issue broadly and also explores students' motivation for working as a predictive factor.

Literature Review

Current Thinking on Working Students

The amount of time students spend working has become an increasing concern for the educators who serve them and, in growing instances, the policy makers who wonder what impact working has on persistence and completion (Tuttle, McKinney, & Rago, 2005). This concern has led to a greater interest in research on the effects of working on the college experience—which has resulted in diverse findings (Riggert, Boyle, Petrosko, Ash, & Rude-Parkins, 2006). Many of these studies reinforce the idea from Tinto (1975) and Bean and Metzner (1985) that students need to make an integrating connection to the university and that tasks or activities preventing them from doing so jeopardize

45

their chances of remaining at the institution. Hodgson and Spours (2001), for example, found that working students fail to make significant connections to the cultures of either work or school. The link between a student's integration into collegiate life and off-campus employment has been further explored by researchers Fjortoft (1995) and Lundberg (2004), who found that working students, unsurprisingly, have less time to devote to academic or social activities. Adding to the discussion of academic interruption, Hey, Calderon, and Seabert (2003) found that working students are more likely to have higher levels of academic stress.

The research findings on the impacts of these disconnections from college life have been mixed and contradictory, however. In investigating the results of working on student outcomes, Hunt, Lincoln, and Walker (2004) found that compared to their nonworking peers, employed students have lower GPAs. Canabal (1998), however, reported the opposite effect on GPA. DesJardins, Ahlburg, and McCall (2002) found that working had a positive influence on timely graduation while not impacting graduation rate. Beeson and Wessel (2002) found that working students had higher retention and graduation rates than nonworking students.

Others have posited that the link between working and academic integration is not as straightforward as portrayed in the simple working/not-working dichotomy. Several studies (Harding & Harmon, 1999; King, 2002; Pascarella & Terenzini, 1991; Perna, Cooper, & Li, 2006; Stinebrickner & Stinebrickner, 2003) have found the negative effects of working begin to appear only as the number of hours worked increases (to more than 15 hours per week, for example). This is consonant with evidence that students perceive high levels of working to be detrimental to their academics (Curtis & Shani, 2002; Hunt et al., 2004; Long & Hayden, 2001). For employed students whose time at work is under a given threshold, the impact of working has been found by some researchers to be positively associated with academic outcomes (Choy & Berker, 2003; Dundes & Marx, 2006–2007; Hood, Craig, & Ferguson, 1992; Moore & Rago, 2007b; Rago, Moore, & Herreid, 2005), yet other researchers have found no relationship (Bradley, 2006; Furr & Elling, 2000, Harding & Harmon, 1999; High, 1999; Nonis & Hudson, 2006; Pascarella & Terenzini, 2005).

To navigate this maze of findings, some scholars advocate a broadening of outcomes (Riggert et al., 2006) to help clarify the effects (or lack of effects) of working on students. Others suggest students' motivations for working may have an important impact on their studies. Perna et al. (2006) examine students' motivations for working through four lenses, each focusing primarily on the necessity of paying or defraying college costs. This view is reflected in the findings of some researchers (Curtis & Williams, 2002; Ferguson & Cerinus,

1996; Ford, Bosworth, & Wilson, 1995), while others have found that working students are largely using their income for spending money (Dundes & Marx, 2006–2007), car expenses (Rago et al., 2005), or nonessentials like vacations, clothes, and social events (Lee, Mawdsley, & Rangeley, 1999). Lee et al., however, note that differentiating essential and nonessential expenses is problematic without knowing the details of a student's life. In most of these studies only a small number of students are motivated to work by interest or alignment with future career goals (e.g., Curtis & Williams, Ferguson & Cerinus, Ford et al.). Luzzo, McWhirter, and Hutcheson (1997) found important developmental benefits of this congruence between students' career goals and their college experiences. Further, Loizou (2000), Gleason (1993), and Curtis and Williams note there can be longer term employment benefits for working students, although others discuss contrary findings (Hotz, Xu, Tienda, & Ahituv, 2002). This study builds on these earlier studies to examine further the issues of motivation and engagement in the college experiences of working students.

The Student Engagement Framework for Research
A relatively recent and important addition to the literature on student success in college is the research of Kuh and others on the links between student engagement and student success. Kuh (2003) defines student engagement as "the time and energy students devote to educationally purposeful activities" and as "the single best predictor of [student] learning and personal development" (p. 24). Conceptually, student engagement grows out of the research and theory of several prominent scholars in higher education: Astin (1993), Pascarella and Terenzini (1991), and Pace (1980). Higher levels of engagement among students have been positively linked to gains in critical thinking (Kuh, Hu, & Vesper, 2000; Kuh & Vesper, 1997; Pike, 1999, 2000; Pike, Kuh, & Gonyea, 2003; Terenzini, Pascarella, & Blimling, 1996), in grades (Astin, 1977, 1993), and in persistence (Astin, 1985; Pike, Schroeder, & Berry, 1997).

The student engagement framework also fits well into traditional theories of retention like those of Tinto (1975) and Bean and Metzner (1985) in which students' connection to the university plays a vital role in persistence. This connection develops through a student's engagement on campus. This type of engagement has been operationalized in surveys like the National Survey of Student Engagement (NSSE), which was developed to investigate the extent to which students participate in activities that are signifiers of student-campus relationships (e.g., interacting with faculty and peers, contributing to interactive classroom behaviors, interfacing with people of different backgrounds and beliefs, preparing well for academics, and partaking in educational activities outside the confines of the traditional classroom) as well as to investigate the relationships between these types of interactions and the school environment (Carini, Kuh, & Klein, 2006; Kuh, 2001, 2003; Zhao, Kuh, & Carini, 2005). NSSE has been used with a variety of populations (Gonyea & Moore, 2007; Kuh, Gonyea, & Palmer, 2001; Nelson Laird, Bridges, Salinas Holmes, Morelon, & Williams, 2004; Umbach, Kinzie, Thomas, Palmer, & Kuh, 2007), and NSSE scores have been linked to higher education outcome measures such as GPA and student persistence in college (Kuh, Cruce, Shoup, Kinzie, & Gonyea, 2007; Kuh, Kinzie, Cruce, Shoup, & Gonyea, 2006). Although several of these NSSE studies include working students in their models, none specifically examines the differences between working and nonworking students or the differences between on-campus and off-campus employment.

Methods

Research Questions

This study examines several aspects of the working student experience, specifically addressing the following questions:

1) What are the differences among working students between working on campus and working off campus in the impact on student engagement?

2) Do working students' motivations for working affect the engagement of these students on campus?

Neither of these questions has been addressed in the literature until now. Answers to both have the potential to aid practitioners to better assist students in making more informed decisions about working and to point to practices that would further engage students in their educational environments.

Data Sources and Samples

The data for this study originated in the 2005 administration of NSSE, which is distributed each spring to a random sample of first-year and senior students at participating colleges. As a set of experimental items, the questions about students' motivations for working were distributed to a subset of 30 institutions participating in the larger NSSE project. These schools represent a range of sizes, locations, research orientations, and selectivity. Schools that were midsized (n=10), in the mid-Atlantic (n=8) or the Midwest (n=8) regions, baccalaureate (n=14), and very competitive (n=14) were most common. There were over 6,000 usable student cases and, of these, 64 percent were female, 13 percent were of nontraditional age (over 24 years old), 11 percent were students of color, and 58 percent were seniors.

Variables

The five dependent variables for this study were drawn from the NSSE benchmarks for educational practice. Definitions of these benchmark variables are as follows. Table 3.1a displays a summary of responses to these items.

- Academic Challenge: the extent to which a student feels challenged by in- and out-of-class course work
- Active and Collaborative Learning: the amount of participation a student reports having with other students in and out of the classroom to complete academic work
- Student-Faculty Interaction: the amount and quality of a student's reported contact with faculty on academic and career issues
- Enriching Educational Experiences: the level of a student's involvement in beneficial educational and cocurricular activities such as an internship, community service, or a learning community
- Supportive Campus Environment: the student's rating of the school climate in terms of its support for the student and the quality of the student's relationships with peers, faculty, and staff

Table 3.1a. **Descriptive Statistics for Dependent Variables**

Benchmark Variables	Mean	SD	N
Level of academic challenge	55.348	13.613	6587
Active and collaborative learning	48.440	16.425	6587
Student-faculty interaction	40.551	20.659	6584
Enriching educational experiences	38.481	17.728	6581
Supportive campus environment	59.446	18.458	6584

Independent variables at both the institutional and student levels were included in the analysis. Institutional-level variables included control (public or private), selectivity, urbanicity, Carnegie classification, percentage of students on financial aid, tuition, and size. Table 3.1b displays a data summary for the institutional-level independent variables.

At the student level (Table 3.1c), variables included measures of a student's background and characteristics (i.e., gender, age, parental education, race/ethnicity, and SAT/ ACT score) and collegiate experiences (i.e., transfer and enrollment statuses, Greek life participation, athletics participation, class rank, and major).

Table 3.1b. **Descriptive Statistics for Independent Variables—Institutional-Level Variables**

Institutional-Level Variables	Mean	SD	N
Public	0.556	0.497	6587
Selectivity	3.794	0.757	6587
Urbanicity	3.022	1.848	6587
Carnegie: Doctoral	0.344	0.475	6587
Carnegie: Baccalaureate	0.211	0.408	6587
Carnegie: Master's	0.412	0.492	6587
Carnegie: Other	0.144	0.351	6587
% of Students on Financial Aid	85.928	11.088	6587
In-State Tuition	16.619	8.284	6587
Out-of-State Tuition	20.204	5.228	6587
Total Size	8.012	8.512	6587

Variables related to students working (Table 3.1d) included the number of hours worked as well as whether the work was on or off campus. Regarding students' motivations for working, variables with specific reasons for working were added: to pay for tuition, to pay for books and supplies, to pay back education-related debt, to pay for living expenses (rent, utilities, food), to pay for transportation expenses (auto loans, gas, repair, bus or train costs), to gain experience, to meet an academic requirement, to support family members, to comply with parent/family demand, to pay for entertainment/social expenses (clothes, music, dining out, cable TV), to continue a job held prior to college, to pay back noneducation debt, and to increase savings. Responses for the motivation items were scored on a 6-point Likert scale, ranging from 1 (not at all important) to 6 (very important).

Analysis

The first research question, regarding the differences in impact on student engagement between working on campus and working off campus, was addressed through a series of parallel regressions: one set for students working on campus and one set for students working off campus. A pair of regressions was run for each of the five benchmark variables. Predictor variables in the model included the individual and institutional characteristics found in Tables 1a and 1b as well as the information about number of hours worked. The parallel regressions allowed for a comparison of effects of on-campus versus off-campus employment on student engagement; students who worked both on and off campus were not included in the models.

Table 3.1c. Descriptive Statistics for Independent Variables—Student Background and Characteristics Variables

Student Background and Characteristics Variables	Mean	SD	N
Male	1.635	0.481	6587
Age	1.837	0.917	6579
Transfer Status	1.214	0.410	6587
Greek Life Membership	1.136	0.343	6586
Student-Athlete	1.090	0.286	6585
Enrollment Status	1.926	0.262	6584
Father's Education	3.863	1.756	6545
Mother's Education	3.792	1.596	6559
Race/ethnicity: Other	0.041	0.198	6587
Race/ethnicity: Asian	0.041	0.198	6587
Race/ethnicity: African American	0.042	0.200	6587
Race/ethnicity: Latino	0.044	0.204	6587
Race/ethnicity: White	0.766	0.424	6587
Race/ethnicity: Missing	0.068	0.251	6587
Combined SAT Score	1135.9	157.2	4349
Class Rank	2.724	1.483	6587
Major: Biological Sciences	0.072	0.259	6587
Major: Business	0.159	0.366	6587
Major: Education	0.102	0.302	6587
Major: Engineering	0.090	0.286	6587
Major: Humanities	0.156	0.363	6587
Major: Physical Sciences	0.037	0.188	6587
Major: Preprofessional	0.071	0.256	6587
Major: Social Sciences	0.137	0.344	6587
Major: Undecided	0.021	0.143	6587

Table 3.1d. **Descriptive Statistics for Independent Variables—Variables Related to Students Working**

Variables Related to Students Working	Mean	SD	N
Off-campus Work: 0 Hours	0.506	0.500	6587
Off-campus Work: 1-5 Hours	0.100	0.300	6587
Off-campus Work: 6-10 Hours	0.203	0.402	6587
Off-campus Work: 11-15 Hours	0.103	0.304	6587
Off-campus Work: 16-20 Hours	0.053	0.224	6587
Off-campus Work: 21-25 Hours	0.018	0.133	6587
Off-campus Work: 26-30 Hours	0.007	0.081	6587
Off-campus Work: 31+ Hours	0.011	0.104	6587
On-campus Work: 0 Hours	0.366	0.482	6587
On-campus Work: 1-5 Hours	0.081	0.273	6587
On-campus Work: 6-10 Hours	0.101	0.301	6587
On-campus Work: 11-15 Hours	0.103	0.303	6587
On-campus Work: 16-20 Hours	0.122	0.327	6587
On-campus Work: 21-25 Hours	0.075	0.263	6587
On-campus Work: 26-30 Hours	0.049	0.216	6587
On-campus Work: 31+ Hours	0.104	0.305	6587
Motivation: Tuition and Fees	3.832	2.017	6587
Motivation: Books/Supplies	4.215	1.843	6573
Motivation: Education Debt	3.742	1.990	6539
Motivation: Living Expenses	4.356	1.805	6564
Motivation: Transportation	4.404	1.796	6567
Motivation: Experience	3.623	1.905	6557
Motivation: Academic Requirement	2.337	1.832	6543
Motivation: Support Family	2.433	1.939	6560
Motivation: Parents Demand	2.516	1.769	6535
Motivation: Social/Entertainment	3.936	1.674	6540
Motivation: Job Prior to College	2.321	1.824	6523
Motivation: Noneducation Debt	2.992	1.981	6527
Motivation: Savings	4.029	1.851	6540

To address the second research question, regarding the effects of students' motivations for working on their student engagement, parallel regressions were again run for on-campus and off-campus employment. In addition to all the predictors listed above, the variables related to students' motivations for working were added to the models. For both analyses, the students' time spent working was added as a series of dummy variables to capture potential changes by the number of hours at work, with 16 to 20 hours per week as the reference group.

Results

Working Students and Student Engagement

The models of students who worked on campus and of those who worked off campus (Table 3.2) produced quite similar results and indicated that working had only a marginal impact on students' engagement in college. The five benchmarks, as in other studies of engagement, were found to be highly related to the institutional factors and the factors regarding students' backgrounds, characteristics, and behaviors—once these factors were controlled for, hours spent working were only influential in the extreme positions on two of the benchmarks. Students not working on campus at all (as compared to students working 16 to 20 hours a week on campus) were significantly less involved in active and collaborative learning activities. Students who worked on campus 1 to 5 hours a week perceived the campus environment as significantly more supportive than those who worked on campus 16 to 20 hours a week. Students' perceptions of the supportiveness of the campus environment were also affected by the extreme values for those working off campus. Compared to students working 16 to 20 hours a week off campus, students not working at all off campus rated the campus significantly more supportive, and those working more than 31 hours a week off campus saw the campus environment as significantly less supportive. In terms of other characteristics, students at smaller, private, and more selective schools were generally more engaged. Full-time students, those involved in Greek life, seniors, and minority students were also more engaged.

Student major was also an important factor in student engagement. There was no consistent pattern to the impact of one's major on engagement: compared to arts and humanities majors, students majoring in pre-professional fields had higher scores on supportive campus environment and lower scores on enriching educational experiences, while those in education saw the campus as more supportive and were more likely to engage in active and collaborative learning activities when compared to arts and science majors. The one consistent predictor was being undecided about one's major. Students in this group scored lower on all five of the benchmarks.

Working Students' Motivation and Engagement

There were some noteworthy, although not entirely unexpected, differences between the mean level of importance respondents placed on motivation for working based on whether they worked on campus or off (Figures 1a and 1b). Off-campus workers ranked transportation needs, living expenses, and savings as their three top motivations for working. On-campus workers listed books and supplies, living expenses, and entertainment as most important. As motivations for working for both on-campus and off-campus workers, educationally related expenses were all similarly important, as reflected in the mean scores on these items: tuition (3.77 on-campus, 3.80 off-campus), books and supplies (4.20 on-campus, 4.14 off-campus), and education debt (3.63 on-campus, 3.70 off-campus). The greatest differences between on-campus and off-campus workers in motivations for working were in transportation expenses (3.72 on-campus, 4.80 off-campus), continuing in a job held prior to college (1.63 on-campus, 2.77 off-campus), and noneducation debt (2.48 on-campus, 3.26 off-campus), with off-campus workers ranking each of these as more important. Those employed off campus, in fact, rated each motivation—with the exception of books and supplies—as more important than the on-campus workers did.

When entered into the regression equation, student motivation for working affected several of the benchmark scores (Table 3.3). For example, students who worked off campus and who were more motivated to work to pay for books and supplies reported experiencing higher levels of academic challenge and saw the campus as more supportive. Those that worked on campus reported higher levels of active and collaborative learning. Many of the motivations, however, had no impact on engagement. The one striking exception was students who were motivated to work to gain experience in their field. Whether working on campus or off campus, these students reported higher levels of engagement in all five benchmarks.

Discussion

This study examines the relationships among institutional and student characteristics, working patterns, motivations for work, and engagement across a random sample of several thousand college students around the country.

Table 3.2. Regression Results for Research Question 1: What are the differences among working students between working on campus and working off campus in the impact on student engagement?

	Level of Academic Challenge				Active and Collaborative Learning				Student-Faculty Interaction				Enriching Educational Experiences				Supportive Campus Environment			
	Off Campus		On Campus		Off Campus		On Campus		Off Campus		On Campus		Off Campus		On Campus		Off Campus		On Campus	
	B	Sig.	B	Sig.	B	Sig.	B	Sig.	B	Sig.	B	Sig.	B	Sig.	B	Sig.	B	Sig.	B	Sig.
Public	3.13	*	3.41	*	4.69	**	4.41	*	5.66	**	4.64	*	8.27	***	8.49	***	11.62	***	9.94	***
Selectivity	3.08	***	3.16	***	1.19	*	1.10		1.46	*	0.77		2.49	***	1.79	***	2.73	***	2.46	***
Urbanicity	0.39	*	0.28		-0.47	*	-0.11		-0.33		-0.33		-0.35		-0.16		-0.62	*	-0.41	
Carnegie: Doctoral	-0.38		1.50		1.81		2.63		-0.07		3.60	*	2.49	*	2.60	*	-4.12	**	-1.66	
Carnegie: Baccalaureate	0.15		0.22		1.81		0.06		0.83		1.00		3.32	***	1.67		3.19	**	2.57	*
Carnegie: Other	-2.58	***	-2.40	**	-0.18		-1.09		-2.13	*	-3.86	***	-1.94	*	-3.36	***	1.58		0.77	
% Students on Financial Aid	-0.05	*	-0.04		-0.04		-0.08	**	-0.01		-0.02		0.00		0.00		0.08	*	0.14	***
In-State Ttuition	0.10		0.24		-0.37		-0.04		-0.24		0.09		-0.30		-0.26		-0.78	**	-0.43	
Out-of-State Tuition	-0.02		0.27		0.36		-0.03		0.16		-0.21		0.12		0.05		0.50		-0.01	

Table 3.2 (continued). **Regression Results for Research Question 1: What are the differences among working students between working on campus and working off campus in the impact on student engagement?**

| | Level of Academic Challenge | | | | Active and Collaborative Learning | | | | Student-Faculty Interaction | | | | Enriching Educational Experiences | | | | Supportive Campus Environment | | | |
| | Off Campus | | On Campus | | Off Campus | | On Campus | | Off Campus | | On Campus | | Off Campus | | On Campus | | Off Campus | | On Campus | |
	B	Sig.	B	Sig.	B	Sig.	B	Sig.	B	Sig.	B	Sig.	B	Sig.	B	Sig.	B	Sig.	B	Sig.
Total Size	-0.06		-0.10	**	-0.35	***	-0.32	***	-0.21	***	-0.26	***	0.03		0.01		0.06		0.01	
Male	1.70	***	2.56	***	0.22		0.18		0.11		0.44		2.02	***	2.55	***	1.19	*	1.04	
Age	-0.26		-0.60		-0.64		-0.12		-0.57		-1.45		-1.41	*	-3.22	**	0.44		-1.83	
Transfer Status	0.42		-0.03		-0.94		-0.91		-0.57		0.05		-2.10	**	-2.19	*	-1.86	*	-1.06	
Greek Life Membership	0.00		1.34	*	3.49	***	3.03	***	2.94	***	3.56	***	4.42	***	4.33	***	2.33	**	2.64	***
Student-Athlete	-1.26	*	-1.22	*	-0.26		-0.44		0.17		-0.47		2.95	***	1.62	**	1.48		0.52	
Enrollment Status	4.77	***	3.25	*	5.06	***	3.57		2.86		1.62		4.96	***	4.82	**	3.23	*	2.48	
Father's Education	0.13		0.11		0.17		-0.03		0.06		0.16		0.07		0.15		-0.02		0.20	
Mother's Education	0.12		0.15		0.12		0.47	**	0.20		0.37		0.27		0.35	*	0.15		-0.02	

Table 3.2 (continued). Regression Results for Research Question 1: What are the differences among working students between working on campus and working off campus in the impact on student engagement?

	Level of Academic Challenge				Active and Collaborative Learning				Student-Faculty Interaction				Enriching Educational Experiences				Supportive Campus Environment			
	Off Campus		On Campus		Off Campus		On Campus		Off Campus		On Campus		Off Campus		On Campus		Off Campus		On Campus	
	B	Sig.	B	Sig.	B	Sig.	B	Sig.	B	Sig.	B	Sig.	B	Sig.	B	Sig.	B	Sig.	B	Sig.
Race: Other	2.67	*	2.39	*	1.59		2.91	*	2.81		4.10	*	3.14	**	4.13	***	-0.14		-1.23	
Race: Asian	-0.17		0.70		-0.28		0.29		-0.31		0.03		1.56		2.00		0.44		1.22	
Race: African American	0.11		1.51		2.98	*	3.67	**	2.19		6.08	***	4.28	**	5.92	***	-0.90		-0.33	
Race: Latino	1.02		1.70		1.34		1.86		2.32		3.42	*	6.11	***	6.71	***	4.49	**	3.79	*
Race: Missing	-1.20		-1.00		-0.26		0.35		-0.50		1.12		-0.34		0.83		-7.02	***	-6.31	***
Combined SAT Score	-0.01	***	0.00	**	0.00	***	0.00		-0.01	***	-0.01	*	0.01	***	0.01	***	-0.01	***	-0.01	***
Class Rank	0.72	**	0.83	*	2.62	***	2.59	***	3.57	***	4.28	***	5.44	***	6.47	***	-1.39	***	-0.59	
Major: Biological Sciences	1.29		0.92		0.62		0.53		1.63		0.31		-1.01		-1.48		1.74		1.43	

Table 3.2 (continued). Regression Results for Research Question 1: What are the differences among working students between working on campus and working off campus in the impact on student engagement?

| | Level of Academic Challenge | | | | Active and Collaborative Learning | | | | Student-Faculty Interaction | | | | Enriching Educational Experiences | | | | Supportive Campus Environment | | | |
| | Off Campus | | On Campus | | Off Campus | | On Campus | | Off Campus | | On Campus | | Off Campus | | On Campus | | Off Campus | | On Campus | |
	B	Sig.	B	Sig.	B	Sig.	B	Sig.	B	Sig.	B	Sig.	B	Si g.	B	Sig.	B	Sig.	B	Sig.
Major: Business	-2.22	**	-2.19	**	0.67		0.80		-1.93	*	-2.14	*	-2.87	***	-3.16	***	2.41	*	2.32	*
Major: Education	0.09		0.70		4.24	***	5.07	***	-0.89		1.17		-0.69		-0.64		2.58	*	3.16	**
Major: Engineering	0.79		1.80	*	1.52		3.02	**	-3.37	**	-3.44	**	-2.99	**	-2.49	**	4.63	***	4.40	***
Major: Physical Sciences	-1.09		-0.71		-2.67		0.19		-0.73		0.08		-4.39	***	-4.08	***	1.48		4.18	**
Major: Preprofessional	1.57		0.45		0.47		0.94		-1.06		-2.31		-2.37	**	-2.49	*	2.53	*	3.63	**
Major: Social Sciences	0.98		0.30		-0.64		-0.81		0.68		-0.64		-2.04	*	-1.72	*	0.35		0.34	
Major: Undecided	-3.73	**	-2.98	*	-3.91	**	-5.17	***	-6.79	***	-7.10	***	-6.61	***	-6.02	***	-2.84		-0.58	
Work: 0 Hours	-0.27		-0.14		-0.76		-4.59	***	-0.10		-2.52		-0.89		-2.10		1.89	*	0.21	

Table 3.2 (continued). **Regression Results for Research Question 1: What are the differences among working students between working on campus and working off campus in the impact on student engagement?**

| | Level of Academic Challenge | | | | Active and Collaborative Learning | | | | Student-Faculty Interaction | | | | Enriching Educational Experiences | | | | Supportive Campus Environment | | | |
| | Off Campus | | On Campus | | Off Campus | | On Campus | | Off Campus | | On Campus | | Off Campus | | On Campus | | Off Campus | | On Campus | |
	B	Sig.	B	Sig.	B	Sig.	B	Sig.	B	Sig.	B	Sig.	B	Sig.	B	Sig.	B	Sig.	B	Sig.
Work: 1-5 Hours	-0.32		-0.43		0.19		-0.90		2.25		1.37		-1.03		0.35		1.80		3.29	*
Work: 6-10 Hours	-0.45		-0.40		0.61		-2.37		2.55		1.06		0.48		-0.63		2.22		2.77	
Work: 11-15 Hours	-0.27		0.35		0.26		-0.90		0.05		2.65		-0.68		0.35		-0.26		2.48	
Work: 21-25 Hours	0.80		0.63		0.83		-1.28		-0.31		-0.85		-0.30		-0.26		-1.00		-1.57	
Work: 26-30 Hours	1.13		-0.52		1.60		-3.86		1.21		-5.20		1.24		-3.41		0.10		-1.57	
Work: 31+ Hours	-1.84		-1.58		-0.50		-2.21		-1.73		0.35		-1.63		4.96		-4.03	**	2.97	

Figure 3.1a. Mean Score for Motivation Items: On-Campus Employees

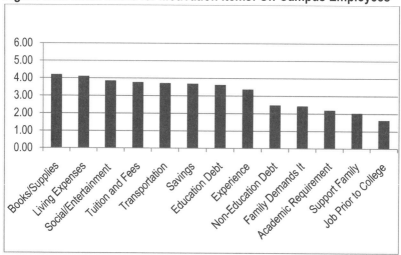

Figure 3.1b. Mean Score for Motivation Items: Off-Campus Employees

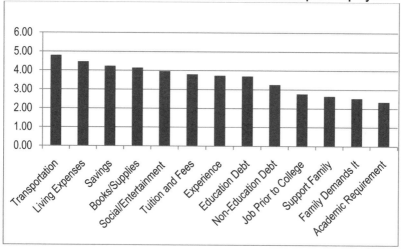

The study's findings generally support the growing body of multi-institutional research suggesting that working does not necessarily have a negative impact on student success in college. In fact, in most cases it appears that even working many hours a week does not impact a student's engagement on campus. Although this finding does not speak directly to a working student's retention or success, the close relationship between engagement and these other measures points to an association between the two that would suggest similar findings.

Table 3.3. Regression Results for Research Question 2: Do working students' motivations for working affect the engagement of these students on campus?

| | Level of Academic Challenge | | | | Active and Collaborative Learning | | | | Student-Faculty Interaction | | | | Enriching Educational Experiences | | | | Supportive Campus Environment | | | |
| | Off Campus | | On Campus | | Off Campus | | On Campus | | Off Campus | | On Campus | | Off Campus | | On Campus | | Off Campus | | On Campus | |
	B	Sig.	B	Sig.	B	Sig.	B	Sig.	B	Sig.	B	Sig.	B	Sig.	B	Sig.	B	Sig.	B	Sig.
Public	2.23		4.92		2.97		4.25		3.6		4.93		8	**	9.4	**	10.44	**	8.51	*
Selectivity	3.14	***	3.34	***	2.04	**	1.52		2.11	*	1.13		3.4	***	2.59	**	2.96	***	3.21	**
Urbanicity	0.6	*	0.35		-0.62		0.35		-0.27		-0.26		-0.39		0.14		-0.94	*	-0.49	
Carnegie: Doctoral	-0.91		3.7		2.28		4.69		-3.01		5.83		3.26	*	3.08		-3.75		5.68	*
Carnegie: Baccalaureate	1.79		0.76		4.82	**	-1.99		1.68		0.28		5.72	***	-0.46		7.36	***	2.87	
Carnegie: Other	-2.08		-1.92		1.5		-1.77		-0.26		-5.11	**	-0.45		-4.32	***	1.99		-0.23	
% Students on Financial Aid	-0.03		-0.04		0		-0.15	**	0.05		-0.03		-0.01		-0.01		0.08		0.15	*
In-State Tuition	0.08		0.34		-0.17		0.54		-0.12		0.52		-0.29		-0.14		-0.7		0.25	

Table 3.3 (continued). Regression Results for Research Question 2: Do working students' motivations for working affect the engagement of these students on campus?

| | Level of Academic Challenge | | | | Active and Collaborative Learning | | | | Student-Faculty Interaction | | | | Enriching Educational Experiences | | | | Supportive Campus Environment | | | |
| | Off Campus | | On Campus | | Off Campus | | On Campus | | Off Campus | | On Campus | | Off Campus | | On Campus | | Off Campus | | On Campus | |
	B	Sig.	B	Sig.	B	Sig.	B	Sig.	B	Sig.	B	Sig.	B	Sig.	B	Sig.	B	Sig.	B	Sig.
Out-of-State tuition	0.15		-0.51		0.24		-0.76		0.18		-0.77		0.17		-0.1		0.63		-0.91	
Total Size	-0.01		-0.14	*	-0.33	***	-0.33	***	-0.1		-0.27	**	0.05	*	-0.03		0.09		-0.19	*
Male	0.36		2.81	***	0.24		-0.38		-1.63		-0.83		1.66		3.13	***	1.29		1.08	
Age	-0.54		-3.39	*	-0.91		-2.86		-0.23		-4.44		-0.58		-5.7	**	2.57	*	-1.16	
Transfer Status	0.72		-0.28		-1.41		-0.4		-2.03		-1.77		-2.71	**	-2.14		-3.08	*	-2.88	
Greek Life Membership	0.31		3.08	***	3.09	**	1.61		2.59		3.53	**	3.84	***	3.48	***	0.79		1.16	
Student-Athlete	-0.41		-0.74		0.51		0.3		2.67		0		4.77	***	1.05		2.84		0.04	
Enrollment Status	4.9	**	3.02		5.78	***	5.35		2.57		-1.21		5.07	**	4.78		3.12		3.33	

Table 3.3 (continued). Regression Results for Research Question 2: Do working students' motivations for working affect the engagement of these students on campus?

	Level of Academic Challenge				Active and Collaborative Learning				Student-Faculty Interaction				Enriching Educational Experiences				Supportive Campus Environment			
	Off Campus		On Campus		Off Campus		On Campus		Off Campus		On Campus		Off Campus		On Campus		Off Campus		On Campus	
	B	Sig.	B	Sig.	B	Sig.	B	Sig.	B	Sig.	B	Sig.	B	Sig.	B	Sig.	B	Sig.	B	Sig.
Father's Education	0.25	*	0.09		0.55	*	-0.02		0.18		0.53		0.21		0.38		-0.06		0.39	
Mother's Education	0.25		0.2		-0.09		0.77	**	-0.08		0.07		0.08		0.08		0.22		-0.27	
Race/Ethnicity: Other	3.47		1.23		1.72		5.03		2.7		4.81		2.47		3.31		2.01		-2.16	
Race/Ethnicity: Asian	-2.28		0.62		-0.97		1.92		-2.87		-0.74		1.56		4.48	*	-3.52		-1.7	
Race/Ethnicity: African Amer.	-1.25		1.99		3.01		3.7	*	-2.59		5.9	*	2.77		6.62	***	-2.96		-0.76	
Race/Ethnicity: Latino	-0.13		-0.2		-0.07		0.23		-1.28		0.34		3.2		3.53		2.31		-0.46	
Race/ethnicity: Missing	-0.65		0.29		0.69		3.24	*	-1.07		3.54		-0.9		2.11		-7.7	***	-6.22	***

Table 3.3 (continued). Regression Results for Research Question 2: Do working students' motivations for working affect the engagement of these students on campus?

	Level of Academic Challenge				Active and Collaborative Learning				Student-Faculty Interaction				Enriching Educational Experiences				Supportive Campus Environment			
	Off Campus		On Campus		Off Campus		On Campus		Off Campus		On Campus		Off Campus		On Campus		Off Campus		On Campus	
	B	Sig.	B	Sig.	B	Sig.	B	Sig.	B	Sig.	B	Sig.	B	Sig.	B	Sig.	B	Sig.	B	Sig.
Combined SAT Score	0	*	0		0		0		-0.01	***	0		0.01	**	0.01	*	-0.01	***	-0.01	
Class Rank	0.92		1.77	**	3.04	***	3.96	***	3.83	***	6.01	***	5.14	***	7.69	***	-1.65	**	-0.09	
Major: Biological Sciences	1.7		0.92		0.2		-0.41		5.06	*	0.88		-1.16		-2.25		1.05		1.35	
Major: Business	-1.95		-2.19		2.01		1.5		-1.97		-3.46	*	-1.68		-2.89	*	2.53		2.53	
Major: Education	0.72		1.96		4.57	**	4.86	**	-2.35		0.85		0.11		-0.32		1.96		3.38	
Major: Engineering	-0.12		3.12	*	0.53		4.17	*	-1.04		-0.67		-3.88	*	-1.07		4.92	*	5.15	**

Table 3.3 (continued). Regression Results for Research Question 2: Do working students' motivations for working affect the engagement of these students on campus?

| | Level of Academic Challenge | | | | Active and Collaborative Learning | | | | Student-Faculty Interaction | | | | Enriching Educational Experiences | | | | Supportive Campus Environment | | | |
| | Off Campus | | On Campus | | Off Campus | | On Campus | | Off Campus | | On Campus | | Off Campus | | On Campus | | Off Campus | | On Campus | |
	B	Sig.	B	Sig.	B	Sig.	B	Sig.	B	Sig.	B	Sig.	B	Sig.	B	Sig.	B	Sig.	B	Sig.
Major: Physical Sciences	-1.5		-1.05		-3.16		1.12		2.11		2.03		-1.93		-2.87		-1.74		4.29	*
Major: Pre-professional	1.43		-1.18		-0.84		0.33		-2.15		-6.15	*	-3.04	*	-4.21	*	0.18		2.69	
Major: Social Sciences	1.93		0.48		0.7		-0.82		1.8		-1.54		0.09		0.15		-0.11		0.1	
Major: Undecided	-4.67	*	-3.85		-0.3		-7.32	**	-4.7		-5.66		-4.58	*	-3.96		-1.17		3.37	
Work: 0 Hours	1.36		0.21		2.64		-3.79		3.34		-1.11		2.89		2.25		5.05		2.08	
Work: 1–5 Hours	0.02		-0.15		0.17		-0.31		2.5		0.37		-0.97		0.29		1.82		2.63	
Work: 6–10 Hours	0.09		-0.26		0.73		-1.53		2.8		1.02		0.86		-0.59		1.57		2.69	

Table 3.3 (continued). Regression Results for Research Question 2: Do working students' motivations for working affect the engagement of these students on campus?

	Level of Academic Challenge				Active and Collaborative Learning				Student-Faculty Interaction				Enriching Educational Experiences				Supportive Campus Environment			
	Off Campus		On Campus		Off Campus		On Campus		Off Campus		On Campus		Off Campus		On Campus		Off Campus		On Campus	
	B	Sig.	B	Sig.	B	Sig.	B	Sig.	B	Sig.	B	Sig.	B	Sig.	B	Sig.	B	Sig.	B	Sig.
Work: 11–15 Hours	0.14		0.48		0.39		-0.38		0.57		2.54		-0.59		0.37		0.1		2.67	
Work: 21–25 Hours	0.58		0.38		-0.07		-0.84		-0.81		-2.03		-0.64		-0.73		-1.24		-1.77	
Work: 26–30 Hours	1.06		-1.56		1.19		-6.52		1.33		-10.64	*	1.11		-7.52	*	0.41		-2.94	
Work: 31+ Hours	-2.25		-0.19		-1.22		-0.56	*	-2.38		-0.1		-2.08		6.05		-4.64	**	3.88	
Motiva-tion: Tuition and Fees	-0.62	*	0.1		0.08		0.03		-0.33		-0.38		-0.21		-0.52		-1.31	**	-0.36	
Motiva-tion: Books/ Supplies	0.6	*	0.31		0.54		0.79		0.65		0.21		0.4		0.53		1.3	**	0.4	
Motiva-tion: Edu-cation Debt	0.71	*	0.14		0.02		-0.29		0.17		0.49		0.01		-0.18		0.31		0.17	

Table 3.3 (continued). Regression Results for Research Question 2: Do working students' motivations for working affect the engagement of these students on campus?

| | Level of Academic Challenge | | | | Active and Collaborative Learning | | | | Student-Faculty Interaction | | | | Enriching Educational Experiences | | | | Supportive Campus Environment | | | |
| | Off Campus | | On Campus | | Off Campus | | On Campus | | Off Campus | | On Campus | | Off Campus | | On Campus | | Off Campus | | On Campus | |
	B	Sig.	B	Sig.	B	Sig.	B	Sig.	B	Sig.	B	Sig.	B	Sig.	B	Sig.	B	Sig.	B	Sig.
Motivation: Living Expenses	0.01	*	-0.2		-0.07		-0.17		-0.22		-0.4		0.01		-0.1		-0.62	*	-0.64	*
Motivation: Transportation	0.29		0.04		0.13		0.29		0.15	*	0.12		0.35		0.21		-0.27		-0.4	
Motivation: Experience	0.49	*	0.71	***	0.62	**	0.77	**	1.11	***	1.61	***	0.98	***	0.86	***	0.75	**	1.29	***
Motivation: Academic Requirement	-0.02		-0.36		0.48		-0.24		0.71	*	0		0.47		-0.59	*	0.75	*	-0.17	
Motivation: Support Family	0.01		0.22		-0.15		-0.14		-0.09		-0.08		-0.3		0.3		-0.29		0.1	

Table 3.3 (continued). Regression Results for Research Question 2: Do working students' motivations for working affect the engagement of these students on campus?

	Level of Academic Challenge				Active and Collaborative Learning				Student-Faculty Interaction				Enriching Educational Experiences				Supportive Campus Environment			
	Off Campus		On Campus		Off Campus		On Campus		Off Campus		On Campus		Off Campus		On Campus		Off Campus		On Campus	
	B	Sig.	B	Sig.	B	Sig.	B	Sig.	B	Sig.	B	Sig.	B	Sig.	B	Sig.	B	Sig.	B	Sig.
Motivation: Parents Demand	0.19		0.16		0.08		0.02		0.28		-0.45		0.21		-0.03		0.01		0.23	
Motivation: Social	-0.17		0.06		0.11		0.24		-0.04		0.04		0.08		0.13		0.36		0.61	*
Motivation: Prior Job	0.17		-0.13		0.19		0.62		0.09		0.76		-0.16		-0.19		0.11		0.59	
Motivation: Noneducation Debt	-0.02		0.23		0.28		0.02		-0.06		0.27		-0.09		-0.03		0.41		0.01	
Motivation: Savings	0.14		0.22		-0.41		-0.08		-0.51		-0.11		-0.37		0.05		0.13		0.13	

Note. * p < .05, ** p < .01, *** p < .001.

A regression identical to that answering the first research question, which had self-reported GPA (one measure of students' success) as the dependent variable, indicated that only working off campus more than 35 hours a week (when compared to working off campus 16 to 20 hours a week) had a significant, negative impact on students' reported academic performance ($\beta = -.355$, $p<.005$).

Overall, this study's results mirror those of Kuh and associates, finding that institutional characteristics (e.g., size, selectivity, control) and student characteristics (e.g., gender, age, enrollment status, Greek life membership) have more influence on a student's engagement than working has. When students' motivations were added to the model, however, a new strong predictor emerged. Students motivated to work by a desire to gain experience in a field were more likely to have higher levels of engagement in each of NSSE's five benchmarks—even when significant school and personal attributes were controlled for.

This study may also shed light on findings from previous research that working students may have better employment prospects after college (Curtis & Williams, 2002; Gleason, 1993; Luzzo et al., 1997). Students who are not only gaining employment experience but also actively making connections between work and school would understandably be more attractive to prospective employers. Perhaps such fostered connections can be productively examined within the context of the linkages between motivation and engagement among working students.

Limitations and Future Research

Further exploration of these findings would be valuable along several lines. First, although diverse institutions were represented in this study, smaller, more selective, private, liberal arts schools were overrepresented. Increasing the representation of larger, public, research-orientated universities would enable a more complete understanding of the impact of students' working.

Another interesting line of research would be to cultivate a better understanding of the motivations for student employment. This study asked students only about how important each factor was in their decision to work. Having students rank items and then applying nonparametric analyses could be productive. Exploring differences in motivation by demographic factors would be particularly useful, for example, to gain understanding about the types of students more likely to connect student employment with future career interests—and the current data set provides some interesting lines to pursue in that regard. Transfer students, Asian and Latina/o students, seniors, and those with higher levels of paternal education were more motivated to work by the connection between student employment and future career interests, while students with higher SAT scores and those majoring in education and the social sciences (compared to the arts and humanities) were less likely to find that motivator important. A deeper exploration could reveal other influences on aspects of motivation.

Another limitation of this study was that it could not explore students' understandings of their motivations. For example, what kinds of connections do students think will be made between work and school? How do students conceptualize their expenses or sort out noneducational from educational debt? Questions like these could be productively explored with students through a qualitative method of inquiry. The model implemented in the study by Hernandez, Ziskin, Gross, Fashola, and Rago (2007), in which they conducted focus groups with working students at a set of urban regional colleges, could be a template for such research. A sharper picture of student motivation from this perspective would serve to create more refined quantitative assessments, better overall models, and richer understandings for those who interact with students.

Implications for Practice

The finding that students who make connections between their present employment and their future work are more engaged on campus is consonant with theory and has important practical implications for individuals who interact with students. That students who are intentional about working and who make connections between their work and their future are likely also intentional in their other activities may provide a window of opportunity for individuals trying to get students more engaged in college life (Chickering, 1969).

Although there may be a common cause of student engagement and motivation for working, it may be possible to help working students to better understand the connections between working and their future careers as well as between career goals and other aspects of their college experience. Tying considerations about current employment to future career aspirations epitomizes what Sedlacek (2004) calls the preference of long-term over short-term goals.

Tracey and Sedlacek (1987, 1988, 1989) have demonstrated that this preference for long-term goals is one of a set of noncognitive characteristics strongly associated with student persistence and success, particularly for minority students. Sedlacek, further, has provided evidence that these non-cognitive characteristics, including the preference for long-term goals, can be cultivated in students (2004; Westbrook & Sedlacek, 1988). This would be especially beneficial in working students less motivated by future career connections.

There are many opportunities to engage students in this effort. First, those that interact with students in advising capacities—faculty, advisors, tutors, and career counseling staff, for example—can help cultivate this preference in students. Several scholars have demonstrated the important role that faculty, serving in an advising role, can have on the occupational and educational decisions of students (Astin & Panos, 1969; Pascarella, 1984; Pascarella, Terenzini, & Hibel, 1978); for example, they can press students on their motivations for work and assist them in making connections between current activities, including work, and future goals. This kind of self-reflection and guided questioning has been shown to be effective in changing student attitudes, self-perceptions, and behaviors in service-learning (Parker-Gwin & Mabry, 1998), career counseling (Meara, Day, Chalk, & Phelps, 1995), leadership development (Cress, Astin, Zimmerman-Oster, & Burkhardt, 2001), and tutoring scenarios (Chi, 1996). To use similar techniques in motivating students to connect current activities to future goals seems promising. Faculty, too, can connect class learning to these same skills (Bradshaw, 1985; Kemp & Seagraves, 1995).

Second, individuals and groups on campus who employ large numbers of students—at the student union, in student activities, and in residence life, for example—can also have a role in helping working students connect their work to their future goals. Even work that is not directly related to a student's future career may be teaching valuable, transferable skills that would be useful in a number of careers. Assisting students to identify these skills and then explicitly and intentionally assigning them work that cultivates those competencies would not only assist them in the future but would begin habituating them to think that way about their academic career (Haigh & Kilmartin, 1999). Employers, also, can structure position descriptions, job responsibilities, and evaluations to conform to a skill development profile (Moore & Rago, 2007a). Allen (2006) outlines a process for thinking about on-campus student employment in just such a way and identifies a common set of abilities for creating a language around those skills (e.g., implementation, initiative, tolerance for risk, situational analysis, relationship building). Educating students on the transferable nature of skills across jobs may begin to orient them away from the short-term benefits of their current positions and toward a more forward-looking perspective.

Third, information on this long-term, skills-based orientation could be provided to off-campus employers of significant numbers of students. Additionally, as many college and university career centers host job postings through their offices, employers advertising for student workers through such a site could be asked—in the process of posting their positions—to indicate both the expected competencies for starting the position and additional competencies to be developed through work in a given position. This would provide students working off campus the same structures for development as on-campus workers. Encouraging students to develop a habit of connecting present activities to long-term goals would improve students' chances of succeeding in college and help them better prepare themselves for future employment (Lucas & Lammont, 1998).

As a final note, although this study gains statistical and predictive power due to its large sample size and its multi-institutional perspective, it may not address the specific issues associated with individual campuses. Institutions interested in knowing more about the impact of working and motivation on their own campuses could replicate this study on a smaller scale with their own students, perhaps uncovering local trends or differences that may be masked in a larger sample. Interventions tailored according to detailed, homegrown information could address the needs of a campus's specific student population.

Conclusions

This multi-institutional study sheds needed light on the impact of working and motivations for working on college student engagement. Student engagement, which has been widely examined across a variety of institutional types and student characteristics, has been shown to be associated with greater levels of student retention and success. Generally, this study found that student employment is not a significant benefit to or hindrance on students' ability to be engaged with their institutions. Students' motivations for working, however, do impact engagement. Specifically, students in this study who were motivated to work to gain experience for a future career were found more likely to be highly engaged in respect to all five of NSSE's benchmarks, even when other significant factors such as age, gender, and institutional type were controlled for. The motivation to work to gain experience for a future career demonstrates a form of preference for long-term goals over short-term goals. Institutions may be able to develop interventions that help students cultivate this preference, make these connections during their time at college, and value such connections and develop them in other arenas of their lives. Such interventions could increase students' engagement with their institutions and thereby increase the likelihood of working students' academic success and degree completion.

References

Allen, K. E. (2006). *Student development: Applying theory to student employees*. St. Cloud, MN: Allen and Associates.

Astin, A. W. (1977). *Four critical years*. San Francisco: Jossey-Bass.

Astin, A. W. (1985). The changing American college student. *The Review of Higher Education, 21*(2), 115–135.

Astin, A. W. (1993). *What matters in college? Four critical years revisited*. San Francisco: Jossey-Bass.

Astin, A. W., & Panos, R. (1969). *The educational and vocational development of college students*. Washington, DC: American Council on Education.

Bean, J. P., & Metzner, B. S. (1985). A conceptual model of nontraditional undergraduate student attrition. *Review of Educational Research, 55*(4), 485–540.

Beeson, M. J., & Wessel, R. D. (2002). The impact of working on campus on the academic persistence of freshmen. *NASFAA Journal of Student Financial Aid, 32*(2), 37–45.

Bradley, G. (2006). Work participation and academic performance: A test of alternative propositions. *Journal of Education and Work, 19*(5), 481–501.

Bradshaw, D. (1985). Transferable intellectual and personal skills. *Oxford Review of Education, 11*(2), 201–216.

Canabal, M. E. (1998). College student degree of participation in the labor force: Determinants and relationship to school performance. *College Student Journal, 32*(4), 597–605.

Carini, R. M., Kuh, G. D., & Klein, S. P. (2006). Student engagement and student learning: Testing the linkages. *Research in Higher Education, 47*(1), 1–32.

Chi, M. T. H. (1996). Constructing self-explanations and scaffolded explanations in tutoring. *Applied Cognitive Psychology, 10*, 33–49.

Chickering, A. W. (1969). *Education and identity*. San Francisco: Jossey-Bass.

Choy, S., & Berker, A. (2003). *How families of low- and middle-income undergraduates pay for college: Full-time dependent students in 1999–00* (NCES 2003–162). Washington, DC: U.S. Department of Education, National Center for Education Statistics.

Cress, C. M., Astin, H. S., Zimmerman-Oster, K., & Burkhardt, J. C. (2001). Developmental outcomes of college students' involvement in leadership activities. *Journal of College Student Development, 42*(1), 15–27.

Cuccaro-Alamin, S., & Choy, S. P. (1998). *Postsecondary financing strategies: How undergraduates combine work, borrowing, and attendance*

(NCES 98088). Washington, DC: U.S. Department of Education, National Center for Education Statistics.

Curtis, S., & Shani, N. (2002). The effect of taking paid employment during term-time on students' academic studies. *Journal of Further and Higher Education, 26*(2), 129–138.

Curtis, S., & Williams, J. (2002). The reluctant workforce: Undergraduates' part-time employment. *Education + Training, 44*(1), 5–10.

DesJardins, S. L., Ahlberg, D. A., & McCall, B. P. (2002). A temporal investigation of factors related to timely degree completion. *Journal of Higher Education, 73*(5), 555–581.

Dundes, L., & Marx, J. (2006–2007). Balancing work and academics in college: Why do students working 10 to 19 hours excel? *Journal of College Student Retention, 8*(1), 107–120.

Ferguson, C., & Cerinus, M. (1996). Students in employment: Learning and working. *Nurse Education Today, 16,* 373-375.

Fjortoft, N. F. (1995, April). *College student employment: Opportunity or deterrent?* Paper presented at the annual meeting of the American Education Research Association, San Francisco.

Ford, J., Bosworth, D., & Wilson, R. (1995). Part-time work and full-time higher education. *Studies in Higher Education, 20*(2), 187–202.

Furr, S. R., & Elling, T. W. (2000). The influence of work on college student development. *NASPA Journal, 37*(2), 454–470.

Gleason, P. M. (1993). College student employment, academic progress, and postcollege labor market success. *The Journal of Student Financial Aid, 23*(2), 5–14.

Gonyea, R., & Moore, J., III. (2007, November-December). *Gay, lesbian, bisexual, and transgender students and their engagement in educationally purposeful activities in college.* Paper presented at the annual meeting of the Association for the Study of Higher Education, Louisville, KY.

Haigh, M. J., & Kilmartin, M. P. (1999). Student perceptions of the development of personal transferable skills. *Journal of Geography in Higher Education, 23*(2), 195–206.

Harding, E., & Harmon, L. (1999). *Higher education students' off-campus work patterns.* Olympia, WA: Washington State Institute for Public Policy.

Hernandez, E., Ziskin, M., Gross, J. P. K., Fashola, O., & Rago, M. A. (2007, November-December). *Making meaning of work for undergraduate students who are employed.* Paper presented at the annual meeting of the Association for the Study of Higher Education, Louisville, KY.

Hey, W., Calderon, K. S., & Seabert, D. (2003). Student work issues: Implications for college transition and retention. *The Journal of College Orientation and Transition, 10*(2), 35–41.

High, R. V. (1999). *Employment of college students*. Rockville Center, NY: Molloy College, Department of Mathematics.

Hodgson, A., & Spours, K. (2001). Part-time work and full-time education in the UK: The emergence of a curriculum and policy issue. *Journal of Education and Work, 14,* 373–388.

Hood, A. G., Craig, A. R., & Ferguson, B. W. (1992). The impact of athletics, part-time employment, and other activities on academic achievement. *Journal of College Student Development, 35,* 364–370.

Hotz, V. J., Xu, L. C., Tienda, M., & Ahituv, A. (2002). Are there returns to the wages of young men from working while in school? *The Review of Economics and Statistics, 84*(2), 221–236.

Hunt, A., Lincoln, I., Walker, A. (2004). Term-time employment and academic attainment: Evidence from a large-scale survey of undergraduates at Northumbria University. *Journal of Further and Higher Education, 28*(1), 3–18.

Kemp, I., & Seagraves, L. (1995). Transferable skills—Can higher education deliver? *Studies in Higher Education, 20*(3), 315–328.

King, J. E. (2002). *Crucial choices: How students' financial decisions affect their academic success*. Washington, DC: American Council on Education, Center for Policy Analysis.

King, J. E. (2003). Nontraditional attendance and persistence: The cost of students' choices. In J. E. King, E. L. Anderson, & M. E., Corrigan (Eds.), *Changing student attendance patterns: Challenges for policy and practice: New Directions for Higher Education, No. 121* (pp. 69–83). San Francisco: Jossey-Bass.

Kuh, G. D. (2001). *The National Survey of Student Engagement: Conceptual framework and overview of psychometric properties*. Bloomington, IN: Indiana University, Center for Postsecondary Research.

Kuh, G. D. (2003). What we're learning about student engagement from NSSE. *Change, 35*(2), 24–32.

Kuh, G. D., Cruce, T., Shoup, R., Kinzie, J., & Gonyea, R. M. (2007, April). *Unmasking the effects of student engagement on college grades and persistence*. Paper presented at the annual meeting of the American Educational Research Association, Chicago.

Kuh, G. D., Gonyea, R. M., & Palmer, M. (2001). The disengaged commuter student: Fact or fiction? *Commuter Perspectives, 27*(1), 2–5.

Kuh, G. D., Hu, S., & Vesper, N. (2000). "They shall be known by what they do": An activities-based typology of college students. *Journal of College Student Development, 41(2),* 228–244.

Kuh, G. D., Kinzie, J., Cruce, T., Shoup, R., & Gonyea, R. M. (2006). *Connecting the dots: Multi-faceted analyses of the relationships between student engagement results from the NSSE, and the institutional practices and conditions that foster student success: Final report prepared for Lumina Foundation for Education.* Bloomington, IN: Indiana University, Center for Postsecondary Research.

Kuh, G. D., & Vesper, N. (1997). A comparison of student experiences with good practices in undergraduate education between 1990 and 1994. *Review of Higher Education, 21*(1), 43–61.

Lee, T., Mawdsley, J. M., & Rangeley, H. (1999). Students' part-time work: Towards and understanding of the implications for nurse education. *Nurse Education Today, 19,* 443–451.

Loizou, N. (2000, April 8). Propping up the student bar could help you find a good job: Even working as a bouncer can be useful in your future career. *The Guardian.* Retrieved November 27, 2007, at http://www. guardian.co.uk/money/2000/apr/08/jobsadvice.careers9.

Long, M., & Hayden, M. (2001). *Paying their way: A survey of Australian undergraduate university student finances, 2000.* Canberra, Australia: Australian Vice-Chancellor's Committee.

Lucas, C. J. (1994). *American higher education: A history.* New York: St. Martin's Griffin.

Lucas, R., & Lammont, N. (1998). Combining work and study: an empirical study of full-time students in school, college, and university. *Journal of Education and Work, 11*(1), 41–56.

Lundberg, C. A. (2004). Working and learning: The role of involvement for employed students. *NASPA Journal, 41*(2), 201–215.

Luzzo, D. A., McWhirter, E. H., & Hutcheson, K. G. (1997). Evaluating career decision-making factors associated with employment among first-year college students. *Journal of College Student Development, 38*(2), 166–172.

Meara, N. M., Day, J. D., Chalk, L. M., & Phelps, R. E. (1995). Possible selves: Applications for career counseling. *Journal of Career Assessment, 3*(3), 259–277.

Moore, J. V., III, & Rago, M. A. (2007a, November-December). *Cultivating engaged student workers: Theories and best practices.* Paper presented at the Reservations and Operations Seminar of the Association of College Unions International, Dayton, OH.

Moore, J. V., III, & Rago, M. A. (2007b, May). *The working student's experience: The hidden costs of working on college student success and engagement.* Paper presented at the annual meeting of the Association for Institutional Research, Kansas City, MO.

Nelson Laird, T. F., Bridges, B. K., Salinas Holmes, M., Morelon, C. L., & Williams, J. M. (2007). African American and Hispanic student engagement at minority serving and predominantly White institutions. *Journal of College Student Development, 48*(1), 39–56.

Nonis, S. A., & Hudson, G. I. (2006). Academic performance on college students: Influence of time spent studying and working. *Journal of Education for Business, 81*(3), 151–159.

Pace, C. (1980). Measuring the quality of student effort. *Current Issues in Higher Education, 2,* 10–16.

Parker-Gwin, R.. & Mabry, J. B. (1998). Service learning as pedagogy and civic education: Comparing outcomes for three models. *Teaching Sociology, 26,* 276–291.

Pascarella, E. T. (1984). College environmental influences on students' educational aspirations. *Journal of Higher Education, 55,* 751–771.

Pascarella, E. T., & Terenzini, P. T. (1991). *How college affects students: Vol. 1. Findings and insights from twenty years of research.* San Francisco: Jossey-Bass.

Pascarella, E. T., & Terenzini, P. T. (2005). *How college affects students: Vol. 2. A third decade of research.* San Francisco: Jossey-Bass.

Pascarella, E. T., Terenzini, P. T., & Hibel, J. (1978). Student-faculty interactional settings and their relationship to predicted academic performance. *Journal of Higher Education, 49,* 450–463.

Perna, L., Cooper, M. A., & Li, C. (2006). *Improving educational opportunities for students who work.* Prepared for the Indiana Project on Academic Success. Bloomington, IN: Project on Academic Success.

Pike, G. (1999). The effects of residential learning communities and traditional residential living arrangements on educational gains during the first year of college. *Journal of College Student Development, 38,* 609–621.

Pike, G. (2000). The influence of fraternity or sorority membership on students' college experiences and cognitive development. *Research Higher Education, 41,* 117–139.

Pike, G. R., Kuh, G. D., & Gonyea, R. M. (2003). The relationship between institutional mission and students' involvement and educational outcomes. *Research in Higher Education, 44*(2), 241–261.

Pike, G. R., Schroeder, C. C., & Berry, T. R. (1997). Enhancing the educational impact of residence halls: The relationship between residential learning communities and first-year college experiences and persistence. *Journal of College Student Development, 38,* 609–621.

Rago, M. A., Moore, J. V., III, & Herreid, C. (2005, June). *Disengaged and ignored: Are working students a lost cause?* Paper presented at the annual meeting of the Association for Institutional Research, San Diego, CA.

Riggert, S. C., Boyle, M., Petrosko, J. M., Ash, D., & Rude-Parkins, C. (2006). Student employment and higher education: Empiricism and contradiction. *Review of Educational Research, 76*(1), 63–92.

Rudolph, F. (1977). *Curriculum: A history of the American undergraduate course of study since 1636.* San Francisco: Jossey-Bass.

Sedlacek, W. E. (2004). *Beyond the big test.* San Francisco: Jossey-Bass.

Stern, D., & Nakata, Y. (1991). Paid employment among U.S. college students. *Journal of Higher Education, 62*(1), 25–43.

Stinebrickner, R., & Stinebrickner, T. R. (2003). Working during school and academic performance. *Journal of Labor Economics, 21*(2), 473–491.

Terenzini, P. T., Pascarella, E. T., & Blimling, G. S. (1996). Students' out-of-class experiences and their influence on cognitive development: A literature review. *Journal of College Student Development, 37*(2), 149–162.

Tinto, V. (1975). Dropout from higher education: A theoretical synthesis of recent research. *The Journal of Higher Education, 45*(1), 89–125.

Tracey, T. J., & Sedlacek, W. E. (1987). Prediction of college graduation using noncognitive variables by race. *Measurement and Evaluation in Counseling and Development, 19,* 177–184.

Tracey, T. J., & Sedlacek, W. E. (1988). A comparison of White and Black student academic success using noncognitive variables: A LISREL analysis. *Research in Higher Education, 27,* 333–348.

Tracey, T. J., & Sedlacek, W. E. (1989). Factor structure of the noncognitive questionnaire revised across samples of black and white college students. *Educational and Psychological Measurement, 49,* 637–648.

Tuttle, T., McKinney, J., & Rago, M. (2005). *College students working: The choice nexus* (IPAS Topic Brief). Bloomington, IN: Project on Academic Success.

Umbach, P. D., Kinzie, J., Thomas, A. D., Palmer, M. M., & Kuh, G. D. (2007). Women students at co-educational and women's colleges: How do their experiences compare? *Journal of College Student Development, 48*(2), 145–165.

Westbrook, F. D., & Sedlacek, W. E. (1988). Workshop on using noncognitive variables with minority students in higher education. *Journal for Specialists in Group Work, 13,* 82–89.

Zhao, C. M., Kuh, G. D., & Carini, R. M. (2005). A comparison of international student and American student engagement in effective educational practices. *The Journal of Higher Education, 76*(2), 209–231.

Section II

Evaluating Persistence/Retention Programs

CHAPTER 4

STUDENTS' USE OF GROUP MATHEMATICS TUTORING AND ITS IMPACT ON MAJOR CHOICE

Leslie J. Robinson

Open a magazine or turn on a newscast today and chances are someone is bemoaning the condition of math and science education in the United States. With the ever-growing demand for employees who are able to function effectively in a more scientifically or technologically based environment, it is vital that colleges and universities play a role in helping students develop these capabilities. Indeed, the proliferation of majors and programs in areas such as informatics and the life sciences illustrates how many institutions of higher education have responded to this societal need.

Yet for many students, obstacles to academic success remain, particularly in areas requiring higher levels of mathematics. Explanations range from math anxiety to lack of academic preparation to different learning styles, but regardless of the reasons for this gap it is important to acknowledge its presence and to work toward finding ways to bridge it. Specifically, researchers and practitioners need to work together to identify the issues and to create appropriate structures that foster more equitable environments for successful student learning.

In response to students' changing needs, many higher education institutions have developed structures such as professional advising, tutoring programs, supplemental instruction, discipline-based organizations, and workshop series. Specifically, for various groups of students interested in science and mathematics, many colleges and universities have created organizations and mentoring programs designed to provide role models and focused support for individuals majoring in areas in which their groups are underrepresented.

The research on the impact of student support programs has been quite inconsistent, however, in part due to the occasional use of less rigorous research methods as well as the challenges intrinsic to the study of student behavior. This study, undertaken as an effort to reach a more accurate and complete understanding of the impact of student support programs, applies a logistic regression to the question of whether the use of a specific support service—in this case, mathematics tutoring during the first year of college—has an impact on students' eventual choice of major.

81

At the large midwestern university where this study was conducted, the availability of advising, tutoring, and other forms of academic support for first-year students has received a great deal of attention in the past few years. A major component of this support is the university's Residential Academic Center (RAC), a collaborative venture begun in 1996. With facilities in three different residence halls, the RAC offers many free services, including first-year advising and tutoring in mathematics, writing, and other subjects. Students can sign up on the same day for two-hour evening small-group sessions tutored by three or four graduate students. Some students drop in for help on a few homework problems while others stay for the entire time to do assignments. As the number of RAC locations has increased, student use of this support resource has also grown, nearly doubling to an annual usage of over 2,000 students making upwards of 13,000 visits—the majority, not surprisingly, for help with mathematics.

Like many other institutions, especially those that are publicly funded, this university faces the question of how to accommodate an ever-growing student population with myriad academic problems. Jones and Watson (1990) discuss the numerous effects of underprepared students at institutions of higher education—direct effects, including the addition of special courses to assist high-risk students, as well as indirect effects. One such effect is the shift toward more courses in majors perceived as "easy," as students "vote with their feet" and gravitate toward disciplines that are seen as less academically challenging.

In his comprehensive work on student attrition, Tinto (1987) articulates his view of the appropriate motivation for assessment: "Retention should not be the ultimate goal of institutional action…Instead, institutions and students would be better served if a concern for the education of students, their social and intellectual growth, were the guiding principle of institutional action" (p. 5). Tinto seems to be calling for a fuller, more comprehensive understanding of how such programs actually function on campus as vehicles by which students obtain access to certain schools within the university and ultimately to successful careers. This study is a preliminary step toward a larger study that uses a mixed-method approach to evaluate this academic support program in greater detail.

Purpose of Study

This research project examined an existing tutoring program at a large midwestern university as a means of uncovering differences in students' choices of major resulting from their math tutoring experiences. The purpose of the study was to investigate whether an academic support program for first-year students, in this case the RAC program, had an impact on students' choice of major, specifically, by allowing them to complete successfully the "bottleneck" or problem introductory math courses and to move toward more math-oriented majors. Examining the degree to which students choose majors in the "hard" sciences, mathematics, economics, computer science, informatics, and business—majors that often lead to more lucrative careers—can also suggest implications for students' long-term financial success.

Research Questions

The primary questions for this study were the following: Does using the group mathematics tutoring offered at the RAC during the first year of college have an impact on students' choice of major? In particular, does such use affect students' selection of a math-oriented major? To begin to address these questions, three areas of research literature were examined: academic support, retention, and major choice. Within the literature on academic support this analysis is somewhat unique in that it applies a relatively more sophisticated quantitative methodology and, as a result of the researcher's access to the extensive data set of the Indiana Project on Academic Success, it considers a relatively large number of cases.

Much of the literature on academic support focuses on first-year students (Abrams & Jernigan, 1984; Commander, Stratton & Callahan 1996; Levin, Levin, & Scalia 1997; Upcraft, Gardner, & Associates 1989), thereby making certain assumptions about the nature of most academic support and its utilization by students. Most of these studies examine first-year student programs that have at their center a desire to promote retention, as the first year of the transition into college is often viewed as the most risky period in terms of attrition.

According to Schuh and Kuh (1991), approximately 80 percent of a student's time is spent outside the classroom, and these out-of-class experiences can significantly impact a student's academic development (Terenzini, Pascarella, & Blimling, 1996). In his examination of learning environments, Terenzini (1999) noted, "the extent to which learning occurs is related in important ways to the extent to which the learner is directly involved in the learning process" (p. 35). Clearly, an indicator of a student's direct involvement would be whether the student visits learning support facilities such as the one under examination in this study.

In her monograph *Lost Talent: The Underparticipation of Women, Minorities, and Disabled Persons in Science,* Oakes (1990) identifies the "pipeline" created for students interested in pursuing a career in the scientific or technological fields. Observing how various groups often seem to drop out of this process at different stages along the way, she writes, "women tend to leave primarily during senior high school and college...if the situation is to be remedied, it will be necessary to intervene at those junctures in the pipeline where students drop out" (p. vii). The RAC is one such intervention.

St. John, Cabrera, Nora, and Asker (2000) have argued for the need to incorporate both economic factors and student-institution fit factors in the study of student departure and academic success, as both sets of factors are important and do not operate independently of one another. Although this study is not about student persistence overall, the economic implications of its focus on students' success and movement in and out of certain fields along with the possible role of a student's financial situation in the major choice process provide the rationale for considering economic factors.

Method

In his role as the original director of the Indiana Project on Academic Success (IPAS), Edward P. St. John was instrumental not only in creating the project's data set but also in designing the framework for postsecondary research guided by the principles of his workable models approach (St. John, 1992). This study takes its research model from IPAS and uses the IPAS data set as its primary source of student data. The framework for the workable models approach to institutional research was conceived as a means of addressing the methodological inconsistencies St. John noted in student financial aid research. One of the chief criteria for the workable models approach is the availability of sufficient data with appropriate variables that can be easily accessed at the campus or university level. This criterion is met with particular strength in this study, where the available data is quite extensive, thanks to IPAS research resources. IPAS amassed a large data set on students attending various institutions of higher education throughout the state of Indiana, including data for students at the particular institution under examination in this study. By adding specific variables related to college experience on this campus, it was possible, as St. John (1992) suggested, to assess how selection of certain student support options has affected choice of academic major on a particular campus.

IPAS is an ongoing inquiry-based project that provides assistance to researchers and practitioners interested in assessing higher education at both the campus level and statewide. The IPAS longitudinal database, constructed from a variety of sources including the College Board, the Indiana Commission for Higher Education, and the State Student Assistance Commission of Indiana, contains information on students who graduated from Indiana's public high schools in 2000 and enrolled in colleges the next academic year.

The IPAS database is the primary source of information for this study because it contains most of the necessary variables, specifically student background and college experience variables such as gender, race/ethnicity, high school GPA, SAT score, family income, financial aid received, major choice (both during the first year and at the end of the junior year), and housing status. After merging the pertinent sections of the IPAS database with data from the institution's mathematics department including this cohort's math placement scores, students who utilized the tutoring services during their first year were identified.

For this study, math-oriented majors include the "hard" sciences (biology, chemistry, physics, biochemistry), astronomy, mathematics, computer science, informatics, economics, and business. The outcome variable is whether by the end of the sixth semester, or third year, of college the student selected a math-oriented major, much in the way discussed by St. John (1992). Majors were clustered into these two categories according to the institution's requirements and the mathematics prerequisites for specific majors. The multinomial characteristics of the outcome variable are observed in the coding scheme. For students who decided on a midlevel math-oriented major, the outcome variable was coded 1; for students who chose a high-level math-oriented major, the outcome variable was coded 2. The comparison group, students who in the third year had a major with a low level of math, was coded 3. Cases with major choice missing in the third year were coded 0.

This study used a multinomial regression approach, with the predictor variables on relevant inputs and experiences entering the model in three blocks: (1) student background and demographic variables such as family income, race/ethnicity, high school GPA, SAT math score, college math skills assessment (MSA) score, and gender; (2) college experiences such as level of math course taken in the first year (developmental or not), first-year college GPA, residence (on- or off-campus), financial aid received, and level of math orientation of the major at the end of the first year (for one of the two models); and (3) utilization of RAC services—entered into the model as a dichotomous variable to discern the unique effects of RAC services on the likelihood of a student choosing a math-oriented major.

The problem of missing data is one of the most pervasive in data analysis and one that must be addressed. As St. John (1992) notes, "the fact is that most quantitative research includes imperfect data" and researchers must develop the best possible model within the constraints of available data (p. 19). Through the inclusion of "missing" as a category for a number of variables, as St. John (1992) suggests, it is possible to use the available data most efficiently while creating an effective model. In fact, the results of the regression for the missing category for the outcome variable—math level of third-year major—may help to further illuminate what variables are most important with regard to academic success.

Limitations of the Study

The use of existing data as part of a workable models study may mean that certain variables that would be useful in an analysis of major choice—for example, some precollege variables—are not available as part of the data set. Yet the SAT and math placement scores should provide adequate information with respect to academic preparation, especially in mathematics, that might influence subsequent major choice.

The timing of the collection of the preliminary major choice information is a little problematic and may serve as another limitation for this analysis since it was collected in the summer after the first year of college rather than earlier in the collegiate career (prior to matriculating, for example). However, even though major choice changes during the first year are not examined in this study, it should still be helpful to look for changes between the first year and later in students' college careers.

Another concern is the potential for self-selection that may occur with regard to RAC use. In short, students intending to choose certain majors, especially those using middle and high levels of math, may be predisposed toward using the mathematics tutoring in their first year. In order to address this issue, a follow-up analysis was done using a linear regression approach with RAC visits as a continuous outcome variable. All remaining predictor variables were included again in this subsequent regression to determine if there was a strong correlation or relationship between math in the first-year major and RAC visits.

Findings

Two separate models were estimated, using all available student data. One model included the first-year major variable (defined as the major declared in the summer after the first year of college) while one did not. The reason for this distinction was to provide a means to examine whether the first-year major variable was highly correlated with the outcome variable (the major at the end of the third year). As usual with these types of multiple-yet-related analyses, comparisons of coefficients and significances of odds ratios for specific variables across models is not advisable from a statistical perspective and thus is not done in this study. Most variables in both models were significant.

There are four possible categories of outcome variable. Because the category of low-level math in third-year major is the comparison group, the following section contains results from the other three categories: midlevel math in third-year major, high-level math in third-year major, and missing third-year major.

All Students with First-Year Major

There were 6,629 valid cases in the data set, representing the majority of students in the 1999–2000 cohort. The outcome variable is level of math in declared major at the end of the junior year. The predictor variables are family income, gender, race/ethnicity, math SAT score, high school GPA, Math Skills Assessment (MSA) score, college GPA at the end of the first year, developmental math course in college, residence, level of math of the major declared, financial aid package, and use of the RAC for math tutoring during the first year. As is the case in this type of analysis, each variable is divided into categories, one of which serves as the comparison group for purposes of the multinomial regression.

The categories for math level of major for either first year or third year are defined by the number of mathematics courses required for successful access and/or progress toward a degree in specific major fields. The midlevel math category includes majors requiring multiple introductory-level mathematics courses (and a statistics course in most cases), while the high-level group consists of majors requiring upper-level mathematics classes. Majors requiring only one introductory-level math course are in the low-level math category.

Students in the low-level math category represented the largest percentages for both the first year (61.9%) and the third year (51.2%). For both cases, this category served as the comparison group. The percentages for the outcome variable in the third year for the other categories were as follows: missing, 18.2 percent; midlevel math, 23.7 percent; and high-level math, 6.9 percent. Figures for the math level in the first-year major were midlevel math, 28.6 percent and high-level math, 9.5 percent. There were no cases with missing math level for students in the first year major.

For family income, almost a quarter of the cases (23.2%) were in the comparison group of $30,000–$70,000, while the largest group (38.0%) was in the over-$70,000 category, and 27.2 percent fell into the missing category. The breakdown for gender in this sample was 56.0 percent female and 44.0 percent male, the latter comprising the comparison group—to investigate from a different perspective the relationship between women and the outcome variable. In terms of race/ethnicity, a large majority of students reported White (86.3%) as their racial/ethnic group, and that served as the comparison group for this variable.

While 26.1 percent of the students in this cohort fell into the low-range math SAT category, the midrange category (30.1%) functioned as the comparison group. Similarly, MSA scores were divided into three categories, with midrange MSA scores being the largest (34.1%) group as well as the comparison group. For both high school and college GPA, students who had a B average served as the comparison group. Of the students who had a reported GPA, these groups were the largest—27.9 percent with a high school GPA of B and 51.7 percent with a college GPA of B. It should be noted, however, that the largest group in the high school GPA category is the "missing" group—at 42 percent—and this may have skewed the results for this particular variable.

Residence and developmental math in college are both "either/or" variables. Students who lived off campus (44.6%) were considered the comparison group for the former variable, and students who did not take a developmental math course in college (90.9%) were the comparison group for the latter. Students who did not receive any financial aid (31.7%) were the comparison group for the financial aid package variable, though the combination of the other categories for this variable indicates that the majority of the students in this population did receive some form of financial assistance. Finally, to examine the extent to which use of the RAC affected major choice, the RAC visits variable was divided into three categories: one to three RAC visits (11.2%), four or more RAC visits (3.8%), and no RAC visits (85.0%)— the last of these being the comparison group.

A discussion follows, with accompanying tables, of each of the three categories of outcome variable (midlevel math major in the third year, high-level math major in the third year, and missing major in the third year). The overall percentage of correctly classified cases for this model was 62.8.

For students who had a midlevel math major at the end of the third year, nine of the twelve variables included in the model resulted in some degree of significance (see Table 4.1a). For math SAT score, the significance is slight ($p<.1$), with a high-range math SAT score having a positive relationship with a midlevel math major in the junior year. Likewise, the relationship between financial aid package, specifically for students receiving grants only or grants and loans, and the outcome variable is positive and slightly significant. Another variable, high school GPA, is highly significant ($p<.01$) for those in the missing high school GPA category, with a negative relationship to the outcome variable. This effect may be explained by the large proportion of female students (approximately 40%) who fell into that category.

The six remaining variables, however, are all significant at the $p<.05$ level or higher: race/ethnicity, MSA score, college GPA, developmental math in college, level of math of major in the first year, and RAC visits. Interestingly, the missing race/ethnicity category has a significant and positive relationship to the outcome variable. A high-range MSA score is highly significant and has a positive relationship (odds ratio 1.441) to the midlevel math major outcome.

Similarly, a high college GPA is also positively related (odds ratio 1.725) to the outcome variable and is highly significant, while having a missing or low college GPA decreased the likelihood of being in a high-level math course (odds ratio .689). Additionally, with a negative coefficient and an odds ratio well below 1, the results indicate that students who took a developmental math course were less likely to end up in a midlevel math major by the end of the third year. Not surprisingly, a declared major with a higher level of math at the end of the first year is highly significant and positively associated with the outcome variable (level of math of the major at the end of the third year); for midlevel majors in the first year the odds ratio is 9.375, and for high-level math majors in the first year the odds ratio is 3.350.

As for the variable that reflects the main question for this study, use of the RAC for mathematics tutoring during the first year of college, the results are interesting. While there is no statistical significance for students in the one-to-three-visits category relative to the outcome variable, students in the four-or-more-visits category are significantly more likely to be in a midlevel math major at the end of the third year than those who did not use the RAC for math help. For students who made four or more visits the odds ratio is 1.620 and is significant at the p<.01 level. In this case, the odds ratios being greater than 1 indicates a positive relation-ship between repeated use of this intervention and an eventual more math-oriented major choice.

For students who had a high-level math major at the end of their third year, nine of the twelve variables resulted in some degree of significance (Table 4.1b), and two of the nine variables—MSA score and financial aid package—are only slightly significant (p<.1). A high-range MSA score is positively associated with the outcome variable to a minor degree. In terms of financial aid package, there is a slight and positive relationship between students who received "other" aid packages and the outcome variable. As in most of the other models, the missing high school GPA group within that variable is very significant and negatively related to the outcome variable.

Six other variables are significant at the p<.05 level or higher: gender, race/ethnicity, math SAT score, college GPA, math level of major in the first year, and RAC visits during the first year. Predictably, a low-range math SAT score had a negative and significant relationship to the outcome variable (odds ratio .668), while a high-range math SAT score has a highly significant and positive relationship to the outcome variable (odds ratio 2.078) as compared to students in the midrange math SAT score group—which, as the comparison category for this variable, has no odds ratio. College GPA presents a similar picture, with a lower average negatively related to the outcome variable and a high average positively so. Moreover, a high level of math in the declared major at the end of the first year is highly significant and positively associated with the outcome variable (math level of the major at the end of the third year). Students who declared a high-level math major in the first year were much more likely to be in the high-level math major category in their third year (odds ratio 27.401) than students who had initially declared a low-level math major.

In terms of use of the RAC for mathematics tutoring during the first year of college, the results are similar to those for midlevel math majors for all students. Students in the one-to-three-visit category were slightly more likely than those who did not use the RAC for math help to be in a high-level math major at the end of the third year. For students who made one to three visits, the odds ratio is 1.378 and is significant at the $p<.1$ level. However, for students who made four or more visits, the odds ratio is 2.611 and is significant at the $p<.01$ level. The significance of gender is also high in this model and suggests that women are less likely to move into high-level math majors.

In the analysis for all students with math level of the first year major included, the Nagelkerke pseudo R2 is .449; in other words, the variables included in this model explain 44.9 percent of the variance in the outcome.

As might be expected for the missing major group, the variables that display a statistically significant relationship are somewhat different than for the midlevel or high-level math major groups (see Table 4.1c). In terms of both high school and college GPA, there is a strong positive relationship between a missing and C or lower average and a missing major outcome.

Furthermore, students from the high family income group (over $70,000) are less likely to fall into the missing major category (odds ratio .648), while students receiving many types of financial aid (loans, grants and loans, and other packages) are significantly more likely to be in the missing major group (1.351, 1.545, and 1.608 odds ratios, respectively). There is a significant and positive relationship between the missing major outcome and the categories of Hispanic ethnicity and missing race/ethnicity. Also, students who have a missing math SAT score are more likely to have a missing major in the third year.

There is a highly positive relationship between the outcome variable of missing major in the third year and declaring a midlevel or high-level math-oriented major in the first year, again at the $p<.01$ level. Finally, there is a negative and significant relationship between one to three RAC visits and a missing major outcome—with an odds ratio of .548, statistically significant at the $p<.01$ level.

Table 4.1a. Impact of Math Tutoring on Major Choice for All Students in First Year of College: Multinomial Regression Analysis of Third-Year Major for Students in Midlevel Math Majors (First-Year Major Included)

Variables	Coefficient	Std. Error	Odds Ratio	Sig.
Family Income				
Below $30,000	0.071	0.133	1.073	
Above $70,000	0.017	0.098	1.018	
Missing	0.139	0.148	1.149	
Gender				
Female	0.065	0.076	1.067	
Race/Ethnicity				
Hispanic, Native American, or Other	0.121	0.208	1.129	
Asian or Pacific Islander	0.094	0.195	1.098	
African American	-0.090	0.188	0.914	
Missing	0.540	0.219	1.716	**
Math SAT Score				
Low	-0.131	0.103	0.877	
High	0.158	0.095	1.171	*
Missing	0.014	0.124	1.014	
High School GPA				
C or Lower	0.182	0.154	1.200	
A	-0.014	0.101	0.986	
Missing	-0.333	0.113	0.717	***
Math Skills Assessment (MSA) Score				
Low	-0.061	0.101	0.941	
High	0.366	0.094	1.441	***
Missing	-0.025	0.120	0.975	
College GPA				
Missing or C or Lower	-0.372	0.104	0.689	***
A	0.545	0.085	1.725	***

All Students, Without First-Year Major

Many of the findings for the model for all students without first-year major were similar to the previous model. The overall percentage of correctly classified cases for this model was 54.9 percent. Each of the three categories of outcome variable (midlevel math major in the third year, high-level math major in the third year, and missing major in the third year) is discussed separately.

Table 4.1a (continued). Impact of Math Tutoring on Major Choice for All Students in First Year of College: Multinomial Regression Analysis of Third-Year Major for Students in Midlevel Math Majors (First-Year Major Included)

Variables	Coefficient	Std. Error	Odds Ratio	Sig.
Developmental Math in College				
Developmental Math Taken	-0.516	0.165	0.597	***
Residence in First Year				
On Campus	-0.071	0.102	0.932	
Math Level of First-Year Major				
Mid	2.238	0.077	9.375	***
High	1.209	0.147	3.350	***
Financial Aid Package				
Grants only	0.178	0.098	1.195	*
Loans only	0.131	0.121	1.140	
Grants and Loans	0.196	0.116	1.216	*
Other Packages	0.243	0.173	1.275	
RAC Visits in First Year				
One to Three	0.166	0.104	1.180	
Four or More	0.483	0.170	1.620	***

Note. Number of cases = 6,629.
Nagelkerke pseudo R2 = 0.449.
*p<.1, **p<.05, ***p<.01.

For students who had a midlevel math major at the end of the third year, nine of the eleven variables included in the model have some degree of significance. Two of the nine variables, math SAT score and high school GPA, are only slightly significant, but the remaining seven are all significant at the p<.05 level or higher: race/ethnicity, gender, MSA score, college GPA, developmental math in college, financial aid package, and RAC visits. As before, a high MSA score and a high college GPA are positively related to a midlevel math major in the third year. Likewise, a low college GPA and taking a developmental math course are negatively related to the outcome variable.

For financial aid package, there is a positive relationship between students who received grants only and the outcome variable. The relationship of gender to the outcome variable is also significant, with a lower likelihood of female students than of male students being in the midlevel math major category.

As for the variable that reflects the main question for this study—use of the RAC for mathematics tutoring during the first year of college—the results are again convincing. There is high statistical significance for students in both the one-to-three-visits and the four-or-more-visits categories relative to being in

Table 4.1b. Impact of Math Tutoring on Major Choice for All Students in First Year of College: Multinomial Regression Analysis of Third-Year Major for Students in Midlevel Math Majors (First-Year Major Included)

Variables	Coefficient	Std. Error	Odds Ratio	Sig.
Family Income				
Below $30,000	0.296	0.207	1.345	
Above $70,000	-0.034	0.160	0.967	
Missing	0.226	0.256	1.254	
Gender				
Female	-0.588	0.125	0.556	***
Race/Ethnicity				
Hispanic, Native American, or Other	0.073	0.323	1.076	
Asian or Pacific Islander	0.358	0.279	1.430	
African American	-0.135	0.318	0.874	
Missing	1.018	0.357	2.768	***
Math SAT Score				
Low	-0.403	0.196	0.668	**
High	0.731	0.154	2.078	***
Missing	0.342	0.230	1.407	
High School GPA				
C or Lower	0.088	0.266	1.092	
A	-0.004	0.162	0.996	
Missing	-0.606	0.199	0.546	***
Math Skills Assessment (MSA) Score				
Low	-0.113	0.194	0.893	
High	0.288	0.154	1.333	*
Missing	0.322	0.199	1.380	
College GPA				
Missing or C or Lower	-0.585	0.180	0.557	***
A	0.516	0.141	1.676	***
Developmental Math in College				
Developmental Math Taken	-0.321	0.318	0.725	

a midlevel math major at the end of the third year. For students who made one to three visits for math help during their first year, the odds ratio is 1.515 and is significant at the p<.01 level. For students who made four or more visits, the odds ratio is 2.187 and is also significant at the p<.01 level.

Table 4.1b (continued). Impact of Math Tutoring on Major Choice for All Students in First Year of College: Multinomial Regression Analysis of Third-Year Major for Students in Midlevel Math Majors (First-Year Major Included)

Variables	Coefficient	Std. Error	Odds Ratio	Sig.
Residence in First Year				
On Campus	0.167	0.171	1.181	
Math Level of First-Year Major				
Mid	-0.512	0.223	0.599	**
High	3.311	0.142	27.401	***
Financial Aid Package				
Grants only	0.009	0.170	1.009	
Loans only	0.064	0.203	1.067	
Grants and Loans	0.098	0.194	1.103	
Other Packages	0.476	0.271	1.610	*
RAC Visits in First Year				
One to Three	0.321	0.181	1.378	*
Four or More	0.960	0.256	2.611	***

Note. Number of cases = 6,629.
Nagelkerke pseudo R2 = 0.449.
*p<.1, **p<.05, ***p<.01.

Table 4.1c. Impact of Math Tutoring on Major Choice for All Students in First Year of College: Multinomial Regression Analysis of Third-Year Major for Students with Missing Majors (First-Year Major Included)

Variables	Coefficient	Std. Error	Odds Ratio	Sig.
Family Income				
Below $30,000	-0.146	0.131	0.864	
Above $70,000	-0.433	0.105	0.648	***
Missing	-0.143	0.145	0.866	
Gender				
Female	0.111	0.079	1.118	
Race/Ethnicity				
Hispanic, Native American, or Other	0.409	0.206	1.506	**
Asian or Pacific Islander	-0.407	0.221	0.955	
African American	0.233	0.168	1.262	
Missing	0.460	0.216	1.583	**
Math SAT Score				
Low	-0.069	0.105	0.933	
High	0.148	0.108	1.160	
Missing	0.298	0.115	1.347	***

Table 4.1c (continued). **Impact of Math Tutoring on Major Choice for All Students in First Year of College: Multinomial Regression Analysis of Third-Year Major for Students with Missing Majors (First-Year Major Included)**

Variables	Coefficient	Std. Error	Odds Ratio	Sig.
High School GPA				
C or Lower	0.362	0.148	1.437	**
A	-0.143	0.131	0.867	
Missing	1.004	0.113	2.729	***
Math Skills Assessment (MSA) Score				
Low	0.048	0.104	1.049	
High	0.033	0.117	1.033	
Missing	0.211	0.109	1.235	*
College GPA				
Missing or C or Lower	1.567	0.086	4.792	***
A	0.007	0.110	1.007	
Developmental Math in College				
Developmental Math Taken	-0.043	0.129	0.958	
Residence in First Year				
On Campus	-0.027	0.111	0.973	
Math Level of First-Year Major				
Mid	0.446	0.093	1.562	***
High	1.015	0.145	2.758	***
Financial Aid Package				
Grants only	0.099	0.106	1.104	
Loans only	0.301	0.129	1.351	**
Grants and Loans	0.435	0.118	1.545	***
Other Packages	0.475	0.174	1.608	***
RAC Visits in First Year				
One to Three	-0.602	0.147	0.548	***
Four or More	-0.364	0.257	0.695	

Note. Number of cases = 6,629.
Nagelkerke pseudo R2 = 0.449.
*p<.1, **p<.05, ***p<.01.

For students who had a high-level math major at the end of the third year, seven of the eleven variables have some degree of significance: gender, race/ethnicity, math SAT score, high school GPA, MSA score, college GPA, and RAC visits during the first year. Two of the student background variables—gender and race/ethnicity—are quite significant (p<.01). Female gender is negatively related, with women students being much less likely to end up with high-level math majors (odds ratio .498). Within the race/ethnicity variable, Asian or Pacific Islander students are more likely to be in the high-level math major category of the outcome variable (odds ratio 2.207). College GPA presents a similar picture, with a high GPA positively related to the outcome variable.

In terms of use of the RAC for mathematics tutoring during the first year of college, the results are similar to those for midlevel math majors for all students. Students who made visits to the RAC for math help during their first year are more likely than those who did not use the RAC for math help to be in a high-level math major at the end of the third year. For students who made one to three visits, the odds ratio is 1.551 (p<.01). For students who made four or more visits, the odds ratio is 3.438 (p<.01).

As in the previous model, the variables displaying a statistically significant relationship to the missing major outcome are somewhat different than for midlevel or high-level math majors. In terms of both high school and college GPA, there is a strong positive relationship between a missing major outcome and a missing GPA and a C or lower GPA. There is a negative and significant relationship between one to three RAC visits and a missing major outcome—with an odds ratio of .580 (p<.01).

Self-Selection, Correlation, and Regression

As a means of determining whether self-selection played too large a role in the findings for the previous analysis of RAC use and its impact on major choice, a follow-up linear regression was performed to analyze the relationships between the variables in more detail. RAC use was a continuous outcome variable. With RAC use as the outcome variable, the number of usable cases for the data set is 996, the number of students who actually used the RAC for mathematics help during their first year.

According to the ANOVA, the model was not statistically significant (.087) at the p<.05 level, suggesting that the relationship between this set of predictor variables and the outcome variable is not strong. Race/ethnicity is one of the only statistically significant coefficients (significance of .017 for all students) in the model; students of color are more likely to visit the RAC more frequently, a finding supported by ongoing assessment of RAC users.

Although no other significant correlations exist between the outcome variable and any of the predictor variables, there are a number of correlations between the predictor variables themselves (see Table 4.2). For the all-student group, math level in the first-year major is significantly correlated with a number of other variables including gender, race/ethnicity, family income, high school GPA, MSA score, and developmental math in the first year of college.

In most cases, the relationship is a positive one, indicating that a higher family income, a higher high school GPA, or being White makes a student more likely to choose a more mathematically oriented major. However, female gender is negatively correlated with math level in first-year major, again underscoring one of the study's premises that women are not as likely to be represented in the midlevel and high-level math majors early in their academic careers.

Table 4.2. Correlations of Significant Predictor Variables

Variables	Variables	Coefficient	Sig.
RAC Visits	Race/Ethnicity	-0.074	**
Gender	Family Income	-0.082	**
	Developmental Math in College	0.077	**
	Math Level of First-Year Major	-0.295	***
Race/Ethnicity	First-Year College GPA	0.064	**
	Math Level of First-Year Major	0.058	**
Family Income	High School GPA	0.525	***
	Math SAT Score	0.154	***
	Math Level of First-Year Major	0.063	**
High School GPA	Math SAT Score	0.238	***
	Math Level of First-Year Major	0.063	**
Math SAT Score	MSA Score	0.135	***
	Developmental Math in College	0.168	***
MSA Score	Developmental Math in College	0.341	***
	Math Level of First-Year Major	-0.096	**
Developmental Math in College	Math Level of First-Year Major	-0.160	***

Note. **p<.05, ***p<.001.

Summary and Conclusions

As a statewide project using a research-based approach to study how and why students succeed in college, the Indiana Project on Academic Success has served as an extremely useful basis for this study and for many others at various institutions throughout the state. Grounded in the principles of action inquiry, IPAS collaborates with researchers and practitioners from a number of colleges and universities to collect data and conduct research that can further develop initiatives to improve retention and graduation rates statewide. By examining an existing program such as the Residential Academic Center and its potential impact on major choice on a specific campus, this study supports the overall aim of the RAC to improve enrollment, transfer, and retention among public and private colleges and universities across Indiana.

The results from all of the models are striking for the consistency of significance for some of the predictor variables. Student use of the RAC proved to be both positively and significantly related to the various categories of the outcome variable for almost every iteration of the regression analysis. In particular, frequent use of the RAC (four or more visits) is significant for achieving an outcome of either midlevel or high-level math major in the third year, supporting the original hypothesis that by helping students to complete their introductory math course, mathematics tutoring has a positive impact on the choice of a math-oriented major.

Specifically, math-related predictor variables (math SAT score and MSA score) are frequently significant in the different variations of the model. For the high-level math major outcome, math SAT score is often significant, with a low math SAT score being negatively associated and a high math SAT score being positively associated with a high-level math major. For the midlevel math major outcome, MSA score is more statistically relevant, with a high MSA score suggesting a higher likelihood of achieving a midlevel math major in the third year. Finally, the category of missing high school GPA, which contains a large number of cases in the student cohort, is negatively related to the outcome at a high degree of significance.

These findings not only contribute to the growing body of theory on academic support but also have useful implications for higher education practitioners. Indeed, they exemplify how theory and practice can work effectively together—in this instance, through the efforts of a researcher interested in evaluating a program in her role as its director. The use of an appropriate quantitative approach, one well established in higher education research, may provide a template for other researchers/practitioners in academic support. Further, the incorporation of institutional program data in a larger, statewide data set is another means by which more complicated analyses can be performed; in so doing, a more accurate picture of college student behavior can emerge.

From a practical perspective, the results of this study are heartening, as they support the working hypothesis that RAC use during the first year of college has real and significant effects on a student's subsequent academic success. Students are encouraged when they see that math tutoring provided at the proper time and place can have a positive impact on their ability to succeed in a more math-oriented major, supporting one of the original goals of the RAC program: to increase retention of certain student populations. Such results can also be useful in promoting the RAC as a mechanism to assist students in entering and succeeding in STEM fields—an issue of interest on this campus and nationwide.

Future Research

As noted previously in the limitations section, unanswered questions remain that may be addressed in future research. Because this assessment originated in an action inquiry model like that of IPAS, there is an expectation that it be cyclical, allowing for initial findings to inform intervention modifications that are in turn analyzed for impact on student success. Given the complexity of researching college student behavior, a revision of this study may need to include other variables. For example, many campuses have multiple support programs for students in various subject areas, and a future research project might examine use of those programs to better understand how and to what degree students use such forms of assistance.

To capture some of these different types of information, another possible methodology for examining this topic—a qualitative approach—might be useful. Using focus groups or interviews as an assessment tool or as part of a larger, mixed-method study would allow students to describe in their own words how support programs like the RAC have affected their academic progress. With the collaborative nature of the RAC program, it seems logical to employ methods of investigation that permit more interaction between researcher and participants in a shared evaluative endeavor.

References

Abrams, H. G., & Jernigan, L. P. (1984). Academic support services and the success of high-risk college students. *American Educational Research Journal, 21*(2), 261–274.

Commander, N. E., Stratton, C. B., & Callahan, C. A. (1996). A learning assistance model for expanding academic support. *Journal of Developmental Education, 20*(2), 8–16.

Jones, D. J., & Watson, B. C. (1990). *High-risk students and higher education: Future trends*. (ASHE-ERIC Higher Education Report No. 3). Washington, DC: ERIC Clearinghouse on Higher Education.

Levin, M. E., Levin, J. R., Scalia, P. A. (1997). What claims can a comprehensive college program of academic support support? *Equity and Excellence in Education, 30*(3), 71–89.

Oakes, J. (1990). Lost talent: The underparticipation of women, minorities, and disabled persons in science. Santa Monica, CA: RAND.

St. John, E. P. (1992). Workable models for institutional research on the impact of student financial aid. *Journal of Student Financial Aid, 22*(3), 13–26.

St. John, E. P., Cabrera, A. F., Nora, A., & Asker, E. H. (2000). Economics influences on persistence reconsidered: How can finance research inform the reconceptualization of persistence models? In J. M. Braxton (Ed.), *Reworking the student departure puzzle* (pp. 29–47). Nashville, TN: Vanderbilt University Press.

Schuh, J., & Kuh, G. D. (1991, Winter). Evaluating the quality of collegiate environments. *Journal of College Admissions, 130,* 17–22.

Terenzini, P. T. (1999). Research and practice in undergraduate education: And never the twain shall meet? *Higher Education, 38*(1), 33–48.

Terenzini, P. T., Pascarella, E. T., & Blimling, G. S. (1996). Students' out-of-class experiences and their influence on learning and cognitive development: A literature review. *Journal of College Student Development, 37*(2), 149–162.

Tinto, V. (1987). Leaving college: Rethinking the causes and cures of student attrition (1st ed.). Chicago: University of Chicago Press.

Upcraft, M. L., Gardner, J. N., & Associates. (1989). *The freshman year experience: Helping students survive and succeed in college.* San Francisco: Jossey-Bass.

CHAPTER 5

SUPPLEMENTAL INSTRUCTION AND EQUITY: ASSESSMENT OF IMPLEMENTATION AND EFFECTS ON STUDENT PERSISTENCE

Mary Ziskin, Ebelia Hernandez, and Jacob P. K. Gross

Supplemental instruction (SI) stands out as a vital program model for academic support used in colleges and universities across the country. As with many academic support programs, practitioners, faculty, and policy makers face considerable complexity in determining sound approaches to assessing SI programs. Despite the wide adoption of the model, it often remains unclear how institutions should proceed to ensure that these programs are soundly implemented in practice, appropriately assessed, and well supported in policy. This chapter builds on the work of the Indiana Project on Academic Success (IPAS) at one participating institution to propose new directions for the assessment of SI, with particular attention to the potential of SI for supporting equity in postsecondary education.

Academic support programs are part of a broader set of strategies meant to support educational equity in tandem with expanding access in the 1970s (Arendale, 2000; Lissner, 1990; Sadovnik, 1994). As is true of most educational practices, academic support programs simultaneously transform and replicate educational inequalities (Lundell & Collins, 2001; Shaw, 1997). Even while these programs hold potential for social transformation—through supporting broader access to college degrees—they can also further replicate those inequalities produced and replicated in primary and secondary schooling (Koski & Levin, 1998; Lavin & Hyllegard, 1996; Traub, 1994). Supplemental instruction (SI), a type of academic support, is a case in point.

On the one hand, SI has the potential to complicate or loosen the hold of conceptual frameworks—sometimes termed deficit models—that attribute educational inequalities to the deficiencies of individual students and that focus on fixing problems via a change in the student. Thus, SI has the potential to reframe teaching and learning in a way that disrupts or transforms such deficit-model thinking as it plays out in many academic support programs and practices. Some components of this transformative potential are rooted in SI's philosophical and pedagogical emphasis on deep processing within its rationale (Entwistle, 2000; Martin, Blanc, DeBuhr, Alderman, Garland, & Lewis, 1983) and in such structural aspects as the targeting of courses with high drop/fail/withdraw (DFW) rates (Arendale, 2000).

At the same time, perceptions of SI programs among faculty, students, institutions, and administrators often reintroduce the practices and attitudes of the deficit-model paradigm into the daily realities of the programs. SI programs themselves can even internalize the paradigm, undermining their own transformative potential. Transformative and replicative practices—practices that promote and constrain educational equity—occur in this way side by side.

One way to understand this tension highlights the transformative potential of the ideals behind SI and illuminates the complexity through which the replicative potential of programs emerges in practice. Seeking to understand this tension as it is revealed in practice invites us to incorporate it into program evaluation. In pursuing questions about how well programs are working in terms of the goals of SI at a national level, researchers and practitioners must consider both how and under what conditions the program is performing—acknowledging the endemic challenges faced by academic support programs and working to minimize their drag on the programs' performance.

In this chapter we explore these tensions—transformative and replicative, ideal and practical, how SI is practiced and how it is perceived—through a pair of studies focusing on one institution participating in the Indiana Project on Academic Success (IPAS). After a brief overview of previous research on SI, we present an analysis of persistence and grades outcomes related to the SI program at that institution. This gives a glimpse into the possible effects of the program and allows us to raise some questions about the nature and structure of program evaluation as it is typically applied to academic support programs. To expand on these questions and explore them further, we discuss the values folded into the practice of SI as illustrated by SI leaders' discussions of the norms and routines they employ in SI sessions. This section gives a glimpse also into the institutional context within which the program operates. We conclude with a discussion of implications for practice and for the assessment of SI programs.

The Theoretical Framework

In the decades since the Coleman Report (1966), most of the debate surrounding the definition of equal opportunity in education has centered on the question of whether it is possible for the concept to encompass equal results, either as a criterion in itself or as evidence of the presence or absence of equal opportunity. As Coleman's (1966, 1968) history points out, there was some engagement with the question of equal results even earlier. In his "Wanted: American Radicals" (1943), for example, Conant referred to "equality of opportunity, not equality of rewards" as a hallmark of American (as opposed to European) radicalism. Throughout the last four decades, however, principal contributions to this debate show a steadier back-and-forth on the issue of equal results.

In the discussion that follows, we build on the framework forwarded by Howe (1997), who argues that real opportunities (opportunities one can genuinely take advantage of, "opportunities worth wanting") are often based on having already achieved equal results. Using Dennett's (1984) concept of real versus "bare" opportunities, Howe argues that without equal results as a basis for further opportunity, opportunity is opportunity in name only. As a result Howe focuses not on the question of whether to include equal results in the concept of educational opportunity, but rather considers what kinds of equal results must be included and to what extent. Access to postsecondary degrees is one important example of how this dynamic plays out, and this framework supports the link—forwarded by many scholars of student academic success—connecting success in college with broader debates about educational equity (Casazza & Silverman, 1996; Dowd, 2007; Hossler, Ziskin, Kim, Cekic, & Goss, 2007; Turner, 2004).

The Literature on Supplemental Instruction

One important thread within the literature on supplemental instruction is substantially concerned with methods for appropriate and useful assessment of programs. Perhaps the most widely used assessment approach compares outcomes of SI participants and nonparticipants within the same course section. This strategy was used by the original designers of the SI model in the early 1980s, and has remained a prominent approach for assessment in this field (Blanc, DeBuhr & Martin, 1983; Lundeburg, 1990; National Center for Supplemental Instruction, 1994).

Attempting to avoid the problems related to self-selection bias inherent in that strategy, Peled and Kim (1996) instead compared students' test scores in biology course sections that offered SI to sections of the same course that did not offer SI. They found significantly higher mean scores and significantly lower rates of very low scores in the sections offering SI. These differences were more modest than those shown in comparisons of scores within SI sections, and the authors used this contrast to further the argument that within-section comparisons are troubled by self-selection bias.

In response to critiques of self-selection bias in assessment of SI and similar programs, Gattis (2002) found that participation in SI sessions was associated with improved performance. Using a survey of students' interest in SI, time conflicts precluding attendance at sessions, and other factors relevant to motivation, Gattis' results showed further that these differences were not attributable solely to higher motivation among SI participants. Students who reported similar levels of interest and time conflicts scored significantly lower on outcomes, for example.

Congos and Schoeps (1999) outlined multiple approaches to assessing the impact of SI programs, each oriented toward a specific purpose. For situations in which the goal is to determine the effectiveness of SI programs and their impact on retention, the authors illustrate the use of descriptive statistics and ANCOVA. In a study focusing on the long-term effects of SI participation, Price and Rust (1995) used qualitative data to demonstrate the extent to which students continued using specific learning strategies from SI in subsequent courses. Finally, and at a general level, Arendale (2000) has pointed to the need to consider specific practices, particulars of implementation, and how these more nuanced aspects relate to outcomes in the assessment of supplemental instruction. This chapter builds on this debate by broadening it to include the conditions programs and institutions must manage in order to maximize the impact of programs on student learning.

SI at Regional University

Regional University (a pseudonym) is a medium-sized, racially diverse, primarily nonresidential institution with inclusive admissions. While the institution grants master's degrees through several graduate programs, enrollment is heavily concentrated at the undergraduate level. A sizable minority of the student body is enrolled part time. Regional University is home to a small but active SI program, established in 2000. The program provides SI for a range of high-DFW courses in social science, the humanities, and math/science fields. In 2005 and 2006, IPAS researchers worked with the SI program at Regional to conduct multiple program evaluation studies. Two of these studies—one modeling the effects of SI participation on within-year persistence and another in which IPAS researchers interviewed SI leaders—are presented in the sections below.

SI Participation and Persistence: An Evaluation of Within-Year Effects

Using participation data collected by the SI program administrators at Regional University and data extracted from institutional data systems, we were able to paint a richly descriptive picture of SI participation, as well as to control statistically for variables thought to affect persistence including student background, academic preparation, and financial aid, to assess the unique effects of SI participation. Participation in SI was included in the statistical model as a dichotomous variable (i.e., the student did or did not participate) rather than as a count of frequency of attendance. Statistically, there was insufficient variation to include participation as a count variable because most students attended just one SI session.

In this analysis we examined the within-year persistence for all Regional University students enrolled in courses offering an SI component in the fall of 2005—a total of 691 students. Nearly 18 percent of these students participated in at least one SI session. A higher proportion of women than men participated. Although Asian American Pacific Islander (API) students participated at the highest rate of any racial/ethnic group (75%), we remain cautious in interpreting this result because the number of API students enrolled at the institution in fall 2005 was small. Hispanic students participated in SI sessions at the second highest rate (21.7%). Traditional-age students—those under 21— participated at the lowest rate of any age group. Students with "Core 40" (college preparatory) diplomas participated at the highest rate among recipients of all high school diploma types. An examination of how participation varied with respect to course grades revealed that students who earned *A*s in their courses attended SI sessions with the highest frequency (more than five sessions), students who earned *B*s and *C*s attended two to four sessions with the highest frequency, and students who failed their courses attended sessions with the lowest frequency.

To examine the effects of SI participation, we chose to use logistic regression because the outcome of interest was a dichotomous variable capturing students' within-year persistence from fall 2005 to spring 2006. In this case, the use of ordinary least squares would violate Gauss-Markov assumptions that the error term is normally distributed and the dependent variable is continuous. Below, in Equation 1, the general logit model is provided, where *P* is the probability that the student enrolled at the same institution in the second semester.

Equation 1: Logit model

$$\ln\left(\frac{P_i}{1-P_i}\right) = x_i\beta + \varepsilon_i$$

Included in the model (see Equation 2 and Table 5.1, below) were (a) student background variables ($\beta 1$) including gender, race/ethnicity, age, income, and SAT score; (b) precollege academic preparation variables ($\beta 2$) including high school degree type and high school rank; (c) college experience variables ($\beta 3$) including part-time or full-time enrollment status, placement into developmental courses, and major; (d) financial aid variables ($\beta 4$) including independent or dependent financial status, financial aid, and participation in the

Twenty-First Century Scholar program; and (e) participation in SI sessions measured as a dichotomous variable ($\beta5$).

Equation 2: Persistence model

$$Persist = x_i\beta_1 + x_i\beta_2 + x_i\beta_3 + x_i\beta_4 + x_i\beta_5 + \varepsilon_i$$

Table 5.1 shows the structure of the model used in this analysis as well as information about the variables included in the model.

Table 5.1. Logistic Regression Model on Within-Year Persistence

Variable	Type
Block One: Background Characteristics	
Gender	Categorical
Race/Ethnicity	Categorical
Age	Continuous
Income	Ordinal
Combined SAT score	Ordinal
Block Two: Academic Preparation	
High school degree type	Categorical
High school class rank	Ordinal
Block Three: College Experiences	
Part-time/Full-time status	Categorical
Placement into developmental courses in college	Categorical
Major	Categorical
Block Four: Financial Aid	
Independent/Dependent financial status	Categorical
Receipt of grant aid	Dichotomous
Receipt of student loans	Dichotomous
Status as a Twenty-First Century Scholar	Dichotomous
Block Five: SI Participation	
Participation in SI sessions	Dichotomous

Table 5.2. Logistic Regression Results

Variable	Block One Sig.	Block One Odds Ratio	Block Two Sig.	Block Two Odds Ratio	Block Three Sig	Block Three Odds Ratio	Block Four Sig.	Block Four Odds Ratio	Block Five Sig.	Block Five Odds Ratio
SI Participants Compared to Nonparticipants									*	1.39
Men Compared to Women and Missing	**	1.57		1.30		1.26		1.48		1.58
Students of Color Compared to Whites	**	1.66	*	1.50		0.97		1.59		1.56
Compared to Students 21 and Younger										
21 to 24		0.68	**	0.46		0.57		1.10		1.12
25 to 29		0.70	*	0.45		0.45		1.03		1.05
30 and Older	**	0.44	**	0.28	*	0.41		0.61		0.59
Age Missing		1.11		1.19		1.00		0.75		0.72
Combined SAT Score						1.00	*	1.00		1.00
Adjusted Gross Income			**	1.00		1.00		1.00		1.00
Compared to Students Who Completed a Regular HS Diploma										
Honors Diploma				0.79		1.25		0.92		0.98
Core 40 Diploma				0.74		0.99		0.91		0.88
Diploma Information Missing				0.74		0.63		1.13		1.19

Table 5.2 (continued). Logistic Regression Results

Variable	Block One Sig.	Block One Odds Ratio	Block Two Sig.	Block Two Odds Ratio	Block Three Sig	Block Three Odds Ratio	Block Four Sig	Block Four Odds Ratio	Block Five Sig	Block Five Odds Ratio
Compared to Students in the Top Quartile of Their HS										
Second Quartile			**	2.50		1.65		1.31		1.24
Third Quartile			**	2.36		1.20		0.85		0.79
Bottom Quartile			**	3.86		1.50		1.08		1.04
High school Rank Missing			**	3.78	**	3.22		2.29		2.16
Cumulative GPA					****	0.31	****	0.27	****	0.26
Part-time Compared to Full-time Students					****	0.31		0.71		0.70
Developmental Math Takers Compared to Non-Takers					*	0.55		0.59		0.57
Compared to Students Undecided about Major										
Humanities						0.69		0.67		0.64
Arts						0.67		0.81		0.78
Science and math						0.34	*	0.25	*	0.23
Social sciences						0.86		0.95		0.91
Health					**	0.40		0.54		0.50
Business						1.06		0.99		0.98
Education					**	0.40		0.48		0.46
Other majors					**	0.48	*	0.54	*	0.50

Table 5.2 (continued). Logistic Regression Results

Variable	Block One Sig.	Block One Odds Ratio	Block Two Sig.	Block Two Odds Ratio	Block Three Sig.	Block Three Odds Ratio	Block Four Sig.	Block Four Odds Ratio	Block Five Sig.	Block Five Odds Ratio
Compared to Dependent Students										
Indeterminate Dependency							**	0.22	*	0.25
Self-Supporting Students								2.10		2.39
Grant Aid							****	0.70	****	0.70
Loans							****	1.00	****	1.00
Other id packages								0.98		0.97
Aid Recipients Compared to Non-Recipients								1.40		1.47
Twenty-First Century Scholars Compared to Non-Scholars							*	3.16	*	3.12
% Correctly Predicted		79.016		79.016		80.174		82.779		82.923
Nagelkerke		0.041		0.104		0.354		0.537		0.542

Note. N = 16,256; Persistence, fall 2005 to spring 2006.
*p<0.10, **p<0.05, ***p<0.01, ****p<0.001.
Aid and income amounts in units of $1,000.

We conducted several tests to identify possible deficiencies in the models. Checks for multicollinearity and autocorrelation revealed no strongly correlated relationships among the independent variables or residuals. The cut point for classification of cases was set according to the observed prior probability of students' persistence (Chatterjee & Hadi, 2006). As Table 5.2 displays, the model proved a good fit, accurately classifying nearly 82.92 percent of all cases, with a Nagelkerke score of .542.

SI participation showed a significant and positive association to within-year persistence, with students who participated in SI about 40 percent more likely to persist than nonparticipants. Although we have included relevant student characteristics in this model in an effort to control for self-selection of SI participants, these results may be attributable in part to unobserved characteristics of the participants. For example, students who are particularly motivated or engaged may be more likely to participate in SI sessions. Being a Twenty-First Century Scholarship awardee was also significantly and positively related to persistence.

Factors negatively associated with persistence included having a science- or math-related major and having received financial aid. The amount of grants awarded exerted a negative and highly significant effect on within-year persistence in this analysis. With a negative coefficient and an odds ratio near to but less than one, amount received in loans was similarly shown to have a highly significant and negative relationship to the outcome. Somewhat counterintuitively, grade point average showed a negative effect on within-year persistence. As students' GPAs increased, the likelihood of persisting decreased. It may be that some students with higher grades or with an interest in specializing in science- and math-related majors transferred to higher status institutions or to campuses offering programs more closely aligned with the students' specific majors.

The logistic regression results suggest that participation in SI contributes significantly to within-year persistence. As important feedback with regard to how SI supports equity, this appeals to the rigorous standard of "equal results" as a measure of equity in education (Howe, 1997). Descriptive results show that participation in SI is widely distributed across racial/ethnic groups and income categories. Furthermore, students in the sample who placed into developmental math courses participated in SI sessions at rates higher than students who took no developmental courses. The results suggest that participation in SI sessions contributed to the persistence of students of color as well as of White participants and to the persistence of academically underserved students as well as of students whose precollege educational experiences prepared them for freshman level courses. These results echo findings in previous research on SI

(Blanc, DeBuhr, & Martin, 1983; Fjortoft, Bentley, Crawford, & Russell, 1993; Garland, 1987; Kallison & Kenney, 1992).

This analysis is somewhat typical of program evaluation studies and—as we have said—provides information on patterns of participation and the relationship between participation and academic success. As often happens with individual studies, however, these analyses leave parts of the relevant questions about the effects of SI unanswered. For example, the use of within-year persistence as an outcome leaves questions open regarding longer term effects associated with SI participation. Second, while we have controlled for variables thought to be related to persistence, the model does not account for all aspects of self-selection and the effects of unobserved characteristics on the outcome. In a third and related point, this analysis does not illuminate aspects of practice and implementation that are also relevant to an assessment of the program, especially with regard to the programmatic goals of providing academic support that emphasizes critical thinking and deep processing and disrupts deficit-model narratives while supporting equity. Consequently, implications for further research include three immediate steps to clarify these results and make them more useful: 1) extend the analyses to incorporate year-to-year persistence and persistence to graduation; 2) employ a two-stage model to account further for the self-selection effects on SI participation; and 3) gain more information about teaching and learning practices as they unfold in SI sessions at Regional University. The evaluation discussed in the next section of this chapter moves in the direction of this third step, shedding more light on the effectiveness, reach, and potential of the SI program.

SI Leaders' Voices: An Assessment of Programmatic Practice

In the spring of 2006, IPAS researchers undertook a second evaluation of SI at Regional University, this time adopting a qualitative approach aimed at understanding from SI leaders' perspectives what occurs in SI sessions at the institution. In this study we focused on how issues of cooperative learning, deep processing, and deficit-model resistance play out in their work on campus. A total of ten SI leaders, approximately half the total number of SI leaders at this campus, were recruited by SI program directors at Regional University to join two focus groups for this assessment. The participants worked in support of a range of SI courses (e.g., math, sociology, accounting, and geography) and also had varying levels of experience as SI leaders. In analyzing these focus group discussions, conducted by IPAS researchers, we coded transcripts independently and subsequently discussed emerging themes. A second round of coding followed based on these discussions and on the informational and assessment needs voiced by the SI program staff as well.

In the following thematic analysis, we focus on three main areas. First, we explore SI leaders' descriptions of their own expectations and practices related to the cooperative learning approach associated with SI. These descriptions include examples from the SI leaders' training and from their work with participating students and faculty members. Second, we discuss what the SI leaders told us of their encounters with others' perceptions of SI on campus. Third, we explore how the implementation of cooperative learning played out across the curriculum. While implementation varied across course sections, one example illustrates the complexities that arose particularly in courses connected with applied fields of study.

SI Leaders' Practice of Cooperative Learning

Focus group participants reported that a formal training program was first provided on campus to SI leaders in 2006, although the SI program had been in place since 2000. This training created an expectation that SI sessions would be based on the cooperative learning strategy, with discussion and group work for solving a problem or answering a question (Johnson, Johnson, & Smith, 1998). One SI leader's description illustrates this point:

> *The first couple of times that I was in SI, I had no training whatsoever. I had no idea what kind of techniques to use, I really think that probably the first semester I was more tutoring than being an SI leader. It tended to be a little more one-on-one and I wasn't certain, eliciting anything from them as much as I was re-lecturing . . . . Then when we came to this training program, then I really realized that there was a method to the madness. I wasn't supposed to be a lecturer, but that we were supposed to discuss.*

This excerpt illustrates the participant's belief that being an SI leader is strongly linked with the use of cooperative learning strategies. The SI leaders identified techniques they learned during the 2006 training session. Examples of these included redirecting discussions on irrelevant topics, making a room more conducive to student interaction, and encouraging higher achieving students to contribute their knowledge to the SI sessions.

It is important to look as well at how the SI leaders incorporated cooperative learning into their sessions. Several participants in both focus groups described taking on the role of facilitator during sessions and linked their role consistently to the creation of an environment that would encourage students to ask questions and work together to seek out the answers.

SI leaders also described moments when some students attending sessions resisted the cooperative learning strategy and seemed to expect SI leaders to lecture or to simply provide answers to their questions. One SI leader explained how she dealt with these expectations and successfully implemented cooperative learning:

> *They'd always want me to tell them the answers. You know what I'm going to do? I had them break up into groups and say, "Now, I'm not going to tell you the answer but what I want you guys to do is to work together, try to figure it out, because," I said, "I'm not going to be there when you're going to be taking the test."*

One SI leader who understood the cooperative learning focus of SI felt nevertheless that this strategy did not work for her course in an applied subject and felt the training did not give examples of cooperative learning techniques for assignments other than reading or writing tasks. In spite of having this explicit doubt, she described using practices consistent with cooperative learning, such as encouraging students to participate and to share knowledge to solve problems:

> *I tried to do how they [SI training] wanted us to do it in the beginning. It seemed like this isn't working . . . . If they had questions, I would do one but I was always like [as if speaking to the students] "What do I do next?" "What do I do here?" They wouldn't necessarily tell me what I thought I would do next, but if I knew I would get to where I needed to be, I would let them direct me. When we would do it their way, then I would say, "You know. We could have gone back here and done this differently." They are like "Oh." Then we would get to where they would go up and actually work the problems on the board and explain it to each other.*

In making sense of SI leaders' experiences with cooperative learning during sessions, we have drawn on the concept of deep processing as explored in the study strategies literature (Elliot, McGregor, & Gable, 1999; Entwistle, 2000). Deep processing, described in some cases as critical thinking, involves challenging the authenticity of information encountered and attempting to integrate new information with prior knowledge and experience. It is distinct from surface processing, a category including learning processes such as memorization and repetitive rehearsal of material (Elliot et al., 1999, p. 549).

One key characteristic associated with deep processing is the strategy of understanding and relating the new information to personal experiences (Entwistle, 2000). Deep processing occurs when students acquire knowledge by comparing new information to prior knowledge and then integrating it into their own frames and stores of knowledge, thus gaining a richer understanding and appreciation of the content. When asked about their SI experience, the SI leaders consistently referred to their deeper understanding of the course material as one of the greatest benefits of being an SI leader:

> *I think SI, it's all about helping other people but it really helps [the SI leader] as a student too because you had this course earlier and now you're, later on you've learned more about it. And it's stuff that I completely forgot about, and it supplements what I'm learning now, and it's all, like, it goes in the circle*

Deep processing involves applying knowledge learned in one area to another area, which in turn provides a richer understanding to both content areas as one finds interconnections between them. One student described her experience of applying prior business knowledge to leading SI sessions:

> *I have a business background so I think of everything like a sales call. That's how it is. You go and present the information. You make your trial close to see if they're going to buy it. They understand it, then you're good. You made your sale. If they don't get it then you have to go back and adjust. After all that time, that's exactly how I've, that's always like a sales call to me. I'm always like, we have to go back. We didn't get that. Let me see what else I have to say to them. Maybe they can get this.*

Participants' descriptions of and expectations for deep processing in SI sessions come through clearly in these focus group discussions. Examining these perceptions and experiences gives us a glimpse into how SI unfolds in practice at Regional University.

Campus Perceptions of SI

The campus community's knowledge about SI at Regional University was reflected in students' and instructors' perspectives on two points in particular: (a) the purpose of SI and (b) SI leaders' role in the learning process. SI leaders said they encountered perceptions of SI's purpose in interactions with faculty and students. They described their peers' knowledge of SI as limited and the general campus perception of the program as a "remedial" or "tutoring" intervention for struggling students. This reputation was perpetuated, they believed, by well-intentioned instructors who encouraged students to participate in SI but who routinely recommended it only for students who needed help. In the following quote, an SI leader sees this as a central challenge.

> *[W]e also have to talk to the professors and really get them to stop thinking of SI as a remedial program, because a lot of the professors are saying "If you need help. If you have questions, go to the SI program." Instead of saying "If you want a better understanding of what we're learning, then you should go and sort of expand on your experience."*

SI leaders believed that students who were doing well might not consider attending SI because they thought it unnecessary and that other students would avoid SI because they thought it would stigmatize them as remedial students. The fact that there was a misperception of the SI program as only a service for struggling students was borne out further in the attendance at SI sessions. SI leaders reported that some students stopped coming to SI sessions after doing well on their first exam and that attendance conversely increased among some students after they performed poorly on an exam. These findings suggest that low attendance may be attributable in part to a lack of understanding in the campus community about the goals and practices associated with SI.

Cooperative Learning Throughout the Curriculum

In the cooperative learning approach, the content of SI sessions is determined by the course faculty member. Some instructors who fully incorporated the SI program into their courses provided the SI leaders with practice questions and old tests and quizzes. Yet SI leaders reported that other instructors did not see as readily how cooperative learning could be applied in their courses. In addition, using the cooperative learning strategy was difficult for some of the SI leaders assigned to science or math-based courses because the strategy was not demonstrated in the classroom. Moreover, the traditional cooperative learning techniques of discussion and small group activities—even to some SI leaders—did not seem to apply as readily to courses in which the main focus is application of formulas or identification. One SI leader expressed this view in connection with a course in accounting:

> *Mine was basically numbers and concepts . . . . A reading course like I guess anthropology and sociology where you*

actually have to read and like relate back if there's a question like "What does blah, blah, blah ___? What are the different forms of ___?" . . . But with accounting, I mean, this is how it was done and this is how it was supposed to be done and you can't change the words in it or you'll be wrong.

In this passage, the SI leader outlines the differences she sees in how well cooperative learning applies across fields and discipline. These comments shows a view— reflected almost universally in the participants' descriptions of SI sessions— that cooperative learning is central to the SI approach. In addition it illustrates the variation in how SI leaders saw this playing out in practice in sessions. As highlighted throughout our discussion of these themes, the SI leaders who participated in the focus groups defined in practice how the cooperative learning strategy has been utilized in this program. Their descriptions of how they carried out their role as SI leaders—in addition to their expectations both in SI sessions and in the classroom—consistently demonstrated this connection. Moreover, through exploring these questions with SI leaders we are able to shed light on how perceptions of the program, sometimes from faculty and students and sometimes from SI leaders themselves, can complicate the implementation of some central aspects of the SI approach.

SI leaders' perceptions and experiences point to a number of implications for practice. In addition to clarifying to all participants the purpose and strategy of the program's cooperative learning framework, results suggest that activities to improve knowledge on campus about SI, especially for participating faculty and students—using handouts, information sessions, or Web page resources, for example—might be a beneficial and strategic place to begin. Further support for SI leaders who may have difficulty in applying cooperative learning to certain material or fields of study would further bolster SI leaders' practice within the cooperative learning framework, and would promote their successful engagement of participating students.

Discussion and Conclusion

When we controlled for student characteristics, high school preparation, college experiences and financial aid, participation in supplemental instruction was found to have a significant and positive effect on the likelihood of a student persisting from semester-to-semester in the first analysis outlined here. Previous evaluations conducted by IPAS showed similar results for SI's relationship to year-to-year persistence and to persistence across three consecutive semesters as well. However, it should be noted that because students elect to participate in SI, these results may have been attributable in part to self-selection. Students who share distinct and relevant characteristics— strongly motivated students, for example—may participate in SI sessions in larger numbers. Similarly, faculty members who share certain relevant characteristics—teachers in a particular department, for example, or those who adopt a learner-centered approach—may elect to incorporate SI into their courses in greater numbers than faculty members who differ on these points. In either case, it is possible that evaluation results reflect these patterns of self-selection.

The qualitative findings reported in the second analysis here illuminate in part how this self-selection plays out. Faculty and student decisions to participate in the program are influenced in some part by perceptions of what SI is and for whom it is intended. This study may also point to ways to alleviate the extent to which self-selection confounds our understanding of the program's effects. This kind of examination will allow practitioners, policy makers, and researchers to understand more about the effects of SI programs and, therefore, to devote efforts and resources more efficiently to the future development and continued improvement of the program.

This chapter points to the need to re-center evaluation of SI. To be effective, evaluation of these programs should be broad and at the same time in tune with the organic and realistic goals of the programs—conceiving effectiveness on the programs' own terms.

SI is effective. Persistence analyses and other traditional modes of evaluation tell us so, and yet these kinds of investigation are often vulnerable to the question of self-selection bias. Moreover, they sometimes fail to point to actionable suggestions for enhancing the good effects we see through this type of evaluation. Evaluation based on qualitative data provides further information—about what happens in SI sessions and in the courses themselves—and it provides insight into program participation, showing the dynamics and conditions of session attendance. Further study in a similar vein could also illuminate the dynamics and attitudes associated with participation and provide insights into how to increase participation overall. Finally, expanded inquiry can further our understanding of the role of self-selection, thus improving our capacity to learn about program effects from inferential analysis.

Taken together, these studies indicate that we should move forward, as others have recommended (e.g., Congos & Schoeps, 1999), with a multipronged approach to evaluating SI programs. In addition to employing both qualitative and quantitative analysis, we should ground these examinations in the underlying goal of increasing equity in higher education. To do this for SI in particular, practitioners should draw on the transformative elements of the original SI model—elements that are aimed at helping institutions achieve educational equity. Likewise, assessment specialists and institutional policy makers should support individual programs in their efforts to institute this kind of practice within the entrenched and replicative discourses that predictably arise on campus and inform the expectations of faculty and students. These replicative discourses—mischaracterizations of SI's goals or subtle stigmatization, for example—curtail and complicate practitioners' and student leaders' ability to realize the most effective potentialities of the program. In order to draw the best results from SI programs, campus policy makers need to understand more not only about the effectiveness of the programs but also about the conditions under which they operate.

References

Arendale, D. R. (2000). *Effect of administrative placement and fidelity of implementation of the model on effectiveness of supplemental instruction programs.* Unpublished doctoral dissertation, University of Missouri-Kansas City, Kansas City.

Blanc, R., DeBuhr, L., & Martin, D. C. (1983). Breaking the attrition cycle: The effects of supplemental instruction on undergraduate performance and attrition. *Journal of Higher Education, 54*(1), 80–90.

Casazza, M. E., & Silverman, S. L. (1996). Learning assistance and developmental education: A guide for effective practice. San Francisco: Jossey-Bass.

Chatterjee, S., & Hadi, A. S. (2006). *Regression analysis by example* (4th ed.). Hoboken, NJ: Wiley-Interscience.

Coleman, J. (1968). The concept of equality of educational opportunity. *Harvard Educational Review, 38*(1), 7–22.

Coleman, J. S. (1966). *Equality of educational opportunity.* Washington, DC: National Center for Education Statistics.

Conant, J. B. (1943, May). Wanted: American radicals. *The Atlantic Monthly, 171*(1), 41–45. .

Congos, D. H., & Schoeps, N. (1999). Methods to determine the impact of SI programs on colleges and universities. *Journal of College Student Retention, 1*(1), 23.

Dennett, D. C. (1984). Elbow room: The varieties of free will worth wanting. Cambridge, MA: MIT Press.

Dowd, A. (2007). Community colleges as gateways and gatekeepers: Moving beyond the access "saga" toward outcome equity. *Harvard Educational Review, 77*(4).

Elliot, A. J., McGregor, H. A., & Gable, S. (1999). Achievement goals, study strategies, and exam performance: A mediational analysis. *Journal of Educational Psychology, 91*(3), 549–563.

Entwistle, N. (2000). Approaches to studying and levels of understanding: The influences of teaching and assessment. In J. C. Smart (Ed.), *Higher education: Handbook of theory and research,* Vol. XV (pp. 156–218). New York: Agathon Press.

Fjortoft, N., Bentley, R., Crawford, D., & Russell, J. C. (1993). Evaluation of a supplemental instruction program at a college of pharmacy. *American Journal of Pharmaceutical Education, 57*(3), 247–251.

Garland, M. (1987). *Research study on effectiveness of supplemental instruction (SI) with minority students.* Kansas City, MO: University of Missouri-Kansas City, Center for Academic Development.

Gattis, K. W. (2002). Responding to self-selection bias in assessments of academic support programs: A motivational control study of supplemental instruction. *Learning Assistance Review, 7*(2), 26–36.

Hossler, D., Ziskin, M., Kim, S., Cekic, O., & Gross, J. P. K. (2007). *Student aid and its role in encouraging persistence.* New York: Rethinking Student Aid Study Group.

Howe, K. R. (1997). Understanding equal educational opportunity: Social justice, democracy, and schooling. New York: Teachers College Press.

Johnson, D. W., Johnson, R. T., & Smith, K. A. (1998). Cooperative learning returns to college: What evidence is there that it works? *Change, 4,* 26–35.

Kallison, J. M., & Kenney, P. A. (1992). *Effects of a supplemental instruction (SI) program in first-semester calculus courses.* Paper presented at the annual meeting of the American Educational Research Association, San Francisco.

Koski, W. S., & Levin, H. M. (1998). *Replacing remediation with acceleration in higher education: Preliminary report on literature review and initial interviews.* Stanford, CA: National Center for Postsecondary Improvement. (ERIC Documentation Reproduction Service ED 428 589)

Lavin, D. E., & Hyllegard, D. (1996). Changing the odds: Open admissions and the life chances of the disadvantaged. New Haven, CT: Yale University Press.

Lissner, L. S. (1990). The learning center for 1829 to the year 2000 and beyond. In R. M. Hashway (Ed.), *Handbook of developmental education* (pp. 127–154). New York: Praeger.

Lundeberg, M. A. (1990). Supplemental instruction in chemistry. *Journal of Research in Science Teaching, 27*(2), 145–155.

Lundell, D. B., & Collins, T. (2001). Toward a theory of developmental education: The centrality of "discourse." In D. B. Lundell & J. L. Higbee

(Eds.), *Theoretical perspectives for developmental education* (pp. 49–61). Minneapolis, MN: University of Minnesota, Center for Research in Developmental Education and Urban Literacy.

Martin, D. C., Blanc, R. A., DeBuhr, L., Alderman, H., Garland, M., & Lewis, C. (1983). *Supplemental instruction: A model for student academic support.* Kansas City, MO: University of Missouri-Kansas City, ACT National Center for the Advancement of Educational Practices.

National Center for Supplemental Instruction. (1994). *Supplemental instruction.* Kansas City, MO: University of Missouri-Kansas City, Center for Academic Development.

Peled, O. N., & Kim, A. C. (1996). *Evaluation of supplemental instruction at the college level* (Research Report). Chicago: National-Louis University.

Price, M., & Rust, C. (1995, May). Laying firm foundations: The long-term benefits of supplemental instruction for students on large introductory courses. *Innovations in Education and Training International, 32*(3), 123–130.

Sadovnik, A. R. (1994). Equity and excellence in higher education: The decline of a liberal educational reform. New York: Peter Lang.

Shaw, K. M. (1997). Remedial education as ideological battleground: Emerging remedial education policies in the community college. *Educational Evaluation and Policy Analysis, 19*(3), 284–296.

Traub, J. (1994). City on a hill: Testing the American dream at City College. Reading, MA: Addison-Wesley.

Turner, S. E. (2004). Going to college and finishing college: Explaining different educational outcomes. In C. M. Hoxby (Ed.), *College choices: The economics of where to go, when to go, and how to pay for it* (pp. 13–56). Chicago: University of Chicago Press.

CHAPTER 6

THE INDIANA PROJECT ON ACADEMIC SUCCESS IN PRACTICE: BRINGING ORIENTATION TO A COMMUNITY COLLEGE CAMPUS

Pauline J. Reynolds, Melanie A. Rago, and Roderick S. Brown

The Indiana Project on Academic Success (IPAS) and its action inquiry model can be likened to a journey. On this journey, IPAS provided maps, legend, and compass, and then each of the campuses involved with the project chose its own destination, route, mode of transport, and those who would come along for the ride. A host of unique variables shaped the project as a whole, with each campus engaging in the project on its own terms and in its own way. Contrary to any rigidity that may be inferred from the step-by-step nature of the model, as detailed in the section on IPAS action inquiry in Chapter 7 of this volume as well as in other publications (e.g., St. John & Wilkerson, 2006), in practice these campuses worked creatively within the model and adapted it. As a result, IPAS became a very different project at each participating institution.

Of the different types of institutions participating in IPAS, some of the most invested in the process were the state's community colleges. Campus leaders, administrators, and faculty at some of these institutions took full advantage of their engagement with the project in their dedication to the success of their diverse student bodies. The campus of Ivy Tech Community College in Richmond, Indiana, proved to be one of those institutions.

This chapter illustrates the IPAS process at work on a single campus and highlights the practical aspects of involvement in this process as well as the research endeavors embarked upon as part of committed participation in the project. It introduces the challenges chosen for inquiry by the campus and its IPAS team, the manner in which the team engaged in the inquiry process, and the ways the team interpreted the model. Earlier writing on IPAS has recognized the value of qualitative research as part of an institution's efforts to learn more about its student body, students' needs, and the efficacy of programs provided for them (St. John, 2006). This chapter presents part of the qualitative work conducted during the project by focusing on a description and evaluation of the pilot undertaken to address areas to enhance student success at Ivy Tech Richmond. It also illustrates the value of using pilot programs as a means of testing solutions for our students.

121

Ivy Tech Richmond and IPAS

Institutional Context

Ivy Tech Community College–Richmond (ITCCR) is one of Ivy Tech Community College of Indiana's 23 campuses in 14 regions. Established in 1963 by the Indiana General Assembly, Ivy Tech (then Indiana Vocational Technical College) began with a modest $50,000 charter. In 1995, the college changed its name to Ivy Tech State College; ten years later, the institution redefined itself and rewrote its mission statement to address its more comprehensive role in the state. As Ivy Tech Community College of Indiana, the state's only community college, the institution seeks to serve as "a statewide, open-access, community college that provides residents of Indiana with professional, technical, transfer, and lifelong education for successful careers, personal development, and citizenship" (http://ivytech.edu/about/mission).

Ivy Tech Community College of Indiana has recently experienced tremendous growth, thanks in large part to its affordable tuition and its commitment to Indiana's workforce development. Between the academic years 1999–2000 and 2005–2006, Ivy Tech's full-time enrollment surged by 71 percent statewide, making it the second largest college in Indiana. Reflecting those trends, ITCCR, an Ivy Tech campus since 1968, now serves over 3,000 credit students each year and over 300 noncredit students through its Workforce and Economic Development division. At the end of fall 2006, the reported headcount at ITCCR had increased by almost 19 percent from the end of fall 2005.

The student body of Ivy Tech has started to mirror that of other community colleges nationwide. Consistent with national trends, the diversity of the Ivy Tech student body has changed significantly over the college's short history. Originally the school enrolled predominantly adult students and those desiring to hone their technical skills; however, the college's new identities— first as "state college" then as "community college"—have enticed students right out of high school as well as those considering transferring to other institutions. Minority enrollment continues to increase; at ITCCR, ethnic minorities comprise less than 6 percent of the population in the region's service area but make up over 8 percent of the student body. Like students at most community colleges, the majority of Ivy Tech students are employed and enrolled part time. Also, the overwhelming majority of incoming first-year students at Ivy Tech require remediation in at least one of the following areas: mathematics, reading, or writing.

The Project at ITCCR

The IPAS process is divided into four main stages: Assessment, Organization, Action Inquiry, and Evaluation. Together, these stages provide an ongoing means of systematically managing institutional efforts to assess, improve, and test programs or initiatives intended to assist students. ITCCR diligently followed the guidelines provided by IPAS on the structure and activities of these stages. On the basis of this advice they assembled faculty, staff, and administrators to discuss critical challenges at their institution by comparing ITCCR assessment results with statewide results.

According to project guidelines, each IPAS partner campus was to assemble a team of faculty and staff representing the following areas: administration, institutional research, student development, and academic programs. "Team Richmond," as ITCCR's team was eventually dubbed, consisted of four high-profile employees with myriad job responsibilities: the dean of student affairs, the registrar, the director of student services, and the department chair of liberal arts and academic services. The composition of this group would prove to be both a blessing and a burden to ITCCR's process; while each member was committed to the project, the daily demands of the respective positions of these individuals sometimes resulted in IPAS being a low priority.

Based on internal and IPAS-generated persistence data, Team Richmond identified in the assessment of their students' needs the following challenges: financial aid, first-generation students, and academic support. Each team member convened a diverse workgroup to address one of these challenges. Coincidentally, ITCCR's retention committee had recently distributed two surveys to the campus community—one version for students and the other for faculty and staff. These surveys, based on the National Student Satisfaction Report developed by Noel-Levitz, attempted to measure student satisfaction with the institution, the importance that different demographic groups of students placed on various experiences at ITCCR, and the performance gap— i.e., the difference between the importance score and the satisfaction score. The surveys provided further internal evidence for the team members as they considered the relation of their chosen challenges to student success. The results of these surveys indicated that while students were satisfied with faculty, extracurricular activities, and campus security, they desired improvements in services such as tutoring, financial aid, advising, and orientation. Faculty and staff noted that students needed more resources to facilitate their self-efficacy.

Using this variety of qualitative and quantitative data, generated both internally at ITCCR and as part of the IPAS process, Team Richmond discussed ways to address all three challenges effectively and efficiently. A revamped orientation program soon emerged as the best way to address each challenge. The team also postulated that students with these challenges might not persist because they might not understand the college culture, the way higher education works, or the language of the academy. In other words, first-generation students, academically underprepared students, and students on financial aid at ITCCR might lack the requisite cultural capital to be successful in college and to remain enrolled. Hence, Team Richmond formed two hypotheses: (1) a revamped orientation program, required for all new degree-seeking students, would facilitate greater *academic literacy,* defined as knowledge/ information students need to make appropriate decisions and to find help at college; and (2) an increase in academic literacy among students with these needs would result in higher persistence rates among them.

Orientation

The choice of orientation as a possible solution to ITCCR's challenges is supported by the recent literature. Mullendore and Banahan (2005) write:

> Orientation can be the defining moment in the transition to college for the student—a time in which basic habits are formed that influence students' academic success and personal growth—and marks the beginning of a new educational experience.

Orientation programs have been in existence for as long as students have needed support in their transition to the college experience, dating back to the founding of Harvard and its program to match new and returning students (Upcraft & Gardner, 1989). Programs resembling those we know today began after World War II, when the introduction of the G.I. Bill drastically increased enrollment and diversity on college campuses, thereby creating a need to assist first-year students in a more systematic, less individualized way (Barr & Upcraft, 1990).

Programmatically, four-year and two-year college orientation programs include many of the same components. Although orientation programs may vary greatly from one institution to another based on the institution's mission, most orientation programs have the common goal of promoting academic success for and retention of their students. Upcraft and Farnsworth (1984) state, "orientation is any effort on the part of the institution to help entering students make the transition from their previous environment to the collegiate environment and to enhance their success in college" (p. 27).

There is a growing body of research that supports the value of orientation programs for first-year students at community colleges (Cuseo, 1997). In 2005, the National Survey on Student Engagement (NSSE) reported that students who attended an institution-sponsored orientation program:

- participated in more educationally enriching activities,
- perceived the campus environment to be more supportive,
- reported greater developmental gains during their first year of college, and
- were more satisfied with their overall college experience.

Student orientation, with its long history of proven success in aiding student transition, may be one of the most viable and cost effective measures a community college can undertake in its effort to serve a broad and diverse student population that increasingly includes first-generation and first-time-in-college students. In addition to the typical transition needs, these students may have limited resources to aid them in their college transition (Tinto, 1987). The financing of programs will always be a concern for the tightly budgeted community college; however, except for human resource expenses, orientation is one of the few programs that can be done at little or no cost.

Ivy Tech Richmond and Orientation

ITCCR did have an orientation program before the one piloted with IPAS. In this prior program, new students were invited to participate in a brief, informal, voluntary meeting where they were introduced to the campus, some staff members, and a couple of key services, like the campus computer network. In comparison, a more robust, comprehensive program would have resource implications, including human resource impacts from the staff's development and provision of the program as well as financial impacts on the campus budget.

Some ITCCR stakeholders wondered if a mandatory student orientation could best address the transition needs of new college students by providing students with increased academic literacy, including the skills necessary to navigate financial aid procedures. After reviewing the literature and research, the ITCCR team decided that an orientation program was the most viable and efficient way to reach as many students as possible with immediate and lasting effects. The consensus across the Team Richmond workgroups was that an orientation program could have a positive impact on persistence rates but that it should not be promoted or perceived as a panacea for all retention ills at ITCCR.

The Action Inquiry stage of the IPAS model specifies that each campus workgroup will look internally at institutional resources and externally in research and literature in the field for solutions to their challenges. Following the IPAS guidelines, they would then assess possible solutions, develop an action plan, and implement and evaluate a pilot project. Accordingly, Team Richmond, in collaboration with IPAS staff, coordinated student focus groups to discuss their financial aid and academic support experiences. Data from each focus group confirmed Team Richmond's hypothesis on the need for enhanced orientation. Students in the financial aid focus groups confessed their ignorance about the financial aid process; bemoaned the lack of clear, accurate financial aid information; and expressed the need to develop their financial management skills. Students in the academic support focus groups cited the Learning Resource Center as the campus's sole source of academic support and made specific recommendations for a comprehensive, new student orientation (e.g., academic advising, introduction to the campus and electronic resources, meetings with faculty).

Armed with data generated from both internal and external sources, Team Richmond submitted a proposal to their chancellor for a mandatory new student orientation program to develop academic literacy among new degree-seeking students at ITCCR—a program they hoped would ultimately increase persistence among these students, by helping students navigate services and requirements such as those contingent with financial aid eligibility. The proposal also recommended that students be required to take a class to develop skills and strategies for their successful adjustment to college. While the second part of the proposal was rejected, the orientation program recommendation was adopted.

The Pilot Orientation Program

The ITCCR team developed a new orientation program that featured components they believed would meaningfully increase students' chances for success at their institution. Success, for the purposes of this pilot, was broadly defined as a student completing and passing his or her classes, possessing the necessary skills to navigate the processes and procedures of higher education, and having a full understanding of academic requirements and the consequences of action or inaction on the fulfillment of academic goals.

The Pilot Program

The orientation program was designed as a series of independent, consecutive sessions over a half day of orientation. Each session during the program concentrated on a different area. Different departments were asked to design different segments of the program, which allowed for some flexibility in the order of sessions and the timing across the program as a whole. The main program features addressing the new orientation recommendations were a success skills workshop, an instructional and informational technology workshop, a tour of the institution, the opportunity to meet faculty, and the provision of important student management information.

In the instructional and informational technology workshop, new students were introduced to the ITCCR computer network and the computing services available to ITCCR students. During this workshop, students set up their own network identification and learned how to access services vital to their progress at ITCCR, such as e-mail, online grades, and online registration.

Information about financial aid deadlines and requirements were a large part of the student management information session. This session also included information about other important dates and "school management" issues, with the goal of helping students become fully aware of the consequences of their actions; for example, the consequences of dropping classes on financial aid eligibility.

The success skills workshop aimed to enlighten new students on strategies that could help them start their college career successfully. Advice on the importance of attending classes, preparing for classes, and taking notes was provided in this session, as well as guidance on where students could find further assistance at ITCCR. Students were also encouraged to take a first-year seminar as one of their first courses to further help them adjust to college and learn the skills for success.

Because ITCCR has a small campus, the orientation program's tour of the institution could take the students to most of the locations important to the ITCCR community, including the Learning Resources Center, the administrative offices, and the common areas. Students also had the opportunity to interact informally with faculty and staff. Lastly, each student received a computer flash drive as a gift for attending the orientation program.

Implications of the Pilot Program

Developed, planned, and implemented as a strategic endeavor to improve the way students interact with services and policies in their institution of higher education, the new orientation program at ITCCR had a feature that the ITCCR team believed to be integral to the success of the program: Attendance was mandatory for all new students. Although several Ivy Tech campuses throughout the state of Indiana offer a brief, voluntary orientation program akin to the one previously offered by ITCCR, none of the campuses has made orientation mandatory, due to the concern that such a requirement might negatively impact enrollment. The chancellor at ITCCR, however, was persuaded to allow the pilot orientation program to be mandatory in the summer and fall of 2005 to test the ITCCR team's hypothesis about the beneficial consequences of a mandatory orientation program. The new orientation program also tested an institutional assumption that requiring more of students initially would mean seeing fewer of them in the classroom.

The ITCCR team prepared for possible resistance to the mandatory orientation sessions by offering many opportunities in the weeks before the start of the semester for new students to attend the half-day program, with attendance at each capped at a total of 20 students. In comparison with the earlier program, this orientation program was a much larger undertaking, requiring substantial funding for food, attendance materials, and the flash drive gift. In addition to the increased financial demands, the program also demanded considerable extra time and energy of campus professionals who already had full schedules.

Monitoring and Evaluating the Efficacy of the Pilot Program

Working collaboratively, IPAS staff and the ITCCR team originally envisioned several forms of program evaluation. Due to campus administration concerns that a required orientation might have a negative impact on enrollments, it was essential that the pilot be effectively scrutinized. Thus, administrators kept a careful watch on enrollment management indicators as the semester started. Student participants were tracked and compared with previous cohorts to determine if orientation had had a positive impact on persistence. Impressions of the impact of the orientation program were collected and analyzed through a series of student focus groups and interviews with faculty and administrators. Additionally, pretest and posttest evaluations for the orientation program itself were developed and administered to measure what students immediately retained from the sessions. Unfortunately, the student information system at ITCCR was not sufficiently robust for the quantitative components of the assessment, but it was possible to carry out the pretest, posttest, and qualitative components of the evaluation.

Formal Program Evaluation

Methods

The data for the qualitative portion of this study were collected from a variety of sources. Two focus groups were held with a total of 12 students new to ITCCR who had participated in the new orientation program. Interviews were conducted with faculty and administrators to gain a better understanding of the observed changes in student behavior. Additionally, there were nine interviews with administrators who interact with new students and eleven phone interviews with faculty who teach courses taken predominantly by first-semester students. These faculty and administrators, several of whom had been involved in the development and implementation of the orientation program, represented a variety of disciplines and administrative areas.

The transcripts from the interviews were analyzed with an inductive, emic approach to identify emergent themes (Denzin & Lincoln, 2003). An emic approach allows a more complete understanding of the question of study. Rather than bringing preconceived notions or theories to the data, as in an etic approach, the researcher using an inductive, emic approach is firmly focused on the data as the source for codes and themes, thus permitting more understanding than just the verification or contradiction of established theories (Denzin & Lincoln, 2003).

The data was analyzed by coding the interviews with labels that distilled the meaning or relevance of portions of text into one or a few words (Carspecken, 1996; Miles & Huberman, 1994). These codes were developed into themes across the interviews as a whole. The coding of the data was limited to meaning and issues pursuant to the broad research question regarding orientation. For example, even though the data might reveal insights about nontraditional students, the function of faculty at community colleges, or the feminization of the community college, this analysis focused solely on meaning pertaining to the effects and efficacy of orientation.

A simple pretest and posttest were developed by the departments and individuals responsible for different facets of the orientation and members of the IPAS team. Questions were generated that distilled the information Team Richmond wished students to know, containing aspects they believed would increase the students' *academic literacy*. Unfortunately, due either to miscommunication or to reluctance from ITCCR, and despite repeated reminders, identifiers were not put on the tests. As the pretests and posttests could not be matched, more sophisticated measures of the effectiveness of the orientation could not be employed. Therefore, this evaluation could only generate simple percentage differences between the pretest and the posttest.

The Pretest/Posttest Results and Enrollment Management Information

The assessments administered to students at the beginning and end of the orientation program were based on the information presented during the program sessions and were developed in a collaboration of the ITCCR team and IPAS staff. The ITCCR team was heartened by the general improvement between pre- and posttest scores, with the average pretest score of 55.7 percent rising to the average posttest score of 80 percent.

The ITCCR team was also encouraged by the information from enrollment management. The numbers of students enrolled had not dropped as feared. In fact, in the first-year seminar, "College Life and Success Skills" (IVY 070), enrollment had noticeably risen—almost doubling from 45 in fall 2004 to 83 in fall 2005. The mandatory orientation program had apparently not deterred new students from enrolling after all.

Administrators also noticed that class attendance increased after the new orientation program began. For financial aid purposes faculty were required to report student attendance after the first two weeks of a course, and students who did not attend were administratively withdrawn. For summer 2005, the first academic session impacted by the new orientation program, no students who attended the orientation were administratively withdrawn although students had been in prior semesters. We have no way of knowing, however, whether in the semesters prior to the new program students who were administratively withdrawn had attended the then voluntary orientation program. This change in behavior compared to previous semesters might suggest that orientation had led students to understand the implications of simply vanishing. Making orientation mandatory might increase students' incentive to stay by getting them personally invested.

Results from the Focus Groups and Interviews

The students involved in the focus groups were fairly representative of students at ITCCR: young mothers, laid-off workers retraining, young people who may have struggled in high school, students needing to stay close to home, and proud first-generation college students. Using a language of difference and struggle, they talked about themselves, their experiences at ITCCR and with orientation. Describing themselves as different from the nation's typical college student, they felt special—with unique needs. This self-perception of special need and exceptionalism framed the students' conversations about orientation. One student candidly articulated the difference she perceived between students at ITCCR and students at other colleges:

I know a lot of big universities are about the money. They're
about getting the rich kids there. And with a small school like
[this], everybody here is working for the same goal. They're
not just here because their mommy and daddy are paying for
it. We're all here because we have a goal. We have things we
are working for, and everybody understands. Even the adults
understand that, because a lot of them were like us and went
through similar situations. They struggled before they went to
college; they've had burdens while they were doing it just like
every person at this school.

Like the woman quoted above, some participants spoke of having an affinity with other students and generally with faculty and administrators at ITCCR, describing ITCCR as both different from "big" universities and as a positive place to be—a place where people care and things are happening. They talked about having a fear of the unknown and feeling unable to manage college before orientation. At the time of the focus groups, however, they described the opposite feeling, saying that ITCCR felt safe and familiar and that they now felt they had the skills and knowledge to navigate their way at college. Students described orientation as an essential part of the journey from fear to familiarity, from being unable to being able.

There are three major, salient themes that emerged from the data, providing some insight into the impact of orientation on the participants: students' self-efficacy, the "personal touch," and orientation as "the start."

Self-Efficacy. The students experienced and expressed an increased confidence and awareness that they attributed in some part to their attendance at orientation, demonstrating that the program had emotional as well as informational benefits. One student said, "[It] helped me not be so scared, and they showed you what [college] was all about." Another student reinforced this sentiment: "It gave me the confidence just to know what I was doing."

Firsthand experience and knowing a bit more about what college was about gave them the courage to return to ITCCR when classes started. Rather than deterring students from enrolling, as some had feared, orientation gave them what they needed to enroll. It demystified and personalized their start at college, whether they were fresh out of high school or returning to college to retrain after being laid off.

Students were enthusiastic about what they had learned at orientation— some about the computer training they received, others about financial aid information. Most were now checking their grades on the e-learning system at ITCCR and using other resources orientation had exposed them to, such as the learning resource center. As demonstrated by the following dialogue, most important was the students' confidence that, "Maybe there were still questions, but if I had a question. . ." (first student) "You know who to go to" (second student).

Administrators described changes in the behaviors of students who had the new orientation compared with returning students who did not. They described the new students as acting more self-sufficient demonstrated by appearing better prepared and more informed about college processes and requirements than students in past years. Several administrators said students were contacting them less for information or assistance; if they did seek help, they were asking better, more sophisticated questions. As one administrator recalled, "Students that did not go through orientation are the students calling us on a regular basis—'I don't know how this works,' that sort of thing. New students—we're not getting those questions from them, or very few."

Administrators also spoke of the impact that orientation had on their own work. Some said they could work more efficiently due to decreased student traffic during normal hours. Those involved with admissions claimed they were able to organize their work better, as orientation allowed them to meet with students at set times rather than at odd appointments that students often missed or rescheduled.

Faculty also saw differences in their new students, some reporting that attendance improved and that these students seemed better informed about college life. Faculty said their first-year students were taking more initiative, for example, in their increased use of online resources. Many faculty members said they had noticed students using the online e-learning resources far more than any previous year to check their grades and assignments. Evidence of this came through students' reminders to post things on the site as well as through the system's log-in sheet. One faculty member gave this account:

> *The questions that I get I think that are indicative of their paying attention in the orientations is if I'm behind in posting grades they'll say, "Hey, Steph, you didn't get my grade for chapter seven homework up there. What's up?" That's really unusual because usually students have no knowledge of the online grade book and the fact that they can get stuff online too.*

Another faculty member commented, "I get far fewer questions about the e-learning Web site. I used to get hammered with those." With noticeably fewer such questions, this faculty member could focus more on the class content.

Students' accounts of their experiences and the evidence from administrators and faculty indicate that orientation had shaped the way students were negotiating college. After starting classes, these students seemed to be doing things for themselves rather than asking staff, taking initiative to keep on top of their class progress, and using services more than new students had in the past.

The "Personal Touch." Of huge importance to students is what may be called the "personal touch." Staff and faculty at ITCCR were described glowingly by most of the students in the focus groups for the way they interacted with students. As one student pointed out, the positive interactions started at orientation: "The staff was all there, so they came in and said 'hi.'"

Simple things, like calling professionals by their first names and having faculty home phone numbers, are significant to the students. As suggested in the student quote above, having so many people attend orientation "just for them" was noticed and appreciated by the students, who valued being able to talk with faculty and staff that one student described as "really friendly." Another student elaborated further,

> They talk to you, they work with you about a lot of things, and they don't just sit there on a business level. They try to get down to your level and work with you on everything, just so you're not on your own.

For these students, thanks to the investment of ITCCR faculty and staff, college came to be about community and family instead of about fear and lonely struggle. Most of these students expressed themselves in a way that portrayed they felt connected, communicated with, and joined to a community of care. The orientation program was the way they were welcomed into this community.

Feeling part of a community of care was manifested in the way several students described how people at orientation and at ITCCR in general made them feel. One student described it this way: "You're not just a number at Ivy Tech. There are people that truly care." Another student echoed this feeling: "You can tell right off the bat that they were there for you. They went above and beyond."

Students attributed this community of care to an impression that ITCCR was doing more for students and that as a small college it was able to be more attentive to students than other, larger colleges. In some ways the students interpreted the orientation program itself and the way it was designed as an expression of care. The care of students was not only espoused at ITCCR through orientation and beyond but was enacted—and the students saw and valued that.

Orientation as "the Start." Importantly, the focus group discussions indicated that orientation was just the start in helping students adjust to and negotiate college—without offering false promises. The students said that ITCCR faculty and staff reinforced the lessons they learned in orientation and that support from the services and people introduced to them in orientation carried on after the program. Several students mentioned, for example, the continuing help they received from staff in the financial aid office.

We might safely conclude from their own descriptions that these students felt prepared to start college. Indeed, orientation may have given the participating students a head start in comparison with former students at ITCCR. Interestingly, a few faculty and staff noted that students were helping each other more and would reference what they had learned in orientation when doing so.

One of the most tangible examples of orientation as being seen as "the start" is that all of the new degree-seeking students in one of the focus groups was taking the first-year seminar class because during orientation it had been promoted as especially helpful. As one student candidly stated with the affirmation of other students, "Orientation was the reason I took this class." This suggests that orientation affected these students' choices and that the students valued the study-skills sections of the program.

This qualitative evidence shows that the ITCCR team met its goal of preparing students to be more academically literate and more able to negotiate the demands of college. The new orientation also affected ITCCR in a few unanticipated ways, including increasing students' self-efficacy. Some administrators believed they could work more efficiently because of this, and some faculty felt this freed them to focus on teaching their classes rather than helping new students use ITCCR services. Students said orientation was a success not only because of the information they received and utilized but because of the way orientation made them feel: cared for and important. Key to this dimension were the ITCCR people involved in orientation and their availability to the students, which helped the students feel comfortable and supported in their new academic environment. The most influential aspect of the orientation and its impact on the students was the cohesion that ITCCR and its staff had between the espoused and enacted. Genuine care and support was a hallmark of their work and a major factor in the success of orientation.

ITCCR Orientation Today

New Student Orientation continues to thrive at ITCCR, with student responses remaining overwhelmingly positive. The program has maintained its mandatory status with no threat to enrollment. However, many components of the original program have changed. Today, an orientation session can accommodate up to 100 students instead of 20. Fewer and larger sessions are offered to alleviate the demands on student services staff and to encourage more faculty, deans, and the chancellor to attend. Effective fall 2007, all degree-seeking students at Ivy Tech campuses are required to take a College and Life Skills course, a suggestion rejected in the initial proposal to the chancellor of ITCCR. Perhaps to some extent the inclusion of a course of action previously dismissed recognizes the success of this program and the acceptance of the continuing relevance of its material by campus administrators. Team Richmond has also ensured that ongoing evaluation continues to assess the effectiveness of the program for students.

Limitations

This study illustrates the impact of orientation on students' initial experiences and interactions with ITCCR and possibly with higher education in general; however, the study may not provide stakeholders at ITCCR with measurable outcomes. This research does not provide a correlation between orientation and success indicators such as student retention.

One student focus group's decision to enroll in the first-year seminar demonstrated the influence of orientation and may indicate the potential of some bias in this study. However, the responses for this group did not appear to be substantially different in content or affect from those of students in the other focus group.

Students and staff found it hard, if not impossible, to predict negative effects of the orientation program or to think of ways it might be improved. Although that sounds like good news for the program, it may suggest a biased view.

Concluding Thoughts

This research and ITCCR's engagement with IPAS offer implications that align with persistence literature and that could influence institutional practice, particularly pertaining to the assessment and implementation of new programs. Although we did not perform a robust mixed-methods evaluation to assess the effectiveness of this program, the outcomes and subsequent action at ITCCR appear positive. Lots of changes have occurred as a result of taking a calculated risk and preparing a pilot orientation for prospective students, even though the conventional wisdom at the community college warned that such a requirement would hurt enrollment. Not only have changes occurred, but they are still going on. Part of IPAS's critical inquiry model encourages continuing evaluation so that assessment and reflection become integral to the way decisions are made about planning services at institutions as well as about determining the effectiveness of established services. As the evaluation for the pilot shows, not only was enrollment not negatively affected, but students seemed to have some immediate benefits from the program, as evidenced in the posttest results. The qualitative study also indicated some unexpected lasting effects from the program, such as the new student behaviors referred to by administrators and faculty. Admittedly, with this evaluation we do not know for sure if the new orientation produced results by enhancing measures of success such as higher GPAs or if it actually increased persistence. Future studies may be able to assess any impact orientation has on these success indicators.

This chapter practically demonstrates the potential power of components of the IPAS model. The proposal for the new, mandatory orientation was successful due to careful preparation supported by multiple sources of assessment. By proposing a pilot program rather than a permanent program, Team Richmond allowed the chancellor to take a calculated risk in incremental steps toward the kind of services his colleagues wished for their students. Community colleges often do not have the financial resources of four-year institutions. Pilot programs can provide community colleges a fiscally viable way to determine what services best suit the needs of their students. This pilot program clarified institutional misconceptions about the impact of a mandatory orientation on enrollment and paved the way for the provision of services proposed in the original proposal, but initially rejected by the chancellor. By following the IPAS guidelines and involving many colleagues in the workgroups to discuss, assess, plan, develop, and implement the orientation, the ITCCR team also garnered buy-in from staff.

Because the pre- and posttest interviews could not be linked, it may not have possible to confirm Team Richmond's hypothesis that increased academic literacy and more comprehensive orientation would increase student persistence. However, ITCCR's journey with IPAS demonstrated the importance of preparation, pilots, and people as institutions plan, develop, and implement new programs for students. Although it describes only one journey and one destination, this account of the IPAS activities at one campus hints at the diverse possibilities for other campuses.

References

Barr, M. J., & Upcraft, M. L. (1990). *New futures for student affairs: Building a vision for professional leadership and practice.* San Francisco: Jossey-Bass.

Carspecken, P. H. (1996). Critical ethnography in educational research: A theoretical and practical guide. New York: Routledge.

Cuseo, J. B. (1997). Freshman orientation seminar at community colleges: A research-based rationale for its value, content, and delivery. (ED411005). Unpublished manuscript.

Denzin, N. K., & Lincoln, Y. S. (2003). *The landscape of qualitative research: Theories and issues.* Thousand Oaks, CA: Sage.

Miles, M. B., & Huberman, A. M. (1994). *Qualitative data analysis* (2nd ed.). Thousand Oaks, CA: Sage.

Mullendore, R. H., & Banahan, L. A. (2005). Designing orientation programs. In M. L. Upcraft, J. N. Gardner, & B. O. Barefoot (Eds.) *Challenging and supporting the first-year student: A handbook for improving the first year of college* (pp. 391–409). San Francisco: Jossey-Bass.

National Survey of Student Engagement (NSSE). (2005). *Student engagement: Exploring different dimensions of student engagement.* Bloomington, IN: Indiana University Center for Postsecondary Research.

St. John, E. P. (2006). Lessons learned: Institutional research as support for academic improvement. In E. P. St. John & M. Wilkerson (Eds.), *Reframing persistence research to improve academic success: New Directions for Institutional Research, No. 130* (pp. 95–108). San Francisco: Jossey-Bass.

St. John, E. P., & Wilkerson, M. (Eds.). (2006). Reframing persistence research to improve academic success: New Directions for Institutional Research, No. 130. San Francisco: Jossey-Bass.

Tinto, V. (1987). Leaving college: Rethinking the causes and cures of student attrition. Chicago: The University of Chicago Press.

Upcraft, M. L., & Farnsworth, W. M. (1984). Orientation programs and activities. In M. L. Upcraft (Ed.), *Orienting students to college: New Directions for Student Services, No. 25* (pp. 27–38). San Francisco: Jossey-Bass.

Upcraft, M. L., & Gardner, J. N. (1989). The freshman year experience: Helping students survive and succeed in college. San Francisco: Jossey-Bass.

Section III

Informing Reflective Practice

CHAPTER 7

INQUIRY IN ACTION IN THE INDIANA PROJECT ON ACADEMIC SUCCESS: A FORMATIVE EVALUATION OF ACTION INQUIRY IN A MULTICAMPUS CONTEXT

Nate J. Daun-Barnett, Amy S. Fisher, and Krystal L. Williams

In *Moving from Theory to Action,* Tinto and Pusser (2006) describe a comprehensive model for guiding institutional action intended to facilitate student access, persistence, and success. The authors summarize and analyze various issues and in their findings suggest that to achieve the goals of persistence and success institutional commitment is primary and essential. They give particular attention to the role of presidents and chancellors, while also recognizing the importance of deans and directors in creating a campus climate committed to the success of all students. Tinto and Pusser acknowledge the important role of policy at three levels—federal, state, and institutional—and suggest that in promoting student access and success institutions must respond to their unique local context while adapting to the existing political climate.

The launching of the Indiana Project on Academic Success (IPAS) preceded the Tinto-Pusser report by a few years, yet it may be the first statewide initiative to do exactly as Tinto and Pusser suggested: to consider the complex interplay of federal, state, and institutional policies while crafting institutional strategies to improve student persistence. IPAS provides great promise for other states attempting to deal with the complexities of facilitating student success in college. In this chapter, we look at IPAS from a formative evaluation perspective to examine the implementation of its strategic planning process. The IPAS approach involves the use of strategic inquiry by campus administrators and faculty to address specific challenges related to student persistence and success. In our formative evaluation of IPAS, we paid particular attention to how the IPAS inquiry process was implemented at five campuses that had participated in the project since its inception. Our evaluation results are organized in a series of case studies illustrating both common challenges and keys to success as well as the unique and individualized approaches adopted by each campus.

141

In a lecture on her conceptualization of the strategic paradigm in contemporary higher education and the rationalist assumptions upon which it is built, Gumport (2006) suggested that four assumptions dominate how campuses approach strategy and planning: (1) colleges and universities can and should adapt purposively to a changing environment, on which they depend for many types of resources; (2) rational intentions can be articulated, shared, and carried out; (3) decisions and actions are consequential, in that they set processes in motion to bring about desired changes; and (4) campus leaders are expected to generate visible, strategic initiatives; in doing so they acquire legitimacy and are seen as appropriately forward-looking, even visionary. Gumport recognizes that in current organizational discourse, strategic approaches legitimate institutional decision making in the eyes of key stakeholders, but she argues that strategy and institutional planning practices must find ways to recognize the uniqueness of campuses as observed across institutional missions and campus cultures. In its utilization of a strategic inquiry process, IPAS provides a viable model for changing the way higher education administrators and researchers approach the planning process.

Indiana Project on Academic Success (IPAS)

The Indiana Project on Academic Success (IPAS) is a significant statewide effort to help institutions (1) develop an inquiry-based methodology and a language for understanding the challenges they face with respect to student success, (2) identify promising practices or interventions, (3) test those approaches, (4) evaluate the outcomes of those approaches, and (5) learn from those experiences along the way. Working with 16 campuses of mostly public institutions across the state of Indiana to develop better strategies to help their students succeed, IPAS provided training on this new methodology, conducted large-scale statewide research, shared research findings with the participating campuses, and provided technical support to the campuses. Action inquiry (described in detail in the next section) was used to elevate the importance of evaluating intervention strategies and to focus campus efforts on developing a broad and shared understanding of the challenges.

IPAS was initiated in 2003 with a grant from the Lumina Foundation for Education soon after two important developments in Indiana education— the adoption of the Core 40 curriculum, with more challenging high school graduation requirements for college-bound students; and the creation of the Twenty-First Century Scholars program, with a guarantee of funding for college for qualified low-income students (St. John, Musoba, Simmons, &

Chung, 2002). Both developments were designed to improve educational outcomes and future opportunities for students in Indiana, and it appeared that such changes were under way. This point is underscored by the fact that Indiana had moved from 40th to 17th in the nation in college participation shortly after the onset of these developments (St. John, Musoba, & Chung, 2004). Part of the IPAS task was to explore statewide data to evaluate the effectiveness of these efforts.

There was also a third development in the state prior to the initiation of IPAS that impacted the degree to which IPAS participants utilized the action inquiry process. As one participant noted, in 2000 the Board of Trustees for Indiana University (IU) and its extension campuses passed a one-percent tuition increase to fund programs specifically designed to improve student retention. Part of the IPAS task was to evaluate these programs at participating institutions: Some campuses took this opportunity to utilize the inquiry process to evaluate the success of their retention projects and to inform their planning processes accordingly. This was a considerable benefit to campuses that did not have the capability to conduct program evaluations to the extent that IPAS did with its access to data and its research team. All three statewide developments provide important context for understanding the implementation of IPAS because, in many ways, it was this confluence that made change possible.

This evaluation was an attempt to learn the extent to which the inquiry process was understood, adopted, and implemented at participating campuses. Bringing about change in organizations and institutions is complicated, and even the most promising changes can be successful only to the extent that they are well designed and properly implemented. As in a summative evaluation, a formative evaluation of IPAS will determine the utility of the action inquiry process and appropriate modifications and adaptations of that process for individual campus needs. Before evaluating the action inquiry process, however, it is important to understand the process and the steps that comprise it.

Action Inquiry

St. John and Wilkerson (2006) have been developing and testing a strategic planning process for campuses that uses an inquiry approach to understand the nature of a problem at a particular institution, develop steps toward addressing the problem, craft and implement intervention strategies, evaluate the intervention efforts, and utilize evaluative data in a continual process of planning and adapting (see Figure 7.1).

The steps through the action inquiry process begin with an honest and thorough examination of relevant data and the identification of critical challenges at the institution. The institutional planners then *build a shared understanding* of each challenge. To effect change, it is important to determine why the problem exists. The data used to identify challenges may also serve to test hypotheses for why the challenge exists. If the challenge is recurring, decision makers must consider previous attempts to resolve the challenge and the results of those attempts, looking for what might have been previously overlooked.

In the second step, planners *identify possible solutions,* considering both internal and external sources. In order to expand the options, it may be useful to consider solutions that have been applied to related challenges, even if they do not precisely match the current challenge.

Figure 7.1. IPAS Campus Inquiry Model

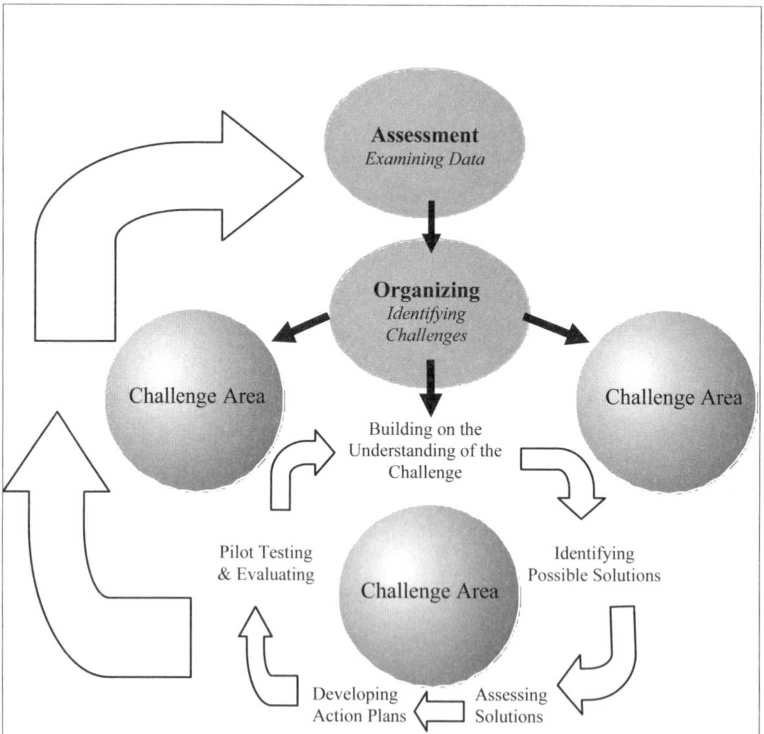

Source: St. John, McKinney, & Tuttle, 2006.

Once possible solutions have been identified, the team proceeds to the third step to *assess possible solutions*. How might each possible solution address the problem? What solution is supported in the literature? What solution fits the unique local and state context of the institution? What information is needed to evaluate the appropriateness and effectiveness of the strategy?

In the fourth step, the team *develops an action plan* for the pilot implementation of the proposed solution for the challenge. Can this solution be implemented by current staff? What are the internal and external budget considerations? What is the time frame for implementation and evaluation?

In the fifth step, the team *pilot tests and evaluates* the implemented solution, collecting data to evaluate the solution and, on the basis of that evaluation, reject or refine it. These evaluation results may be used to seek additional funding from internal and external sources.

As shown in Figure 7.1, the action inquiry process is a continuous loop, designed to generate a full understanding of challenges and the implementation of the most effective solutions possible. This process may be applied to each critical challenge identified in the initial assessment and may continue in subsequent iterations through the steps of the process as initiatives are piloted and evaluation results are fed back into planning.

Interview Method

Although IPAS is a centrally coordinated effort, it can also be viewed as a series of campus-specific intervention strategies. For this evaluation we employed a case study methodology to examine the unique approaches followed by five campuses that participated in IPAS. Over a period of four months a team of three researchers conducted 20 interviews with 35 faculty and administrators. Most of those interviewed either (a) were directly responsible for one of the retention strategies employed by the campuses, (b) served as top-level administrators who were directly involved or who gave approval for participation in the project, or (c) were campus coordinators or IPAS scholars with specific responsibilities to employ strategic inquiry as a planning tool for the campus and the evaluation of pilot tests of campus programs. Several interviewees had less direct contact with IPAS or the inquiry process but were involved in programs related to the institution's retention efforts. For example, two faculty members in the Regional Community College System (RCCS) had no direct knowledge of IPAS but they taught the freshman seminar that was the focus of IPAS activities at that campus.

Our analysis is presented below in five case studies—three are institution specific, one combines the activities of two institutions, and the last is a collaborative effort among three neighboring regional institutions that arose from participating in IPAS-sponsored meetings. Each case begins with a brief description of the institutional context and considers several of the following questions:

1. At what point in the change process did the campus begin participating in IPAS?
2. How did the campus utilize the action inquiry process?
3. How did institutional structures adapt to the new planning process?
4. What problems occurred, or what could have been changed to better meet the needs of the campus?
5. What role did IPAS technical support play in the experience of the campus in its adaptation of action inquiry?

Our initial description of each case addresses the first two questions above, and the remaining questions are addressed in the context of several salient themes that emerged from the interviews. Many of these themes were common across multiple campuses and in some cases across all five institutions. For example, Regional Community College System (RCCS) and Single Campus Community College (SCCC) are both in the same two-year community college system and, as such, their data and research capabilities are somewhat similar. At the end of the discussion of each case, we return to the questions above and to the related themes.

A theme was assigned to a given campus because it was particularly prominent in the campus's interviews or because it was cogently illustrated in the assets or needs of the campus. The benefit of this case-by-case analysis is that it explicitly demonstrates what happens when any sort of change strategy is adapted to a local community and campus context. The themes were not unique to each case, but the prominence of those themes, coupled with the combination of the assets and deficits of each institution, suggest that a strategy must be flexible and adaptable to be effective.

St. John (2008) considered the same set of interview data in his examination of the relationship between individual praxis and higher education professionals' organizational context. That work, which explored how professionals frame problems and develop strategies for addressing them, served as a validity check for this evaluation. St. John found that at campuses engaged in the inquiry process professionals demonstrated elements of reflective reasoning. While the individual was not the primary focus of our evaluation, we similarly found that institutions' adaptations of strategic inquiry changed the nature of the strategic planning process in some way on all five campuses.

This evaluation is not intended to determine the success or failure of implementation; to do so would be to suggest that success could be clearly defined by a static set of metrics consistent across all campuses. Each of these five campuses is in some way a success story in that each was active in IPAS and each utilized elements of the inquiry process. Success, then, in the context of this formative evaluation, is measured in terms of the extent to which a campus implemented the IPAS process as intended while adapting it as necessary to local conditions.

Analysis of Cases

The interviews at the five campuses participating in the formative evaluation illuminated our understanding of the implementation of the inquiry process. All of these institutions adopted the inquiry process, but each institution's utilization of the process depended on factors ranging from institutional support to the commitment of those responsible for implementation. Although IPAS was centrally coordinated, the adaptations for implementation were unique to each campus. For that reason, we approached the analysis of interview transcripts as a series of case studies, generally grouped by institution, with two exceptions. First, two institutions, identified as Regional Technical University (RTU) and Regional Comprehensive University (RCU), below,[1] were similar in terms of their experience with the IPAS process and were combined as a single case in our evaluation. Second, one IPAS effort grew out of regional cooperation among three institutions facing a common challenge—how best to serve a population of students that had to work while in school. We discuss this collaboration last.

We organized our analysis in cases because some process difficulties and benefits were more clearly evident at some campuses than others, although many of these themes were found across other campuses as well. We hope to illustrate that campuses varied in the extent to which they adopted the inquiry process, but we do not mean to suggest that one campus was more or less effective than another. Individuals are responsible for bringing about institutional change and it is they who must adapt any process to the existing institutional conditions. A successful process in this context, then, is one that is useful and accessible to those responsible for creating change in their particular context.

We begin our analysis by presenting the critical challenges identified by each campus. At the beginning of each case, we provide a brief

---

[1] The naming conventions for each institution are borrowed from St. John (2008).

description of where the process began, how it proceeded, and where the process was at the time of the interviews.

Case 1—Regional Community College System (RCCS)

Regional Community College System (RCCS) is comprised of four comparably sized institutions with a combined full-time equivalent (FTE) enrollment totaling nearly 5,500. One chancellor is responsible for the four coordinated campuses, and one campus is identified as the main campus. Although the campuses are separated by as much as 20 miles, each serves a similar population of students who are largely lower-income, first-generation, and under-prepared for college-level work. RCCS was an enthusiastic adopter of the IPAS approach in general and the inquiry process in particular. The year before IPAS was initiated, RCCS piloted programs for both faculty and student orientation. A dean of the institution reported the one or two hours of orientation were not adequate for students to learn what was necessary to succeed, so RCCS also developed a freshman seminar that was not compulsory but was recommended for all students who needed basic skills courses. During the pilot phase, a number of free-standing freshman seminar sessions were offered in addition to a number of sections linked to other courses. At the time of our interviews, the campus was still waiting for the results of the evaluation of the pilot program.

Access to Data. Early in the first interview at RCCS, a top-level administrator contextualized RCCS's participation in the IPAS process by stressing the importance of the project team being granted access to the state higher education data system:

> *The IPAS group at Bloomington has offered to do some of that [analysis] because they have access to our computer structure. They were granted that at the beginning of the process. I think that was a really smart move on the part of the state to allow them to get involved in that way. Because we have always been very closed to having another institution of any kind have access to our data . . . it was very smart on the part of the people on the Commission for Higher Education and everybody to open that up to the IPAS group.*

For the two-year institutions in particular, access to state data was an important incentive for participation because these institutions lacked adequate systems to run data for even many basic descriptive reports. We learned during the interviews that RCCS was investing in a statewide data system, but at that time it was still in the planning stages.

Table 7.1. Campuses and Identified Critical Challenges

Campus	Critical Challenges
Regional Community College System (RCCS)	First-year experience Working students Tutoring
Single Campus Community College (SCCC) Regional Technical University (RTU)	First-year experience Working Students Working students Supplemental instruction Academic recovery program
Regional Comprehensive University (RCU)	Undecided students Supplemental instruction Critical literacy program (remedial students) Working students
Private Christian University (PCU)	Undecided students
Collaborative on Working Students (CWS)	Working students

Source: St. John, McKinney, & Tuttle, 2006

Top-Level Support. At least three interviewees at RCCS identified the importance of the support of deans, directors, and the chancellor to the successful implementation of the freshman seminar program initiated as part of their IPAS efforts. In response to the question, "What were the two or three major challenges at RCCS?" a dean responded:

> *Well, the buy-in of the top administration. If the chancellor and the dean of student services and myself had not been willing to say we are willing to invest time, money, and*

> *effort because it has cost money to give downloads for courses, it costs money for travel . . . we came back from the Indy trip [the first IPAS meeting] we sat down and wrote up what it meant if we committed to this, what it was going to mean.*

Commitment meant two things to the dean of the college. First, the freshman seminar program was going to cost money, and they had to be willing to find the resources to support it. Second, and less explicit in this comment, the institution would need to be committed to participating in the inquiry process. For RCCS this meant considering the assessment data from IPAS, crafting a strategy to improve retention on campus, pilot testing the program, and evaluating the results. One member of the RCCS team responsible for much of the implementation of the freshman seminar noted the importance of top-level support as well, but conveyed a slightly different perspective:

> *You know, as the person in charge of most of the details, I found that part of the road [top-level support] really frustrating. At one point I was told by the academic dean to go through her and that was fine. I did not care. I just wanted a person to go to . . . now we have these assistant deans and when I tried to go to her [the dean] this semester, she referred me back to the assistant dean even though this is a division-wide project.*

The message of this comment was not that top-level support did not exist, but rather that the organizational structure could be difficult to navigate and that top-level support could be stronger. Top-level support may pose a larger problem for a multicampus system than for a single-campus institution. The chancellor of RCCS was supportive of the IPAS initiative and was willing to commit institutional resources, but successful IPAS efforts on each RCCS campus required buy-in from the dean of each campus. During the course of the interviews, we spoke with two of the four deans and both expressed their support for the project, but as the comment above suggests, that support did not always make the implementation process more effective.

External Legitimacy. Creating the perception of legitimacy was an important theme during a number of interviews and across most of the campuses, but views on this issue depended largely on one's role in the organization. One administrator, for example, viewed the IPAS process as creating legitimacy for their college success intervention strategy in the eyes of faculty:

> *They [faculty] will be more involved in it or impressed with it [intervention strategy] . . . once some statistical data comes out and says we have improved from where we were or we didn't improve and we are looking at changing it to see what else we can do with it.*

To a faculty member involved in the freshman seminar, the issue of legitimacy was framed in the context of both upper-level administration as well as peer institutions within the region:

> *You know [x] and [y] are big schools and we are just little [z] and so it is giving it a little more credibility so when the data come in, I think the whole thing will be more credible than if I had just worked on it. If this was my own project, I do not think it would have as much credibility as it does, but because I am working with the big boys. . . .*

For the chancellor, external legitimacy was cast in terms of validating what was already known by those at RCCS:

> *I think the opportunity to have the independent reviewer come in and work with us to kind of focus some of those areas to affirm what we thought was going on is actually going on and then how do we address it.*

Each of these perspectives on external legitimacy recognizes the fact that each of these individuals is accountable to various stakeholders and that a process like that offered by IPAS would be viewed as more legitimate than other approaches they might have utilized in the past.

Communication. The final important element of the RCCS adaptation of the IPAS process was the issue of communication up and down the RCCS institutional hierarchy and across campuses. The fact that the four campuses were spread over 20 miles and that each campus had separate coordination for its participation in IPAS may mean that communications at RCCS were more complicated than at other IPAS institutions. One aspect of the complications was illustrated above in the discussion of top-level support. In order for top-level support to be effective, that support must be communicated throughout the organization. In some cases, communicating across the organization can be difficult. Early in an interview at one of the campuses, a group of faculty and administrators suggested the communication between this campus and those coordinating the IPAS process could be improved. When asked how, one participant said "Well, I think just keeping the lines of communication open." This participant's later comment was more specific:

> *I think the problem was that because we were already doing the learning communities, I do not think it was an intentional exclusion . . . well I think it was intentional but not for bad purposes. It was because they were already doing something with the learning communities and we were never asked if we were interested [in the freshman seminar].*

This campus elected to pilot the freshman seminar but postponed the start-up for a year—until they had tested their learning community program. RCCS did not substantively change its institutional structures during its IPAS activities. The freshman seminar was added and linked to a number of basic skills courses, and the dean delegated additional IPAS participation responsibilities to their IPAS scholar, but RCCS did not add positions, substantially change the roles of existing staff members, or otherwise alter existing organizational arrangements. Most of the themes described in this case address the benefits of participating in IPAS but they imply that without top-level support, access to state data, and the external legitimacy of a statewide project led by the project team at IU Bloomington, this strategy for change might not have been possible at RCCS.

Communication is the one area that continues to present problems for RCCS. This stems in part from the fact that the institution is spread across four campuses, and the majority of individuals connected to the inquiry process are located at one of the campuses. Technical support was not a focus of the themes identified in the RCCS case, but the project team was instrumental in the success of RCCS's efforts. Providing access to state data was one critical role of the technical support team and this was directly beneficial in the assessment and planning stages of the process.

Case 2—Regional Technical University (RTU) and Regional Comprehensive University (RCU)

While Regional Technical University (RTU) and Regional Comprehensive University (RCU) are distinct, separate institutions with slightly different though overlapping critical challenges, their approaches to and adoption of the IPAS inquiry process were similar. Also, individuals on each campus reported similar benefits and difficulties in participating. Because of these similarities, it is useful to consider the two campuses together here. Both are regional affiliates of larger public universities, are located in the same region of the state, and as such draw from the same pool of students. The IPAS efforts at RCU are led by a faculty member, whereas at RTU an upper-level administrator fills this role. Both campuses already had several retention-related efforts under way when their association with IPAS began, and they elected to use those programs for participation in the project. These existing programs were evaluated as pilot programs by the IPAS team, and that data was used in further planning for the projects. Both campuses had experienced or were about to experience turnover in staff, which can influence the degree to which the inquiry process is understood and utilized.

    Evaluation Capacity. St. John (2008) has noted that a number of campuses participating in the IPAS process did not have on-campus institutional research capabilities and, therefore, they saw participation in IPAS as an opportunity to receive support in this area. A senior administrator at RCU made the point directly that, "our prime purpose was to get the IPAS expertise and assistance with evaluating these programs." He continued,

> *The evaluation is the main purpose [of our participation] and they've been helping us, but we have not gotten all of the data . . . so I think IPAS is serving a very important purpose because we really need that help in terms of deciding what works and what doesn't work and they're providing that help to us.*

A staff member responsible for the implementation of one of the three projects at RCU reiterated the importance of the evaluation role:

> *That is one of the things I've really wanted to look at is how we evaluate these programs and prove they are working—because I think they are. But right now the data isn't . . . . it hasn't been run yet to show us all of that.*

During the interviews a number of people pointed out that they were still waiting for the results of the evaluations of their pilot projects. Pilot test data from RCU and RTU, as for most of the IPAS campuses, had just been sent to the IPAS staff, so these comments were more statements of fact than critiques of the process.

Staff Turnover. The continuity of any program depends on the stability of staff and the ability of the institution to familiarize new staff with the existing models of operation. RCU experienced two entirely different problems affecting program continuity. First, key administrators indicated they were either new to their position or new to the IPAS process. One director stated, "I have been with RCU for [x] years doing another position, but I have been working with the special retention programs since September first and had not heard much about IPAS until I was hired." Another administrator's responsibilities shifted in the same office, so that person was familiar with IPAS but had not participated in the initial training sessions or meetings. A second potential problem affecting program continuity at RCU was revealed during an interview when an administrator predicted the consequences of a staff member's departure:

> *My gut reaction is that it will fall apart . . . whoever is going to come over is going to wanna run it their way. Change is always difficult. People are going to be resistant. I am not far behind [x] to be leaving . . . and I do not know what IPAS can do about that; I don't think there is anything they can do.*

Staff turnover was lower at RTU, but the director of the IPAS program there had taken the position after the early IPAS meetings and training sessions. One administrator at RTU noted, "One of the things we notice is that, ya know, as people come and go, we are reinventing the same thing." These remarks express the anticipation that, as a result of turnover, those entering the project without knowing its history or having memory of it would run it as they envisioned it, rather than how it was originally designed. Evidence from the interviews indicates staff turnover can be managed to maintain the continuity of the project and the inquiry process, but engaging and training new staff in the project requires special effort.

One interviewee suggested that the key to dealing effectively with problems like turnover is to change the institutional culture:

> *IPAS has helped us look at change in our culture. We haven't had a culture of assessment. And so I see that changing within the university. We were probably doing it administratively, but now we are trying to talk with the faculty about that.*

When inquiry and decision making based on assessment and evaluation are adopted by the organizational culture and become the practice of its individuals, individuals entering the organization will be introduced to that approach to planning and will be expected to participate in kind.

Role Confusion. One complicating factor with any new project is that expectations and roles frequently change. St. John (in press) notes for example that when IPAS was initiated, an assumption was made that campuses had institutional research offices to assist with assessment and evaluation. When it became evident that a number of campuses lacked this capacity, the role of the IPAS team changed. Two individuals at RTU noted that one potential improvement would be clearer expectations of what was done by whom:

> *I think it would be helpful to have a clearer set of explanations about what IPAS is about and what they would like to help with. At the first few meetings, lots of people had lots of confusion. It wasn't very clear. The purpose was clear, but how and what services would be provided to the campuses was unclear.*

Another campus administrator suggested, ". . . maybe a clear line for who is responsible for that project so that we can forecast the progress of the project." The RCU and RTU cases illustrate a number of issues discussed across all five campuses that were particularly salient here. Individuals at both RCU and RTU suggested that while they valued and understood the inquiry process, it did not apply to them because they were already well into their persistence efforts. Their participation was more utilitarian in the sense that IPAS offered a mechanism to evaluate programs affiliated with the one-percent tuition increase for retention efforts. It is unclear if either of these campuses adapted existing structures to create the programs evaluated through IPAS, but it is clear that they did not make these sorts of changes as a result of participation in IPAS. In terms of difficulties, staff turnover and role confusion were prominent and perhaps even related. Most campuses experienced some turnover from the inception of the project to the time of our interviews, but the differences among campuses may have been related, in part, to how each campus brought new members into the process. If new participants were not formally introduced to the IPAS process or the capacity-building seminars, it is likely that roles were less than clear. Technical support at RCU and RTU were still valued highly, but more of the comments from interviewees suggested that they were waiting to see the advantages of the technical support. The reason is that both campuses were participating specifically at that point with evaluation in mind and were still awaiting results from their program evaluations.

Case 3—Single Campus Community College (SCCC)

Single Campus Community College (SCCC), a smaller community college than RCCS, is one campus and serves about 1,000 students. In many ways, SCCC is the one institution that followed the inquiry process as it was developed by the IPAS team. A campus team was assembled by the chancellor of the institution, participated in the earliest conferences and meetings hosted by IPAS, and utilized the early assessment studies conducted by IPAS to identify the three critical challenges specific to its institution. Then, the team organized, brought together necessary staff from across the institution, and decided where to focus its energy and how to design a pilot project. SCCC pilot tested an orientation program strengthened with a set of incentives (food and flash drives) and consequences for failure to participate (academic holds). At the time of the interviews the team was waiting for the pilot study results but reported a sense that the pilot program was an improvement.

Investing Time in the Process. SCCC may be the strongest example of a campus adopting the inquiry process. Their experience, as echoed by one SCCC campus administrator, is that the process can take a great deal of time if done correctly:

> *I am not sure I would use the inquiry process again. It took a lot of work and a great deal of time to do. I think it is valuable but it may not be practical.*

Adopting a new approach to strategic planning requires additional thought and effort to avoid reverting to practices that are more familiar and ingrained. Consider this insight from an upper-level administrator: "We kept jumping to the solution and their [IPAS staff] words would echo in our heads . . . we had to force ourselves not to jump to the solution." In the case of SCCC, their inquiry process training appears to have influenced their planning.

A second reason the process takes more time is that it involves the consideration of assessment data. The SCCC data, provided by IPAS, involved the pilot testing of an intervention strategy and the evaluation of that strategy. As mentioned earlier, at the time of our interviews at least four of the campuses were waiting for evaluation data. The process of evaluating existing efforts extends the planning process in two ways. First, campuses in this study did not commonly evaluate their programs, in part because they lacked the capability. Second, and related, the data had to be gathered and then sent to the IPAS technical support team to be analyzed, extending the time between the pilot test and inserting the evaluation results into the larger loop of the strategic planning process.

The Value of Evaluation and Assessment. Perhaps the clearest, most consistent finding across all five campuses was that the campuses valued the evaluations and assessments conducted by IPAS. This finding may be best illustrated at SCCC. Staff at both RCU and RTU clearly articulated that the data analysis capacity of IPAS was their primary reason to participate in the project. In reference to the assessment conducted by IPAS, the SCCC administrator summarized,

> *The IPAS folks had done a logistical regression on a cohort from 2000 and something and looked at what things had impacted their persistence, from one fall semester to the next fall semester . . . we used that, we looked at that. We had ourselves had a previous retention advisor position who had gone through a retention type thing . . . we looked at the things that impacted persistence along with again some research IPAS provided us with getting into our critical challenges.*

Staff at SCCC was diligent in following the model precisely. During an interview, a staff member pulled out her training manual and said she referred to it frequently throughout the process. Administrators and staff at each of the campuses recognized the availability of the training manual, but this SCCC staff member was the only one to indicate regular use of it.

An upper-level administrator at SCCC spoke of the important role IPAS played in evaluating their orientation program, implying that the data IPAS provided was valuable for their process:

> *We have a lot of information on if they [students] participated [in orientation]. We are looking for those folks that leave to see using the same regressions . . . IPAS can do these things for us. In addition, along the way there have been more focus groups with other faculty and staff and that is put together with an evaluation of the program, then we will look at what has been accomplished and see if there is something else we need to do.*

SCCC is unique not only because that team valued the evaluation and assessment conducted by IPAS but also because members of the team clearly articulated the importance of this information to their planning process.

Transforming Practice through Leadership. Like many innovative strategies for change, IPAS is intended as an approach to strategic planning that will continue beyond the project timeline. A dean at SCCC illustrated how strategic inquiry could be more fully incorporated into the institutional fabric. First, she applied the approach in her management style. When asked how she got buy-in from staff not trained in the process, she quipped, "Was it buy-in or did I just tell them?" In a follow-up, when asked how strategic inquiry had influenced how she runs her organization, she explained,

> *It is probably a combination of things. It [inquiry] fits my style anyways. As far as the inquiry process, they are always giving handouts and the student affairs staff specifically were given that and asked to talk about it during staff meetings.*

This particular dean committed herself to the process and took responsibility for training others in the planning process. She also saw the importance of sharing the process with the larger campus community, recognizing that few of the critical challenges facing the campus were exclusively student or academic affairs:

> *We had to sell everybody . . . our chancellor allowed us to do a presentation at our all-staff [meeting]. We bored them to tears, but then they got excited toward the end. And so everybody knew about it.*

There are certain direct benefits of participation in IPAS that result from the of role IPAS staff in supporting each campus, but a key goal of IPAS is to create a sustained and transformative process that lasts beyond the duration of the funded project. SCCC demonstrates as clearly as any campus that this sort of transformation is possible and has occurred. SCCC made an important structural change by creating a mandatory orientation program for all incoming students. In the past, the program had been voluntary and of relatively short duration. The scope of the program grew in participation and costs. The campus provided flash drives to all participants to encourage participation and to promote the use of technology.

SCCC was the single example of an institution that worked through the entire process from assessment through the identification of critical challenges to the creation of a pilot project and its evaluation. It was a time consuming process. Like RCU and RTU, technical support at SCCC was a less prominent theme, but there was evidence of its importance in the training and capacity building seminars. While it was not an identified theme in the study, if we disaggregate which elements of technical support campuses valued, SCCC would rate the project high on the professional development and capacity building pieces. They also spoke about the important role IPAS played in conducting the early assessment studies. Those results became leverage for the project team to develop campus buy-in and financial support.

Case 4—Private Christian University (PCU)

Private Christian University (PCU) provides a unique example that illustrates the transformational potential of an action inquiry process, although it is difficult to know the degree to which participation in IPAS contributed to that success. PCU engaged in a process of transforming its institutional culture several years prior to the inception of IPAS, but chose to participate in IPAS partly because of the technical support it received in the evaluation of its efforts to better serve students who have not declared majors, "undecided" students. According to those interviewed on campus, PCU is the fastest growing institution in Indiana. Approximately 3,500 students attend its main campus, and these are mostly traditional-age students. More than twice as many students (10,000) attend 10 other campuses across Indiana, Ohio, and Kentucky. PCU students overall tend to be older than the traditional 18–24 year old, to attend part-time, to enroll in online courses, and to have families. The institution has piloted a number of strategies on the main campus to help undecided students find their life calling. As part of its participation in IPAS, PCU chose one of two courses created to serve this population of students because of the availability of a comparison group of students who attended the institution before the course was offered. The project team was awaiting results of evaluation data at the time of the interviews and was in the process of planning for the expansion and adaptation of their work for the satellite campuses.

Changing Institutional Structures. PCU was unique in its approach to IPAS and one of its distinctive differences was the scope of the change it adopted to improve student retention. Like other campuses, PCU created courses to better serve students. This was a modest structural adaptation, but they took it a step further. PCU created an entire "Center for Life Calling and Leadership," hired a director for the center, and created a staff of life coaches to serve a different and complementary role to the academic advisors.

The first structural change occurred shortly after the center director was hired. The position had been advertised as reporting to the vice president for student development, but within six months of being hired, the director proposed a change that would give the position greater legitimacy:

> *We sat down [director and two VPs] and said how can we best structure this? The VP for student development . . . was very unselfish about the project. So we sat down and said this would be better off structurally if it were in academic affairs than it would be in student development . . . within six months I was reporting to academic affairs.*

In addition to the creation of the center and the shift from student development to academic affairs, the director strategically chose to seek an appointment as associate professor and take on the responsibility of chairing the general education committee. He understood, in the context of his institution, that the program would succeed best as an academic unit because that was valued more than student development.

Developing Institutional Capacity. Administrators at PCU understood the importance of building institutional capacity for the work they were doing as part of IPAS, and their commitment to developing capacity began before their involvement with the project. The director of the Center for Life Calling and Leadership demonstrated this commitment clearly when he described the center's genesis. PCU recognized that grants for the center, from the Lilly Foundation and other sources, were seed money and that the long-term success of the center rested on the demonstrated value of the center's services to the campus community; in essence, it had to become self-supporting. PCU administrators viewed participation in IPAS the same way and were trying to figure out how,

> *to do the research on our own beyond IPAS, that would be quicker and easier. IPAS has it all set up in the IU systems and things like that. So take that whole thing and their models and synthesize it and make it easier for where it can be more transportable into another institution [like PCU].*

On no other campus was structural adaptation so pronounced. As discussed above, PCU created an entire center, hired a director, shifted the unit from student development to academic affairs, and hired a team of life coaches who were entirely new to the campus. These changes were substantial and transformative because they were undergirded by a strong conceptual approach to serving students better at PCU. The only drawback articulated by interviewees at PCU was the lack of a comparison group in the evaluation of the impact of one of their courses. Administrators at PCU recognized that one of the important features of IPAS was its provision of research and technical support. They also recognized that this sort of support would not continue indefinitely, and they would need to find ways to conduct the same sorts of analyses with available data. So while not framed as a challenge, PCU was eager to take what IPAS provided and find ways to incorporate that into the institution's capacity—something that appeared difficult to do from their perspective. In some ways, PCU is an even stronger example of the successful adaptation of an inquiry process than SCCC, but so much of PCU's work occurred prior to the creation of IPAS that it is difficult to ascertain precisely what circumstances they faced and what the process looked like when the approach was first adopted.

Case 5—Collaborative on Working Students (CWS)
     The Collaborative on Working Students (CWS) is a unique case because it is not a campus-specific initiative. Rather, it involves the collaboration of three campuses in a region of the state where the participating institutions share a common set of challenges and serve a similar population of students. The CWS is an important case to consider for two reasons. First, it is an unforeseen but positive outgrowth of the capacity building and technical support efforts of IPAS. The three coordinators of the respective campuses began a working relationship as a result of the training meetings and conferences hosted by the IPAS staff. The IPAS technical support person assigned to the region identified the issues overlapping on the three campuses. Second, unlike the campuses that typically began by evaluating an existing program, this collaborative work group began the inquiry process by first identifying its common challenge, working students, and then crafting an approach to better understand or assess this challenge. The team developed a plan and a student survey to be administered at each of the three participating campuses. The pilot test of the survey was scheduled to occur near the time of our visit to campus and the results were to be used to develop a strategy or multiple strategies to better assist working students.
     The Synergy of IPAS Capacity Building Conferences. The Collaborative on Working Students can be described as an unintended benefit of participation in IPAS. As discussed earlier, part of the IPAS strategy was to host training sessions and topical meetings pertaining to

persistence. During these meeting, the three campus coordinators from RCCS, RTU, and RCU developed a working relationship and a shared understanding of the challenges common across their region. During our interview with the group, the evolution of the Collaborative on Working Students was discussed:

> *It was part of meeting at IPAS. I think it started with the financial aid workshop we were planning for last spring. The chancellors dictated they wanted a three college workshop and we got involved with that at the beginning. It [the Collaborative on Working Students] is really kind of [X's] idea and she can say better how it evolved. Based on our relationships we worked well together.*

Later in the interview, another member of the group pointed out that the IPAS technical support person for the region was involved in connecting the campuses on the issue of working students:

> *At some point, [Y] became our contact person . . . he told me that RTU was beginning this working students' survey. So they initiated it, no doubt about it. So when I had to choose a project as the IPAS fellow I wanted to do something on retention of minority students . . . but I realized mastering the literature would be a challenge . . . so I decided why not join the study and RTU.*

The conferences and meetings were designed as opportunities to train campus representatives in the process and to open up dialogue on the pertinent issues facing Indiana colleges and universities. These forums created the added advantage of bringing campus representatives together to learn from one another and to facilitate collaboration. The Collaborative on Working Students was the most concrete outgrowth of these meetings.

Regional Cooperation and Shared Challenges. On some level, every campus in the state of Indiana faces challenges related to their ability to help students succeed and earn degrees. However, as was the case with most of the campuses we visited, participants joined IPAS with campus initiatives ready to be evaluated, without having spent much time understanding the problems the initiatives were supposed to address. In the case of the working students' survey, the IPAS forums gave the coordinators from the three campuses the opportunity to explore and discuss their shared challenges. Through that work they discovered they were all serving students that worked while in school. One coordinator summarized it this way: "The discussion about working students made such an impact on other campuses because we are all facing the same issues. If it had been another issue like freshman seminar or something like that we might not have kept that coalition going." Another coordinator immediately interjected, "Absolutely, we all have the same problems . . . the students at any one of our campuses, in terms of work, it's kind of the same issue. We are commuter campuses."

It was not an explicit goal of IPAS to create regional work groups per se, but it was a positive outgrowth of a well-defined and adaptable process. This region is not the only one in the state with multiple institutions in relatively close proximity to each other. There are several other locations where initiatives like this might have made sense, but they did not materialize. The synergy experienced in this region was a result of the hard work and commitment of the three coordinators coupled with the alignment of many of the challenges and benefits described in prior cases. The teams at these institutions had top-level support to do their IPAS work, and they received a great deal of technical and research support from IPAS staff. The coordinators understood and utilized the inquiry process. They communicated well and established legitimacy for the program, even raising money to fund the working students' survey. All of these factors contributed to the success of this collaboration.

Research Support. In many ways, research support complements the value of assessment and evaluation discussed earlier and may be the second most frequently cited benefit of IPAS mentioned among those interviewed. The IPAS technical support staff was integral to each campus in terms of conducting and analyzing research. This role included analyzing statewide assessment data, conducting campus focus groups, and evaluating the pilot programs (this work was still under way at the time of our interviews). One coordinator discussed the benefits of the research in this way:

> *I will just go back to the fact that we are not used to research. But I think the chancellors getting together and that meeting with you guys have given this some credibility. If this was my own personal project, I do not think it would have as much credibility as it does.*

One advantage of the technical support model employed by IPAS was the provision of consistent personal technical support and campus-specific counsel. Another coordinator discussed the role of the technical support person for the region, "He comes up whenever we need him. He has gotten us literature review lists." Reviews of relevant literature became important for individuals interested in addressing the challenges related to persistence who did not have higher education or student affairs administration backgrounds. A coordinator at RCU who was also a faculty member in another discipline explained that it is difficult to explore and understand the complexities of a problem if professionals are not steeped in the relevant literature.

The CWS's needs for research support were slightly different from other cases in that they extended to include the creation of a survey, a sampling strategy, an analytic approach, and access to supplemental data. The following comment illustrates the importance of the research support provided by IPAS staff:

> *What they are going to do for us that is powerful is connecting the surveys to the state database. It's got course taking patterns I think, and other background data and their financial aid.*

Campus administrators and nonacademic units are less capable of conducting independent research. Among these five campuses, all but one lacked an institutional research office that could assist in this sort of work. As a consequence, for the participating campuses to follow the inquiry process it was critical that IPAS prioritize research support, evaluation, and assessment as the essential functions they provided. Without this, it would have been difficult for campuses to fully utilize the strategic inquiry process, which uses assessment to understand critical challenges and evaluation research to make decisions about the continued viability of intervention strategies.

The creation of the Collaborative on Working Students, with three administrators, reflects a "structure" or a mechanism for improvement that did not previously exist. The difficulties faced by this group stemmed largely from the absence of a template for successful collaboration among these campuses. However, the lack of precedents may explain why the inquiry process was so useful for this group. A particular challenge articulated very clearly was the difficulty of conducting research on three campuses simultaneously. Only one of the three team members was a "researcher" by training. The creation of a valid survey instrument, the development of a sampling design, clearing the project through an Institutional Review Board (IRB), and finding funding for the project were all new to the members of the group, but these difficulties were overcome with support from IPAS. The IPAS technical support team was integrally involved in the formation of this collaborative, and they have remained an essential part of the continued progress of the group. As in its other efforts, IPAS was planning to conduct some of the analysis once the survey was completed and processed.

Themes Across Cases

These cases provide useful illustrations of the key themes discovered in the course of our interviews, and they remind us that each campus must adapt a process like inquiry to the existing local and institutional conditions. However, it has been important to explore these cases because some themes were more consistent across them than others. For example, technical support was consistently regarded as a valuable benefit of participation and a critical element for success. Three interviewees valued the literature reviews and a number of top-level administrators across the campuses valued the evaluation component, even though the results were not yet tabulated. CWS utilized the technical support the most, conducting a new research project vis-à-vis the working students' survey.

Some campuses utilized the strategic inquiry process more fully than others. PCU had been engaged in a process very similar to the inquiry process for several years before the project began, whereas RTU and RCU only adopted elements of the process as it suited their perceived needs and existing circumstances. Only SCCC seems to have followed the full planning loop subsequent to its initial work with IPAS, and the CWS reflects an unintended benefit of IPAS that may reap long-term benefits for all three campuses involved in that effort.

The fact that some institutions formally adapted institutional structures and systems as a result of IPAS may be more a reflection of the critical challenges they identified than a statement of which campuses are more likely to adapt. For example, the greatest structural changes occurred at PCU, where they chose to focus on undecided students in the persistence puzzle. Making their efforts a reality through the creation and staffing of the Center for Life Calling and Leadership was as much a reflection of institutional values and the leadership of administration as it was a result of an analysis of strategic approaches to serving undecided students well. Equally, the fact that there were few changes at RTU or RCU may be due to effective changes made prior to the participation of these campuses in IPAS. The fact that structural changes were made at three of the campuses suggests a heightened level of institutional support at those institutions, as such changes require additional resources.

Finally, in some ways, many of the themes described above indicate the difficulties individuals on each of the campuses faced in their respective roles. In the cases of these five institutions, however, these difficulties did not deter progress. They may have added time to the process or created some confusion or concern along the way, but all of these campuses found ways to adapt. Some difficulties—for example, staff turnover—strain the resources and resilience of any organization, irrespective of participation in an inquiry process such as that of IPAS. It happens that this formative study caught two campuses at a particular moment in time when the repercussions of staff turnover were playing out. Another legitimate difficulty for the campuses may have been the amount of time it took to conduct evaluations of pilot projects and to incorporate the evaluation results into the larger planning loop. This is not to suggest, however, that these evaluations could have been done faster or that the campuses themselves should have conducted them. In fact, one of the motivations of campuses for participating in IPAS was to draw on the technical support and research expertise from the IPAS office.

Conclusion

Many of the themes underscored in each of these cases resonate across campus boundaries. Considering the cases separately enabled us to recognize the uniqueness of each campus and the need for campus administrators, faculty, and staff to adapt the inquiry process to maximize the assets of their respective campuses and community contexts and to address the particular issues inherent in each. No one campus or collaborative arrangement has adapted the process entirely as envisioned, but the inquiry process itself was being tested to see how it can be applied in actual institutional settings. In some cases, only elements of the process were replicated, while in other cases an inquiry process appeared to have been under way before IPAS came along. In the end, our study found that it is possible to integrate strategic inquiry into the strategic planning of campuses if the appropriate training is provided, if there is a particular focus on developing institutional capacity to conduct the requisite research, and if there is institutional support in terms of money and other resources. When these conditions are in place and campus representatives believe the process can work, changes can occur that will positively influence students' persistence in college.

Today there is a growing sense of urgency for institutions of higher education to adapt to changing conditions. Simultaneously, there is a need for institutional change processes to be viewed as rational and, by extension, legitimate. Throughout this study, we found that strategic inquiry was a useful though in some ways more time-consuming alternative to common rational planning approaches. IPAS attempted to move campuses away from traditional planning approaches to broader thinking about the challenges institutions have in common while also recognizing the unique local and institutional contexts within which each college operates. Our findings suggest that practices changed, at least in terms of these specific efforts related to student persistence and retention. But perhaps more promising for longer term success, and consistent with Gumport's thoughts on the future of strategy in higher education, IPAS and the inquiry process developed a new set of capabilities in campus leaders and administrators who appear to think differently now about their roles in planning and change.

Strategic inquiry may challenge contemporary assumptions regarding institutional planning in higher education and may require even more time and resources to implement well. Because it is research driven and provides mechanisms for evaluation and continual improvement, however, strategic inquiry may provide the change process greater legitimacy—an important theme throughout our interviews. Administrators indicated it was worth the time and energy it took to rethink how their campuses develop and adapt institutional practices to better serve students.

References

Gumport, P. (2006, December). *Organizational studies in higher education: Insights for a changing enterprise.* Organizational Behavior and Management Lecture in the Distinguished Scholar Lecture Series at the Center for the Study of Higher and Postsecondary Education's 50th Anniversary Celebration, University of Michigan,   Arbor.

St. John, E. P. (2008). *Action, reflection, and social justice: Integrating moral reasoning into professional development* (Language and Social Processes series, L. Rex, Ed.). Cresskill, NJ: Hampton Press.

St. John, E. P., McKinney, J. S., & Tuttle, T. (2006). Using action inquiry to address critical challenges. In E. P. St. John & M. Wilkerson (Eds.), *Reframing persistence research to improve academic success*: *New Directions for Institutional Research, No. 130* (pp. 63–76). San Francisco: Jossey-Bass.

St. John, E. P., Musoba, G. D., & Chung, C.-G. (2004). *Academic preparation and college success: Analysis of Indiana's 2000 high school class* (IPAS Research Report No. 04–03). Bloomington, IN: Indiana Project on Academic Success.

St. John, E. P., Musoba, G. D., Simmons, A. B., & Chung, C.-G. (2002). *Meeting the access challenge: Indiana's Twenty-First Century Scholars Program* (New Agenda Series, Vol. 4, No. 4). Indianapolis, IN: Lumina Foundation for Education.

St. John, E. P., & Wilkerson, M. (2006). Reframing persistence research to improve academic success: New Directions for Institutional Research, No.130. San Francisco: Jossey-Bass.

Tinto, V., & Pusser, B. (2006, July). *Moving from theory to action: Building a model of institutional action for student success*. Washington, DC: National Postsecondary Education Cooperative.

CHAPTER 8

THE INDIANA PROJECT ON ACADEMIC SUCCESS PAPER TRAIL: AN ANALYSIS OF DOCUMENTS AND REFLECTIONS OF THE IPAS STAFF

Pauline J. Reynolds and Don Hossler

A central purpose of the Indiana Project on Academic Success (IPAS) was to support college campuses in the deliberate and consistent assessment of efforts to benefit students. IPAS encouraged institutions to look carefully at their own programs and policies through evaluation and introspection and to thoughtfully follow the IPAS inquiry process (described in Chapter 7) when considering additions to or changes in services to students, particularly in areas identified in the inquiry process as challenges. If such an endeavor is considered valuable, if a process of systematic evaluation and ongoing assessment is important and worth replicating at other institutions, then understanding the dynamics of the IPAS initiative from the perspective of the IPAS staff is every bit as important as understanding the insights those institutional efforts produced. In this regard, IPAS staff would be remiss if they did not follow their own advice and thoughtfully evaluate the progress of the project at the participating institutions.

Some of these considerations have already been broached in St. John and Wilkerson's (2006) *Reframing Persistence Research to Improve Academic Success,* particularly in St. John's chapter "Lessons Learned: Institutional Research as Support for Academic Improvement." However, those lessons focus on ways institutions can inform practice and conduct actionable research rather than on the conditions that affect the participants' engagement. Our study, in contrast, examines IPAS staff interactions with IPAS campus partners and the IPAS staff's perceptions of this three-year consultative process.

Following the authors' systematic analysis of documents and communications generated and recorded throughout the IPAS effort including the personal reflections of some of the IPAS staff, this chapter identifies conditions, choices, and events that positively or negatively impacted project involvement. This chapter and Chapter 7, based on interviews of IPAS campus participants and IPAS staff, together provide a comprehensive summative perspective on the project in practice.

Arguably the most significant of IPAS's implicit and explicit expectations of participating campuses was that campuses establish their own teams

169

dedicated to working with IPAS through the action inquiry process. IPAS provided clear recommendations on the formation of teams but, naturally, once they had agreed to participate, the campuses themselves were solely responsible for selecting personnel for their teams. Other expectations included participating in meetings with IPAS staff and with other IPAS campus teams, making an effort to move through the IPAS process by identifying challenges on campus, and engaging in the processes of assessment and action inquiry. For the IPAS staff, campus activities in these broad areas provided a framework of tacit indicators that made it possible to evaluate the success of each campus' engagement with the project. The analysis presented in this chapter was founded on our understanding of the choices or parameters that allowed the participants to fall short of, fulfill, or exceed these broad project expectations.

Method

This chapter reports the findings of a qualitative analysis of the internal documents generated as the work of IPAS was carried out. These documents consist of:

- Agendas designed by IPAS staff before meetings
- Notes/reports written by IPAS staff detailing and commenting on meetings
- Notes written by IPAS campus team members reporting on meetings conducted at their campuses
- Progress reports from IPAS staff
- IPAS staff notes on telephone calls with IPAS campuses
- E-mails between IPAS staff and IPAS campus team members

These documents contain a variety of pertinent information, including reflections from IPAS staff about the state of the project at individual campuses, discussions between IPAS staff and campus team members about the project, information on the progress of the project, and confirmation of actions planned and taken by campus teams. In addition, we drew on some of the personal reflections of the IPAS staff on the nature and outcomes of their engagement with participating campuses. Van Maanen (1988) observes that researchers engaged in ethnographic fieldwork often find they need to introduce impressionistic or even confessional insights derived from their efforts. Writing this chapter, we found at times that reflecting on our personal experiences helped to illuminate the findings we were reporting about the campuses' participation. Thus, in preparing this chapter we employed multiple case sampling (Miles & Huberman, 1994) and drew on Van Maanen's insights to examine ourselves and our efforts in the IPAS process.

Our analysis of existing documents focuses on materials created by four of the fifteen campuses initially invited to participate in the project. These documents include institutional reports, e-mails, and memos created during the three years of the IPAS project period. The main benefit of using multiple cases is the confidence this method generates in the findings, as the different sources of inquiry can confirm or contrast with each other—and can thereby strengthen "the precision, the validity, and the stability of the findings" (Miles & Huberman, p. 29).

Consistent with this type of sampling, the cases in this study are exemplars of points along the continuum of engagement demonstrated by the institutions in the project and were chosen for this study for two main reasons. First, these cases are representative of the range across campuses of involvement in the project, as four broad manners of engagement were evident among the campuses. Two of the campuses chosen for this study remained engaged in the project until its conclusion, although one clearly followed IPAS's guidelines, while the other picked the suggestions they would follow. One campus ceased engagement after quite a lot of work had been done with the team. Another dropped out of the project fairly early on without having done any research. The second reason these cases were chosen for this study was the availability of documents, as the main source of data for the study was internal documents. The activities of these four campuses were well documented throughout the project, even through changes in IPAS personnel.

To protect the anonymity of the campuses, no potentially identifying information, such as demographic data, is presented in this chapter. Due to the small total number of campuses involved in the project and the fact that care was taken to involve a variety of institutional types, even basic information about the campuses, such as whether they are public or private, might have the potential to identify the institutions and individuals in this study. Also, specific information about the campuses' project activity, such as the challenges campuses chose to study, cannot be divulged as these have previously been associated without anonymity in other publications (e.g., St. John & Wilkerson, 2006). For the purpose of facilitating this chapter's discussion, we have assigned these campuses the following aliases, which have no relation to their actual locations: North University, South University, East University, and West University.

The following analysis of documents and personal reflections approaches this inquiry through a process outlined in Carspecken's (1996) guide to critical ethnography. Using this hermeneutic process, our analysis recursively assigns codes and organizes codes into themes, using pragmatic horizons assumed by subjective, objective, and normative positions to make sense of the material and to bring forth the implicit from the explicit. In this qualitative analysis, codes are shorthand labels for descriptive characteristics or inferential insights gleaned from the data (Miles & Huberman, p. 56). The process as a whole is emic and inductive, with findings arising from the data themselves rather than being predetermined by codes or themes derived from theory or concepts formed before seeing the data (Denzin & Lincoln, 2003).

Findings

This analysis highlights themes and revealing moments that can contribute to an understanding of the ways people and institutions—and their choices—hampered or supported the involvement of these campuses in IPAS. Perhaps unsurprisingly, continued engagement in the project was impacted by existing campus dynamics, by the personalities of individuals at the participating campuses and on the IPAS staff, and by the ways campuses chose to structure their involvement. The findings divide into the ways campuses made IPAS work for them and the ways campuses' progress with IPAS was impeded. Interestingly, the evidence for these broad divisions does not correspond exactly to the data regarding the continuation or attrition of campuses in the project. In fact, all campuses had features that would have been expected either to encourage or to discourage continuation. The findings of the study—on the ways institutions and people participating in IPAS were hampered or supported in their involvement with the project—are presented below within the framework of two main themes: organization and interaction.

Organizing for Success?

The first decisions campuses made after agreeing to participate in IPAS exerted the most influence, according to our findings, on the extent to which these campuses evidenced sustained engagement. IPAS staff provided guidance on the types of commitments that campus stakeholders needed to make to effectively participate in the project, but individual institutions naturally made their own decisions for their own reasons. Among the four campuses we consider in this study the composition of teams exerted a significant influence on campus involvement in the project. Two campuses, West University (WU) and South University (SU), followed the IPAS guidelines and established teams with people who had institutional functions resembling those IPAS suggested, including senior administrators from both academic and student affairs, institutional researchers, faculty members, and practitioners. One of the campuses even included an adjunct faculty member on their team. None of the four campuses included students in their teams, although an IPAS staff member recalls that during discussions both WU and SU considered including students. The other two campuses in this study, East University (EU) and North University (NU), did not follow the suggestions provided by the project when considering the composition of their teams. These initial decisions held layers of implications that had unforeseen ripple effects on the progress of the project.

Contrary to the IPAS guidelines, EU and NU assembled teams of staff members who lacked the power and position essential for the success of the project. One of the teams, for example, was compromised mainly of entry-level student affairs practitioners. Despite the investment of some of these individuals in the project, they did not have the clout at their institutions to involve the necessary parties or to make final decisions about the challenges, something which was immensely frustrating for the team members themselves, as they expressed in conversations with IPAS staff members. In fact, rather than doing what the IPAS process indicated was needed, the teams at EU and NU were "told" by senior administrators what they could do; thus, the intent of the inquiry model was hampered. For example, a team member at NU wrote, "Our chancellor would like for the IPAS team to work on the following areas . . . ."

Each of these two campuses had delegated a person to be responsible for the project but, sadly, as their commitment was unsupported they became frustrated. These unempowered "lone crusaders" recognized the untenable nature of their positions. The EU team leader expressed fears to IPAS staff members who reported that ". . . their efforts or participation will be futile" due to the lack of more than verbal support from senior administrators. After a conversation with this EU leader, an IPAS staff member wrote in a report, "The provost had assured . . . 100% support, but nothing had happened since then." The notes and e-mails for this campus consistently stressed the need for additional members to participate in the project, with the team leader becoming increasingly overwhelmed and isolated and with frequent references to meetings with the provost to try to get needed human resources. "The team will talk with the provost to discuss future team members," was a typical remark in campus documents. In fact, at one point the team decided to try to recruit senior administrators themselves, including the provost, to take an active part in the project, as they realized they could not make any meaningful progress without such institutional investment. An EU meeting brief notes, "Participants were uncertain of the level of commitment from the upper administration. This is why they chose to select a team as their first task to judge the commitment level of the administration." Their various attempts to garner more institutional support fell on deaf ears as no discernable changes were made to the EU team.

IPAS staff members experienced similar frustrations when working with NU, spending considerable time and effort preparing an institutional report for them, for example, only to discover sometime later that no one on the campus had looked at it. This came to light when one of the NU team members suggested IPAS assist them by supplying some data—data contained in the report previously hand-delivered to the team point person by an IPAS staff member. Although frustrating, from this and other similar incidents with campuses IPAS staff learned that the manner in which data was presented to a diverse campus audience was crucial to its digestibility and utility for IPAS campus partners. Fueled with this knowledge, IPAS staff spent considerable time presenting the information NU had requested in a more digestible manner. Yet nothing happened after the team was presented with this information. Not only did the campus not engage in decision making for inquiry related to their challenges, it became apparent to IPAS staff that the new report probably had not been read either. Due to the lack of institutional commitment, and the absence of any institutional reward for participation in the project, members of the NU team had little incentive to give and take in the project.

The feeling of isolation and constraint expressed at EU was also expressed at NU, where the point person said he felt he was "bearing the burden of the project." Indeed, he called himself "the Lone Ranger of IPAS" in one e-mail and was reported in project meeting notes as seeming "discouraged and tired." IPAS progress reports also indicated that what should have been teamwork at NU was really the work of one person. IPAS staff members grew increasingly frustrated as the attendance of campus team members at meetings gradually dropped and the only person participating in inquiry efforts became completely overwhelmed.

Due to how their teams were organized, both EU and NU were unable to involve appropriate others or to get meaningful buy-in from senior administrators. It was quite a different story at WU and SU, however, where the individuals responsible for the teams, who interacted regularly with IPAS staff, were "champions" for the project rather than ineffectual "Lone Rangers." These latter teams, whose membership included senior administrators such as a dean of students or a vice chancellor of academic affairs, were able to surround themselves with appropriate people, delegate tasks, and make IPAS a sustainable, effective tool for institutions to use to explore the challenges facing them and their students. The ability to delegate and involve others meant that no one person was "burdened" by the project.

The title "IPAS Scholar" was given to individuals at participating campuses appointed by their institution to take more responsibility in their campus' IPAS endeavor. As suggested and encouraged in IPAS guidelines, IPAS Scholars were rewarded with reduced institutional obligations to make it possible for them to more fully engage in the IPAS process. SU's "champion," for example, was assigned a lighter teaching load. "I just received some exciting news," this individual reported to the IPAS staff. "Our Dean has approved a one-course download for me to serve as our campus' IPAS scholar."

Both WU and SU had adequate human resources to sufficiently plan and conduct research before petitioning the president or chancellor for fiscal resources and permission to start programs or to change established institutional practices. Having such persons involved at participating campuses was a boon for the IPAS staff members and led to a sense of collaboration, joint endeavor, and shared accountability. For example, communications between the IPAS staff and the SU team went both ways—IPAS staff members sent the SU team e-mails about project progress, and SU's IPAS Scholar e-mailed the IPAS staff about the progress of reports or arrangements for meetings.

Each of the four campuses delegated a person who was invested and hard working to rally institutional forces and to be responsible for interactions between their campus and the IPAS office in Bloomington. What made the vital difference to project engagement and success among these campuses was that the individuals at EU and NU were not empowered with the human resources to succeed, were not in positions with sufficient power to get the human resources they needed, and, thus, were essentially given responsibility for a project that could never flourish. In other words, they were set up to fail. It is interesting to note that the individuals given responsibility for IPAS at EU and NU both left their institution during the project. At NU this resulted in the abandonment of the project, as IPAS members received no responses to their attempts to continue engagement. At EU the project was halfheartedly started again by a person who had no previous involvement with the project. Like his predecessor, the new leader was constrained by campus politics—perhaps even more so, as this person was politically cautious and evidently unable or unwilling to implement suggestions from IPAS staff members that might have energized and validated the project. "Concerning next steps," as written in IPAS staff notes, "[the IPAS staff member] asked Mr. [Y] if he was in a position to delegate people to workgroups. He replied that positionally 'yes,' but in actuality 'no.'"

IPAS staff members faced continual blocks like this at EU. During visits to the campus interactions with EU team members were positive, but it seemed the interactions were taking place with the wrong people. The team members either were not in a position to further the project or did not wish to do so. As reflected in the above quotation, reluctant and even obstinate responses came from the second elected leader of this team.

Campus culture and climate had an impact on the organizational choices of the participating institutions. Both WU and SU were places that already boasted adherence to a culture of evidence, as substantiated in internal reports and data that team members brought to the discussion of their challenges. In fact, a staff report outlining WU's progress claims, "The campus has the sense that they are already engaging in behaviors promoted by IPAS and are ahead of the game in some respects." A pre-existing climate of collaboration at WU and SU between academic affairs and students affairs also impacted the organization of the campus teams, which had a mixture of professionals from these areas that included practitioners, faculty, and administrators who appeared to work well together.

At EU, however, the team was composed of student affairs professionals in entry-level positions and an institutional researcher. This team, at the request of their provost, embarked on a challenge that IPAS staff were later surprised to learn was also the focus of an already existing committee at the institution comprised of faculty and senior administrators—with obviously significantly greater institutional clout. Despite attempts to involve and liaise with this committee, the EU's IPAS team and their input were effectively ignored. Team members spoke to IPAS staff of being frustrated by how they were being treated, saying that even though they were not faculty or senior administrators they could offer valuable insights on developing solutions for this challenge. Documents indicate that the administrator leading the pre-existing committee was becoming characterized as a gatekeeper for the success of the IPAS effort: "Dr. [X] has appeared to be the dominant player on campus and it seems to be necessary to get him involved with IPAS or to delegate people to be involved for the project to be successful at [EU]." Also according to documents, Dr. X had agreed to let the IPAS campus team meet with his committee, but there is no evidence of the content of this meeting or even whether it took place. Whatever the outcome, EU's involvement with IPAS ended after the second round of IPAS training. Under institutional conditions like this IPAS could never have been a force for change. It could only be a burden to the unfortunate, ignored staff delegated to move the process along.

Although an inquiry model cannot account for losing personnel and having too much to do in too little time, all campuses participating in IPAS suffered from institutional impediments, most typically the fact that the campus team members were all busy professionals whose IPAS duties did not impact their day-to-day obligations and for whom IPAS was often a lower priority. This became an insurmountable obstacle to engagement for some campuses. EU, for example, lay fallow until polite pressure from IPAS staff led to meetings that were sadly ineffectual and did not inspire future efforts. WU and SU, however, despite the stresses of their existing responsibilities which were no less than those of their co-professionals at unengaged campuses, managed to stay engaged.

The four institutions in this study all agreed of their own volition to participate in IPAS, yet the choices these institutions made while organizing for the project give a truer indication than these initial agreements of the value they anticipated the project would have for their campus communities. One might reasonably conclude that it was more important to campuses to be seen to participate in the project than to actually participate. All four campuses espoused commitment to the project, but only two made choices that fully enabled them to enact their verbal commitment. Therefore, the institutional choices at these campuses could be considered to reflect the extent to which the campuses actually wished to be involved in IPAS. As there was no compulsion—or any material incentive—to be involved, it is intriguing to speculate what the motivations might have been for participation that was predictably half-hearted, lukewarm, and unempowered. Perhaps the campuses simply wished for the benefits of the IPAS process but were unprepared, unwilling, or unready to do what was necessary to have them.

In IPAS We Trust?

The components of the second major theme that emerged in the document analysis were impacted by the efforts the institutions made at organizing their participation in IPAS, and vice versa. Issues related to partnership and trust/legitimacy are the two major areas for discussion within this broad theme of interaction between the campuses and IPAS staff.

Partnership. Particularly at WU and SU, partnership was a vital component of the engagement of campuses in IPAS. Rather than expecting all needed resources, human and fiscal, to be provided to them, these campuses acted as true partners in research endeavors. They conducted their own meetings without the presence of IPAS staff, they kept their commitments, and they took initiatives that advanced their progress in the project. SU's team members were especially exemplary partners. They developed an ambitious timeline for their research, which they maintained by involving numerous colleagues who participated in the development of a solution to their challenges and the implementation of a pilot program. Being organized for success, team members were allocated appropriate tasks they could be realistically expected to carry out. For example, SU's IPAS Scholar rather than IPAS staff wrote a report of some early focus group discussions of their challenges. Such reports for EU and NU were all written by IPAS staff. Also, the institutional researcher on SU's team conducted analysis with SU data and provided copious amounts of their institution's data to the IPAS staff for further analysis. To IPAS staff this involvement indicated a real investment in the process at multiple levels. The team at NU was partners up to a point; their leader definitely tried to partner with IPAS but was hampered due to his "Lone Ranger" status. WU partnered IPAS in the development of research and also was able to include the right people. However, EU did not develop any partnerships at all. After initial attempts by their "lone crusader" to involve the right people, no meetings were held about the project unless instigated by IPAS staff, and then reluctantly before they withdrew from the project. IPAS staff was also asked by their second team member not to develop relationships with EU senior administrators, such as the aforementioned "gatekeeper"—which might have put the project at the forefront of efforts to address institutional needs. This request presented a dilemma for IPAS staff members who wished to respect the wishes of the EU point person but found it hard to reconcile such convoluted campus politics with the espoused commitment to the project. With such limitations, IPAS staff did not find the right approach to assist the EU team in this situation before they withdrew from the project.

Trust and Legitimacy. Trust, based in part on the perception of legitimacy, played a large role in the interaction between IPAS and the participating campuses, and indeed in the development of partnerships. Some of the campuses were very open with IPAS and eager to learn from and participate in St. John's inquiry model (1994, 2003, 2006) while others were more restrained and cautious. There were different issues with trust on campuses. Three possible reasons for this revealed in the documents and personal reflections are (1) a reluctance to reveal the campus's challenges to other higher education professionals; (2) a professional wariness due to the unknown aptitude of IPAS staff; and, finally, (3) simply not knowing the IPAS team. WU tackled the last of these directly by inviting team members to campus expressly for the purpose of a "getting to know you" experience. The IPAS staff joined service day activities for faculty and attended meetings that introduced them to the initiatives already taking place on campus. As their team leader wrote, "The main purpose of your attendance here is to come to a better understanding of the complexity of our college, and the forward thinking approach." For the staff members involved, this meeting was highly successful. It provided the foundation for a positive and fruitful partnership between IPAS and campus leaders.

Some IPAS teams never lost their reluctance to talk about their campus in front of outsiders. In this sample, NU seemed to be particularly reluctant and indicated their team met immediately before visits from IPAS facilitators. To IPAS staff, these meetings before their campus visits appeared to be occasions to decide what to say or not to say in front of IPAS outsiders. IPAS staff members recollected observing both reluctance to meet prior to meetings and reticence within them at NU and EU and wondered whether the fact that they worked with several campuses as partners in this process was an added impediment. Whatever the reason, it can be inferred from both the documents and staffs' personal reflections that the IPAS staff was not working with the full trust of these campuses. Perhaps the lack of upper-level institutional support also impeded these teams in this respect, making them feel insecure institutionally or unsafe in sharing with outsiders.

Several IPAS staff members were graduate students, which presented unique trust issues for the campuses and may have affected the way they engaged in the project. The provost and vice president of student affairs at EU alluded during a meeting to previous bad experiences with student-staffed research teams. The IPAS staff present reported feeling the meeting had become a test, as it had included a jibe about outside research teams, for example, that seemed intended to provoke a reaction. Although they left the meeting feeling they had passed the test and had heard assurances of further commitment, perhaps EU's progress would suggest otherwise.

This circumspection was also evident in a reply from EU's so-called "gatekeeper" to an IPAS staff member's e-mail request for a meeting. After learning the identity of some of the IPAS staff involved with the project he wrote:

> *I am very appreciative of your willingness to spend a few minutes with me to talk about the IPAS project and help dismiss many of my apprehensions. Knowing that professionals like you and [other IPAS staff members] are "on the job" is a relief.*

From these examples it is clear that EU team members were uncomfortable working with student staff at IPAS and were hesitant to engage fully in the project with them. Perhaps IPAS staff's inability to alleviate this administrator's apprehensions was reflected in EU's disengagement with the project.

This kind of legitimacy was also a concern at campuses that were more engaged. Yet although EU may have rebuffed IPAS due to concerns over its student staff, these same staff members gradually earned the respect of the professionals they liaised with at the other campuses in this sample. As the IPAS Scholar at SU wrote to an IPAS student staff member, "You and [another staff member] have made our team feel very special—quite a feat considering you're also connected to several other campuses (oh yeah . . . and that doctoral 'thang' too.)"

Aligned with EU's concerns over the use of student staff, an IPAS student staff member working with WU expressed concern that her gender and youth were impacting the progress of the project on that campus. After one meeting she wrote:

> *I felt that the [WU] team may not view me an authority, perhaps due to my gender. I explored this idea over lunch with the one female member of the [WU] team by asking about women and leadership within their institution. . . . She was frank about struggles to be seen as an authority and a valid leader, which perhaps confirmed my feelings about how the team may or may not view me as a facilitator.*

Despite using the word "authority" in this report, it was clear from conversation and reflection that this IPAS staff member was concerned about being part of a meaningful conversation with the WU team and about competently facilitating the team's progress through the inquiry process. In fact, this concern was explored in some depth during a staff meeting with all IPAS staff, who concurred with the staff member about the interaction with her campus partner.

Techniques were employed in an effort to instill in participants the idea of this staff member as a leader. For example, the IPAS staff member observed that after her presentations participants directed their questions not to her but to a male staff member. To try to change this pattern, a male member of the IPAS staff deferred to her in meetings. The issues of gender and the use of student staff were aided by the "blessing of higher education gurus"—which helped markedly in IPAS establishing trust and legitimacy through partnerships. As evidenced in this study, the senior scholar who led the project at this point, Dr. Edward P. St. John, conferred an invaluable sense of legitimacy to the initiative on several levels, and this had two main advantages. First, campus teams appreciated and were flattered by the time and effort a senior scholar took to work with them. Second, by supporting the student staff the senior scholar legitimized those staff members as facilitators in the project.

A major part of trust and legitimacy was also resolved as staff members and campus teams built working relationships. The e-mail communications in this study's data clearly express growing respect, warmth, and familiarity between IPAS staff and three of the sample participating campuses. Participants and staff shared personal stories and friendly greetings in their IPAS-related communications that positively impacted the progress of the project. The "Lone Ranger" at NU, for example, wrote one January early in the project, "I am glad you made it back and hope you had a good time at home. I am energized and ready to take on old man winter and the challenges of my work." Although these kinds of interactions were not evident in communications with EU, which experienced a change in personnel and left the project fairly early, IPAS staff members recollected lively conversations at the few meetings held with that team.

Although the growth in relationships between the IPAS staff and the IPAS campus teams seemed to build trust and strengthen the legitimacy of the project, it may also unexpectedly have somewhat hindered the effectiveness of IPAS efforts at one campus. In discussions of communications with IPAS campus partners, IPAS staff members recollected that e-mails to multiple staff members on the campus teams often resulted in no response and that e-mails to individual members proved to be more successful at establishing communication. Communication with NU was mainly with one person, the so-called "Lone Ranger" of the project there, and was effective as long as he was the NU point person. His departure later in the project essentially signaled the end of NU's involvement in the project, as relationships with other team members had not been established well enough to draw on to complete the project. A different strategy by IPAS staff members in this area may have resulted in greater trust throughout the NU team and, perhaps, NU's continued engagement in the project.

Further influencing legitimacy was the ability and willingness of participants to engage in dialogue about data. In early project thoughts, one of the senior administrators on the WU team pointed out that for humanities faculty to become involved and "in order for them to gain the most from IPAS, they need to become better consumers of data."

An e-mail message to IPAS staff from a WU team member further illustrates the positive impact of such skills and the benefits of openness to explore data: "Thank you for providing the data for persistence/nonpersistence for [WU]. I finally got the opportunity to review it and found it quite illuminating! . . . This indicates that what we are doing . . . is really making a significant difference." The IPAS staff member's response included a reminder: ". . . all the data we gave you was for students enrolled in 2000. If I recall correctly, I think you said that the [program] wasn't in existence then." This reminder did not stop the WU team from discussing the data. In fact, their follow-up reply offered other ideas for collecting data to investigate the program:

> *Thanks for reminding us that this cohort did not have the benefit of [the program]. It effectively burst my bubble about its effectiveness. [We] are planning to take two samples of students . . . and track them through their WU years and beyond.*

Trust and legitimacy, an important part of dialogue about data with IPAS campuses, allowed the campuses to be open with IPAS staff and other participants.

Data had another notable impact on interactions and legitimacy in the project. As well as being a source of conversation and action, data also appeared to result in stalling and possible cessation. In numerous conversations with IPAS staff, campus team members had heard the message that no results were negative results, as any results would help them learn something—even if it was about what was not working. Nevertheless, negative feedback from students on a program that NU staff was proud of and thought was doing well was received with disbelief, and NU team members communicated this reaction to IPAS staff: "Initially there were some concerns about the reliability of the focus group report." Additionally, the focus group report for NU had been written by a graduate student staff member of IPAS, which had strict review procedures for quality control of reports. After reviewing the evidence for the report, the NU team reluctantly had to agree with the report's conclusions, but they had only one more meeting with the IPAS staff, which only two members attended. The IPAS staff member laments in a routine report, "After getting all of this work they have stalled—meetings were hard to get. They may have stalled because they did not like the results from the focus groups analysis." Not long after this, NU's "Lone Ranger" left the project and the institution and the stalled IPAS team at NU became defunct.

Data at SU had the desired impact and spurred that team and institution into appropriate change for the good of their students. However, at WU the impact of positive results appeared to have a stalling effect, as the team seemed to be unable to move past their success. Even their continued efforts seemed to be intended to prolong the status quo through arrangements to continue the same assessment in future years. Of course, a major positive development was that the campus embraced continuing evaluation and intended to promote the IPAS ethos of assessment and information to inform change beyond the end of the project. The only change at WU, though, was the continuation of evaluation efforts.

Discussion

The results of this study have implications that can help alert researchers working with campuses to obstacles they and their project participants may face. Regarding the problem of attrition among research project participants, St. John, McKinney, and Tuttle (2006) speculated, "We expect that the labor-intensive nature of the change process, inconsistent technical support, and lack of resources were reasons for disengaging" (p. 68). As we can see from the findings in this study, all three of the obstacles St. John et al. mentioned were among the conditions at the four campuses in this sample, and yet not all campuses in this study disengaged from the project. The conjecture about campus engagement by St. John et al., although valuable, is ultimately incomplete without considering the relationships with and choices made by campuses. Our analysis illustrates that the path to successful engagement was dependent on the members comprising the IPAS campus teams, particularly in respect to their institutional positions.

The successfully engaged teams in this study had several key, shared features that contrasted with the features of teams that left the project early. Institutionally, the successfully engaged teams were empowered, had the ability to include others, and were heard when they spoke to administrators more senior than they. Perhaps due to this, the interactions between these campus team members and the IPAS staff were partnerships, in which trust and legitimacy were established through the building of professional relationships and the engagement in dialogue about data and research. The first decisions made by campuses were vital in their teams' ability and ongoing willingness to engage effectively in the project. Individuals on the campus teams were vital to campuses' engagement in IPAS. Some individuals hindered while others accelerated the effectiveness of the project in their roles as disinterested or interested administrators, uninvolved or enthusiastic team members, lone crusaders, gatekeepers, or champions. The power of team members within their institutions was a vital retention factor, as the ability to recruit appropriate human resources and gain upper-level support for initiatives were revealed to be significant forces in continued engagement. Timing was also a huge factor in campus retention, as being ready for the project seemed more important than how much the campus wanted to be involved or what commitments had been made to the project. Also, progress was shown to be supported by an already existing culture of evidence at the institution and an open culture of communication and collaboration between different campus groups, such as academic affairs and student affairs.

Some of these findings align with the explorations of Tierney (2006) into the cultural conditions of trust in the work of academics. From this perspective of trust, engagement in IPAS involved the juxtaposition of complimentary as well as contradictory values enacted through the behaviors and choices of both IPAS staff and IPAS campus participants. The individuals involved and the institutional processes and cultures at SU and WU clearly supported the risk-taking, change-oriented, inquiry-driven means promoted by IPAS for addressing challenges on their campuses, while from this evidence and at a variety of levels this was not the case at NU and EU. As demonstrated in their choices and the quality of their engagement, these institutions differed in their enacted values of the project.

The relevance of trust to the success of participating campuses involved in this project suggests it would be worthwhile to examine more closely the role of trust in other organizational change projects similar to IPAS. In this study, for example, it would be interesting to know the assumptions regarding trust of those associated with IPAS. Was the institution's agreement to participate the only meaningful trust hurdle in the conceptualization of the project? Examining these findings and engaging in further work on trust could lead to more effective methods for building trust in research endeavors like IPAS.

For campus administrators thinking about getting involved in a project like IPAS, several recommendations emerge from these findings. First, administrators should make sure that challenges chosen for study by the teams do not duplicate other campus efforts and that all parties concerned are "on the same page" for a concerted, streamlined effort. Second, administrators should make sure the appropriate people are involved. Institutions do themselves or staff members no favor by requiring project involvement from individuals who, due to their position in the campus hierarchy, are not empowered to act. Third, projects like this generate buy-in among many professionals in academia with good intentions toward the student body. For altruistic as well as fiscal reasons, institutions are very willing to support the success and retention of their students, but careful thought should precede involving a campus and staff in such an endeavor. Does the project align with current institutional needs at an actionable level? Can the institution commit the required time, human resources, and financial resources (however limited) to this project? Is the institution willing to support and commit to the findings of the team involved in the project? If an institution cannot answer these questions in the affirmative, it is probably not the right time for it to try to engage in this type of inquiry.

For those already engaged in IPAS-like endeavors, these findings also suggest recommendations for working with campuses. First, establish guidelines for the organizational structure of campus teams and ensure in some way these guidelines are followed. Although IPAS had guidelines in place to help participating campuses form their teams, IPAS staff did not stress sufficiently why such organization was important. Had they done so, institutions may have been more thoughtful about whether they could enact their espoused commitment to the project. Second, regarding the findings on the building of partnerships and the gaining of trust, staff assigned to work with campuses should perhaps be given responsibility for fewer campuses to allow time to build these relationships with the whole team at participating campuses, rather than with just one or two key people. Third, prior to working with participating campuses, project staff members should be adequately trained in areas such as communication, relationship-building, and facilitation skills. If graduate students are among the staff working with campuses, they also should be appropriately trained in facilitation. Role-play activities might help them adjust to their position, listen to the needs of campuses, and be responsive. The supportive involvement of senior scholars is also important to the success of graduate students in the project. Finally, consider personalities when hiring staff members. The findings of this study show that to gain the trust of campus participants and to develop effective partnerships with them in projects such as IPAS, staff members need to be able to relate well with a wide range of people and personalities. As well as being competent emerging scholars, those involved with the project must also have good social skills.

Concluding Thoughts

This study shows that even the best efforts to bring about organizational change are beset by a variety of complications and complexities. People, personalities, institutional culture, timing, politics, intent—all of these factors and others combine and interact to impact an institution's ability to do this type of work. As for the campuses that remained engaged in IPAS, their choices, their institutional environments, and the relationships they established with IPAS staff members allowed them to engage more fully with the inquiry model and to effect sustainable, evaluated change for the good of their students. Projects like IPAS can and do make a difference. Using the findings from this study of IPAS, institutions can be more aware of the importance and implications of certain choices in committing to and sustaining efforts to make changes on their campuses.

References

Carspecken, P. F. (1996). *Critical ethnography in educational research: A theoretical and practical guide.* New York: Routledge.

Denzin, N. K., & Lincoln, Y. S. (Eds.). (2003). *The landscape of qualitative research: Theories and issues.* Thousand Oaks, CA: Sage.

Miles, M. B., & Huberman, A. M. (1994). *Qualitative data analysis.* Thousand Oaks, CA: Sage.

St. John, E. P. (1994). *Prices, productivity, and investment: Assessing financial strategies in higher education* (ASHE-ERIC Higher Education Report, 3). Washington, DC: George Washington University, School of Education and Human Development.

St. John, E. P. (2003). *Refinancing the college dream: Access, equal opportunity, and justice for taxpayers.* Baltimore: Johns Hopkins University Press.

St. John, E. P. (2006). Lessons learned: Institutional research as support for academic improvement. In E. P. St. John & M. Wilkerson (Eds.), *Reframing persistence research to improve academic success: New Directions for Institutional Research, No. 130* (pp. 95–108). San Francisco: Jossey-Bass.

St. John, E. P., McKinney, J., & Tuttle, T. (2006). Using action inquiry to address critical challenges. In E. P. St. John & M. Wilkerson (Eds.), *Reframing persistence research to improve academic success: New Directions for Institutional Research, No. 130* (pp. 63–76). San Francisco: Jossey-Bass.

St. John, E. P., & Wilkerson, M. (Eds.). (2006). *Reframing persistence research to improve academic success: New Directions for Institutional Research, No. 130.* San Francisco: Jossey-Bass.

Van Maanen, J. (1988). *Tales of the field: On writing ethnography.* Chicago: University of Chicago Press.

Section IV

Conclusion

CHAPTER 9

LESSONS LEARNED: A FINAL LOOK

Don Hossler, Jacob P. K. Gross, and Mary Ziskin

Calls for accountability in higher education are certainly not new. However, in the current social and political context—with increasing concerns about economic competiveness, changing demographics, and growing gaps across demographic groups in postsecondary completion rates, along with the advent of No Child Left Behind—policy makers and practitioners are paying more attention to indicators of student success and are searching for mechanisms such as state or national databases to better track students and understand what factors contribute to student success (Ewell & Boeke, 2007; Welsh & Kjorlien, 2001). This volume addresses both of these policy issues. In addition, it provides insights into the complexities of bringing about organizational change in efforts to enhance student success. A striking fact about research on student success is that there are relatively few empirical studies of the efficacy of campus-based efforts to enhance student success, persistence, and graduation. Research is also scarce on the use of state databases to help guide state and institutional policy making.

The evidence in this volume is clear and compelling. When senior campus policy makers as well as middle managers in our colleges and universities deliberately devote time and resources to developing solid programs in tutoring, supplemental instruction, and orientation, these programs have a strong possibility of being successful. Several chapters in this volume suggest that student success, as measured by GPA and/or persistence, can be improved through well-designed programs that are adequately funded, attentively administrated, and sufficiently supported in campus policies. So often in university administration it seems we are looking for "the new study" or "the profound insight" that will enable us to transform unsuccessful student support programs. Our studies in the Indiana Project on Academic Success (IPAS) suggest that the task is both much less complicated yet much more difficult than we might think. Enacting successful targeted interventions—organizing the programmatic interventions and staying on top of them—takes the time, willingness, and commitment of campus administrators and policy makers. It takes administrators who are willing to put in the time—whether in advisory committees or in training paraprofessionals—to deliver the planned programs. It takes senior policy makers who are willing to make orientation programs

189

mandatory or to provide seed funding or to show support by attending planning meetings for targeted interventions. The amount of money required is often surprisingly small, but administrators do have to arrange sufficient time for the staff who will manage these programs to make them successful. Too often in the rush to prove they are doing everything they need to do, administrators initiate more programs than they can effectively oversee or adequately fund. Is it possible that a few well-funded, well-organized student support programs might be better than a wide range of poorly supported programs?

Several of the chapters in this volume demonstrate how action research can be used to inform policy decisions, to improve programs, and to provide data to support the efficacy as well as the funding of successful interventions. The chapters on student transfer and the effects of financial aid on student success provide examples of how state databases can be used to help state and institutional policy makers answer important policy questions. In one case in point, results show that after Latino students move past their second year in college, their use of student loan programs increases dramatically to levels like those of non-Latino students. This provocative finding seems to challenge, at least in Indiana, the prevalent assumption that Latino students are simply less likely to use financial aid. The finding may suggest, for example, that after being enrolled for two or more years Latino students gain greater confidence in the returns on higher education degrees or in the likelihood of acquiring these degrees—and that with this confidence they are willing to take out loans to finance their further higher education. The analysis of transfer behaviors reveals a variety of complex transfer patterns, challenging traditional articulation and transfer agreements based on the model of student transfer in which students earn associate's degrees and only then move on to a four-year college and in which most transfers are from two-year to four-year campuses. By making empirical observations like this possible, state databases can help state and institutional policy makers develop a richer understanding of how students move through our institutions of postsecondary education and, in the process, can inform policies better shaped to enhance access and student success.

The IPAS experience with participating campuses—with its successes and its disappointments—mirrors the busy, turbulent world of college and university administrators as well as the possibilities and the limitations of action inquiry as a vehicle for organizational change. Indeed, this may have been the most discouraging aspect of IPAS over the months and years of the project. Campus administrators would be so stretched that they simply would not have time to engage in IPAS action research or program evaluation. A key member of an IPAS campus team would leave without a replacement. A participating campus would drop out. A program manager would seem to feel threatened by the IPAS process itself, as if worrying, "What happens if the results show my program does not work or if IPAS seems to do a better job of program evaluation than I do?"

Overall, our findings demonstrate that postsecondary educational institutions can take rational, planned, measured actions to enhance student success—but that as typically implemented thus far these efforts are less likely, rather than more likely, to be successful. It goes without saying that this is an unfortunate result for students and for institutions. If student success is going to remain one of the most important public policy issues of the first part of the 21st century, institutions are going to need to find the will, and public policy makers should be prepared to provide the incentives, to encourage serious campus-based efforts to develop and evaluate programs that enhance student success. The work of IPAS provides both a collection of research results that can support and inform such efforts and, by example, a glimpse into the realities and practicalities of linking research, policy, and practice for the enhancement of student success.

References

Ewell, P. T., & Boeke, M. (2007). *Critical connections: Linking states' unit record systems to track student progress.* Indianapolis, IN: National Center for Higher Education Management Systems.

Welsh J., & Kjorlien, C. (2001). State support for interinstitutional transfer and articulation: The impact of databases and information systems. *Community College Journal of Research and Practice, 25(*4), 313–332.

CHAPTER 10

REFLECTIONS AND LESSONS

Edward P. St. John

It is with deep appreciation that I review this volume of *Readings on Equal Education*. This is the sixth for which I have had responsibility as series editor, the term of my agreement with AMS Press. My goal in undertaking this commitment was to engage with other researchers in a process of rethinking the roles of public education policy and public finance in promoting educational opportunities. At the outset of this project I envisioned three critical tasks:

- **Task 1: Assess the Impact of Interventions and Policies on Equal Educational Opportunity.** My assumption was: *It is critical to build an understanding of how educational policies influence equality in educational opportunity.* I thought equity had been largely overlooked in educational policy.
- **Task 2: Examine the Effects of Interventions and Policies on Excellence and Efficiency as Well as Equity.** My assumption was: *It is crucial to broaden the discourse about equal education to consider concerns about quality and the efficient use of tax dollars, with an eye on the risk of creating false efficiencies.* I thought advocates of equity should not overlook calls for excellence.
- **Task 3: Rethink the Role of Policy When Considering Implications of Policy Research.** My assumption was: *It is important to rethink strategies, with an emphasis on illuminating workable changes in education and finance policies that encourage balance in educational outcomes.* This remains a critical and elusive goal.

In combination, the six volumes of *REE* make progress on these tasks but there is still a very substantial distance to travel toward the aim of placing greater emphasis on equity across race and income in K-12 and higher education. In this reflection, I summarize key understandings reached from these six volumes as they relate to each of the tasks, as well as reflect on the possibility of a shared agenda for scholars interested in using research to inform and improve social justice.

193

The Impact of Interventions on Equity

In 2004 when I took on the role of series editor, I was in the process of completing Volume 19 as an issue editor. That volume took on the problem of statistical errors in the reporting of national statistics on education preparation, access, and college success by the National Center for Education Statistics (NCES). The Advisory Committee on Student Financial Assistance, a Congressional advisory body, had commissioned papers by Don Heller (2004) and William Becker (2004) documenting methodological errors in the NCES reports. As Brian Fitzgerald (2004) and John Lee (2004) documented in that volume, the NCES reports had consistently misreported information on the causes of inequality in college access. The errors had resulted in misinformation that underestimated the impact of student financial aid and overestimated the impact of curriculum reforms. *REE* 19 provided compelling evidence of the need to refocus on interventions that promote equity in opportunities to prepare for and attain a college degree.

The Bill & Melinda Gates Foundation has proven an important partner in endeavors aimed at improving equity in opportunity for low-income and minority students. Volumes 20 and 23 of *REE* presented a comprehensive collection of studies on the impact of the Gates Millennium Scholars (GMS) Program. GMS is a long-term intervention that aims to provide 20,000 scholarships to high-achieving, low-income students of color. These generous awards provide last-dollar grants supporting students through their undergraduate education and, if STEM or other high-priority fields are chosen for advanced study, through completion of graduate education. In Volume 20, Walter Allen, William Trent, Sylvia Hurtado, and William Sedlacek contributed papers that documented the impact of the program. It was clear from these papers that the program has supported a new generation of leaders. However, while there is a strong empirical relationship between receiving an award and critical outcomes—engaged learning, completing college, and going on to graduate school, especially in education—proving causality has been difficult, given that preference was given to students who exhibited non-cognitive indicators correlated with these outcomes (Sedlacek & Sheu, 2004).

Volume 23 also contributed substantially to the understanding of the Scholars program. Studies directed by William Trent, Walter Allen, Sylvia Hurtado, William Sedlacek, and myself documented the ways scholars benefited from funding by engaging in academic and social activities, documenting some of the ways these students build social and academic capital during college, overcoming financial barriers that constrained this type of involved learning by their peers (i.e., applicants with similar backgrounds and achievement) who did not enjoy the additional financial support. In addition,

Walter Allen, John Tippiconic, Shirely Hune, and Sylvia Hurtado reported on studies that documented patterns of student engagement among Blacks, Native Indians/Alaskan Natives, Asian Americans/Pacific Islanders, and Hispanics, respectively. They documented the distinctive patterns of engagement, leadership, and learning among students in each group.

The Gates Foundation also provided generous support for the Washington State Achievers (WSA) Program, an intervention in high poverty schools in Washington that funded school reforms and provided last dollar scholarships to low-income students. In Volumes 21 and 22, William Sedlacek, Charles Hirschman, and Shouping Hu contributed studies that documented the benefits for students of attending schools undergoing reform and receiving last dollars scholarships. Since WSA provided scholarships to students from low- and moderate-income families, the studies illustrate that a broad array of students from underrepresented populations could benefit from guaranteed financial aid and increased access to advanced high school courses. These studies further contributed to the understanding of cultural capital formation.

The studies of the Indiana Project on Academic Success in this volume also illustrate that local interventions undertaken by college campuses can enhance collegiate learning outcomes for students from underrepresented groups. Jacob P. K. Gross (Chapter 1) documents the benefits of financial aid for low-income students, Hossler and colleagues (Chapter 2) document that degree attainment often involves lateral transfers within state systems, and Moore and Rago (Chapter 3) document some of the challenges facing working students. These studies illustrate the diverse pathways students traveled in their efforts to achieve academic success and were part of a comprehensive assessment that informed institutional interventions.

In combination, these contributions illustrate that improving equity remains a challenge for high schools and colleges. They also demonstrate that patterns of engagement in academic and civic activities during college may differ for students from underrepresented groups, at least in comparison to the extensive body of research on majority students (Pascraella & Terenzini, 2005).

Balancing Equity with a Commitment to Excellence

When I undertook this editorial responsibility, I was aware that research on equity had frequently overlooked excellence-related outcomes just as researchers who focused on academic preparation overlooked inequalities and the role of financial aid. As I explored these challenges with contributing authors, I realized there was a theory problem. Thus, another of my aims as editor was to encourage studies that contributed to retheorizing the problem of improving educational opportunity. Few researchers examined equity and excellence in balanced ways, in part because there was a lack of theory to guide research and intervention.

Volume 21, published in 2006, engaged colleagues in reviews and new studies that examined the balance between equity and excellence in new way. For example, Kim Metcalf and Kelli Paul (2006) examined the contradictions in voucher experiments: While researchers debated whether or not achievement effects could be measured, the fact that some students could not afford to enroll in private schools even with vouchers went largely overlooked. Other chapters documented the equity and achievement effects of comprehensive school reforms (St. John, Hossler et al., 2006), charters (Eckes & Rapp, 2006), and other education high school reforms (Musoba, 2006). Reflecting on the studies of school reforms, encouragement programs, and postsecondary pathways, I concluded that: (1) the basic right for an education was in the midst of redefinition and now included advanced course work for the labor market and college preparation; and (2) there was inequality in access to this basic standard of education, as the structure of education often denied this basic right to those in the greatest need.

Volume 22, published in 2007, extended this line of inquiry and encouraged others to engage in exploring theoretical framing of the problem. William Tierney and Kristan Venagas (2007) theorized a cultural ecology model to examine how students' educational, social, and family experiences influence the ways they learned about the problem and Ontario Wooden (2007) explored some of these concepts in his examination of barriers to learning in a Black high school. Penny Pasque (2007) reviewed the literature on the public good in higher education and Amy Fisher (2007) examined how the political context in a state influences the shift away from public funding. Louis Mirón (2007) explored how activist research could influence the agenda for rebuilding schools in New Orleans after Katrina. In combination, the studies in this volume illustrated the necessity of revising theories to guide action aimed at improving equity and achievement.

This volume provides a new generation of empirical studies that attempt to reintegrate evaluation and reform within colleges and universities. A review of prior research on interventions in higher education reveals that most strategies to improve persistence have gone unstudied (Patton et al., 2006) but have been rationalized based on persistence research that considers only social and academic integration without examining how interventions influence these intermediate outcomes. Studies in Part II help fill this void while illustrating a method of research informing action within institutions of higher education: Leslie J. Robinson (Chapter 4) examines the impact of math tutoring on women's persistence in science and math majors within research universities; Ziskin, Hernandez, & Gross (Chapter 5) document the impact of engagement in supplemental instruction within a regional university; and Reynolds, Rago, and Brown (Chapter 6) illustrate the uses of action inquiry to inform the redesign of an orientation program in a community college. These studies illustrate that inquiry and action can be integrated in ways that build actionable knowledge in higher education.

When readers glance across these volumes, they will find evidence that the goals of equity and excellence are inexorably linked but not necessarily highly correlated. Educational interventions that promote and expand opportunities for underrepresented students must focus on improving achievement as an integral aspect of extending opportunity. On the other hand, educational strategies that emphasize excellence without considering balance can undermine opportunity. For example, in a chapter in *REE* Volume 22 Inoue and Geske (2007) documented how Louisiana's implementation of merit grants undermined the intent of the state's court-mandated desegregation. The need for theory that integrates consideration of equity and excellence is accentuated by the recurrent patterns of reform that undermine equity.

Rethinking the Role of Policy and Intervention

If the excellence movement has created new inequalities, and there is very substantial evidence this is the case (St. John, 2006; St. John & Mirón, 2003), then there is a need to rethink public policy and intervention methods. My argument has been that action research that is grounded in balanced theoretical frameworks can promote transformation in education that improves equity and excellence (St. John, 1994, 2008). The Indiana Project on Academic Success was designed to enable practitioners to use research to address critical challenges (St. John & Wilkerson, 2006). The studies in this volume illustrate examples of interventions that address both academic and equity challenges.

If some groups in society are underrepresented among high school and college graduates, it is possible that the nation's education system does not serve them well and should be changed to address this challenge. But this may require many ground-level changes instead of—or in addition to— reformulation of public policies on education and public finance. The studies of interventions in the orientation program at a community college, math tutoring in a research university, and supplemental instruction in a research university illustrate expanding opportunities for underrepresented groups involves addressing the challenges students actually face.

The central problem with the excellence movement has been that it was based on the idea that what works for the few must also work for the many. For example, when there was evidence that completing algebra correlated with college completion (Pelavin & Kane, 1990), the majority of states started requiring Algebra for high school graduation. However, the issue was more complex; it required providing instruction in Algebra for students who lacked the foundation for it (e.g., Moses & Cobb, 2001). New action strategies must focus on improving learning opportunities for those who have not been served by the current system. Changing the system to address educational challenges should be given priority rather than tacitly assuming the system that works for some should work for all.

The IPAS action inquiry process provides an example of how research can be integrated with the intervention process to generate new forms of actionable knowledge, but it is a difficult process. The IPAS used that state's student unit record (SUR) data system to conduct studies for the campuses and also provided assistance with aligning inquiry with evaluation. This structural approach to assessment and evaluation was supplemented by technical assistance with an action inquiry process that involved teams of practitioners pondering the implications of the research, gathering more information, designing interventions, and pilot testing the new plans to see if they worked. In this process there should also be a commitment to refine or refocus interventions when they don't work as intended.

In their formative evaluation of the project, Daun-Barnett, Fisher and Williams (Chapter 7) documented that some campus practitioners jumped into reform without considering the research provided from the student unit record (SUR) data system. Not all of the practitioners interviewed communicated a conceptual understanding of the action inquiry process. And only one of the campuses visited as part of that study actually completed a full round of the inquiry process. It is clear that the inquiry process takes time, but it is also evident that there were benefits to campuses from engaging in the process even when they did not complete every step.

Reynolds and Hossler (Chapter 8) dig deeper into possible explanations for variations in institutional engagement using records kept from the intervention process along with insider understandings of the campuses and people involved. There is little doubt from their analysis that action inquiry was a challenging process for assistance providers, as it was for practitioners at the campuses involved. One key finding is that trust played a key role in the willingness to engage in the reform process. Practitioners and researchers are conditioned to follow protocols and using proven pathways to avoid problems seems to be the path of least resistance in research and practice. The problem with following past practices is that past failures are replicated unless people are willing to consider why there were problems in the first place, and they don't design and try out practices that address underlying causes. Opening up these questions places practitioners and researchers in situations that can feel risky because they are unfamiliar and because they involve recognizing and addressing problems and challenges previously overlooked.

The studies of institutional change included in Volume 24 of *Readings on Equal Education* have lessons for policy makers. The process of shifting from replicating a failure—a lesson that should perhaps have been learned from the school reform movements of the past two decades (Mirón & St. John, 2003)— toward investing in interventions that address critical local challenges is explored.

First, there is reason to question whether replication of practices that have worked in one locale—or appear to have worked—might also solve problems in education in other locales. The large SUR data systems can be used to evaluate experiments that can be replicated from one area to another. It is possible this approach can work with new interventions. However, not all interventions are designed with random assignment. In addition, large scales experiments can miss groups who are not served by the current system. For example, a national experiment with need analysis (Long, 2004) is dependent on being able to pay for tax services, a luxury many low-income families cannot afford and may not need.

Second, the SUR data systems can also be utilized to conduct assessment research to identify critical challenges and to integrate technical assistance with evaluation to support local practitioners in the reform process. This approach was used in the IPAS project to engage administrators and faculty members in using research to enable local change. While this process is time consuming, it appears to be a workable approach for addressing local problems. It provides local administrators with opportunities to build expertise and, thus, can be viewed as an integral part of the professional development process.

An Agenda for Research and Action

Two questions emerge from this review that relate to the process of forming agendas for research and action. First, what are the major challenges that merit the attention of researchers and other professionals committed to reducing inequality in educational opportunities for under-represented groups? Second, what methods can and should be used to address these challenges through research and change in practice?

While these questions are essentially an individual matter involving professional commitment to research and service, they are also of significance to the institutions in which professors and other professionals practice. It is easier to engage in reforms—as a practitioner or researcher—when they are aligned with institutional initiatives, another lesson learned from IPAS (St.

John, 2008). Below I address these questions as they relate to the future of *REE* and other publications seeking to inform efforts to improve equity and the quality of educational services.

First, there are many critical issues that merit the attention of researchers and other practitioners who are concerned about reducing inequality. My assumption when taking on the role of series editor for *REE* was that educational equity had ceased to be the focus of educational policy in the United States, and there was a need to bring policy back into balance so that it emphasized both educational improvement and equitable opportunity for all students. The research published here and elsewhere reinforces this assumption: there is still an imbalance in public policy. Yet progress has been made. For example, in part as a consequence of the work of the Advisory Committee on Student Financial Assistance (2002, 2003), the Spellings Commission emphasized increased funding of student financial aid along with increased accountability (U.S. Department of Education, 2006). Although the history of accountability in K–12 education gives reason to question the wisdom of emphasizing accountability after decades of shifting the burden of paying for college from taxpayers to students (St. John, 2006), the fact the increased investment in student aid is now being seriously considered once again is a sign of progress.

A plethora of issues related to educational inequality need to be addressed. For example, the demise of affirmative action in some states and the conservative interpretation of discretion precluding consideration of race in admissions decision is a crucial issue given the very substantial underrepresentation of Blacks and Latinos in public four-year colleges. Since there are persistent inequalities in K–12 schools that limit the ability of admissions officers to provide fair admissions without considering background, new remedies to inequality are needed.

To find remedies to inequality, a new generation of social action is needed in K–12 schools, higher education, and society as a whole. Reducing inequalities in access to education and health services, along with finding ways of reducing global warming, are among the issues that require new forms of action. Current practices are causing inequalities in education, so continuation of the status quo is unacceptable given the orientation to basic rights in the U.S. and in state constitutions. However, the obligation to pursue a path toward just practice is not just legal, it is also moral in a sense that consistent with the major faith traditions (Fogel, 2000; Batan-'dzin-rgya-mtsho, Dhali Lama XIV, 1999). There are many compelling reasons to address educational inequalities. Experiments can help identify *best practices* associated with student success, including practices that increase opportunities for students from underrepresented groups.

Second, since reducing inequality in educational opportunity involves changing current practice, it is necessary to take an activist agenda. One approach involves studying interventions made by institutions and states. This approach has been used for decades to accumulate research on the effects of student financial aid (Leslie & Brinkman, 1988; Heller, 1997; Curs, Singell, & Waddell, 2006). Another approach involves experiments; however, randomizing treatment, a requirement of experimental design, is not always possible.

Best practices can be problematic when there are locally situated challenges or when professional expertise and judgment are part of the solution. For example, one of the solutions to inequality involves providing mentoring to aspiring students. However, requiring that individuals have a mentor to participate in a program or that practitioners serve as mentors does not always solve the problem because of the human factors. The fact is that new and better methods for enabling students from underrepresented groups to find and excel in appropriate educational opportunities—to make informed choices—is not a matter of prescription but of learning and judgment.

The human dimension is critical to social justice. Merely following practices thought to be best can replicate serious problems when there is no critical reflection on the reasons why challenges exist in the first place. There are many terms for the human factors that can inhibit equality or facilitate reducing inequalities. *Cultural capital* refers to closing the gaps in education and functioning that lead to the replication of education and class status across generations. *Social capital* includes processes like mentoring and networking. These human factors are critical to reducing inequality in concert with legal, educational, and financial remedies.

Readings on Equal Education has a vital role to play in building knowledge about methods for reducing inequality in education. This periodic publication and others like it should promote high quality research. In the past six volumes I have taken the approach of encouraging reviews, theory papers, and quantitative, qualitative, and action studies to test new approaches to remedying inequality. There are many outlets for policy briefs and papers that share information on best practices. There are fewer publications that encourage inquiry into the underlying causes of and cures for inequality in educational opportunity. Ultimately readers' interests determine whether publications with this agenda can thrive.

References

Advisory Committee on Student Financial Assistance (2002). *Empty promises: The myth of college access in America.* Washington, DC: Author.

Advisory Committee on Student Financial Assistance. (2003). Review of NCES research on financial aid and college participation and omitted variables and Sample selection issues in the NCES research on financial aid and college participation. Report prepared for ACSFA by D. Heller & W. E. Becker. Washington, DC: Author.

Batan-'dzin-rgya-mtsho, Dhali Lama XIV, (1999) *Ethics for the new millennium.* New York: Riverhead Books.

Becker, W. E. (2004). Omitted variables and sample selection in studies of college-going decisions. In E. P. St. John (Ed.), Readings on equal education: Public policy and college access: Investigating the federal and state roles in equalizing postsecondary opportunity (Vol. 19, pp. 65–86). New York: AMS Press, Inc.

Curs, B. R., Singell, L. D., & Waddell, G. R. (2006). The Pell program at thirty years. In J. C. Smart (Ed.). *Higher Education: Handbook of Theory and Research* (pp. 281–334). Netherlands: Springer.

Eckes, S., & Rapp, K. (2006). Charter school research: Trends and implications. In E. P. St. John (Ed.), Readings on equal education: Public policy and equal educational opportunity: School reforms, postsecondary encouragement, and state policies on postsecondary education (Vol. 21, pp. 3–36). New York: AMS Press, Inc.

Fisher, A. S. (2007). State valuation of higher education: An examination of possible explanations for privatization. In E. P. St. John (Ed.), *Readings on equal education: Confronting educational inequality: Reframing, building understanding, and making change* (Vol. 22, pp. 219–243). New York: AMS Press, Inc.

Fitzgerald, B. K. (2004). Federal financial aid and college access. In E. P. St. John (Ed.), Readings on equal education: Public policy and college access: Investigating the federal and state roles in equalizing post-secondary opportunity (Vol. 19, pp. 1–28). New York: AMS Press, Inc.

Fogel, R. W. (2000). The fourth great awakening and the future of egalitarianism. Chicago: Chicago University Press.

Heller, D. E. (1997). Student price response in higher education: An update to Leslie and Brinkman. *The Journal of Higher Education, 68*(6), 624–659.

Heller, D. E. (2004). NCES research on college participation: A critical analysis. In E. P. St. John (Ed.), Readings on equal education: Public policy and college access: Investigating the federal and state roles in equalizing postsecondary opportunity (Vol. 19, pp. 29–64). New York: AMS Press, Inc.

Lee, J. P. (2004, March). Access revisited: A preliminary reanalysis of NELS. In St. John, E. P. (Ed.), *Readings on equal education: Public policy and college access: Investigating the federal and state roles in equalizing postsecondary opportunity* (Vol. 19, pp. 87–96). New York: AMS Press, Inc.

Leslie, L. L., & Brinkman, P. T. (1988). *The economic value of higher education.* New York: Macmillan.

Metcalf, K. K., & Paul, K. M. (2006). Enhancing or destroying equity? An examination of educational vouchers. In E. P. St. John (Ed.), *Readings on equal education: Public policy and equal educational opportunity: School reforms, postsecondary encouragement, and state policies on postsecondary education* (Vol. 21, pp. 37–74). New York: AMS Press, Inc.

Mirón, L. F. (2007). Activist research, post-Katrina: One tool for renewal? In E. P. St. John (Ed.), *Readings on equal education: Confronting educational inequality: Reframing, building understanding, and making change, Readings on Equal Education* (Vol. 22, pp. 283–316). New York: AMS Press, Inc.

Mirón, L F., & St. John, E. P. (Eds.). (2003). *Reinterpreting urban school reform: Have urban schools failed, or has the reform movement failed urban schools?* Albany, NY: SUNY Press.

Moses, R. P., & Cobb, C. E. (2001). Racial equations: Civil rights from Mississippi to the Algebra project. Boston: Beacon.

Musoba, G. D. (2006). Accountability v. adequate funding: Which policies influence adequate preparation for college? In E. P. St. John (Ed.), *Readings on equal education: Public policy and equal educational opportunity: School reforms, postsecondary encouragement, and state policies on postsecondary education* (Vol. 21, pp. 75–125). New York: AMS Press, Inc.

Pascarella, E. T., & Terenzini, P. T. (2005). *How college affects students: Vol. 2. A third decade of research.* San Francisco: Jossey-Bass.

Pasque, P, A. (2007). Seeing more of the educational inequalities around us: Visions toward strengthening relationships between higher education and society. In St. John, E. P. (Ed.), *Readings on equal education: Confronting educational inequality: Reframing, building understanding, and making change, Readings on Equal Education* (Vol. 22, pp. 37–84). New York: AMS Press, Inc.

Patton, L. D., Morelon, C., Whitehead, D. M., & Hossler, D. (2006). Campus-based retention initiatives: Does the emperor have clothes? In E. P. St.

John & M. Wilkerson (Eds.), *Reframing persistence research to support academic success. New Directions for Institutional Research* (Vol. 130, pp. 9–24) San Francisco: Jossey-Bass.

Pelavin, S. H., & Kane, M. B. (1990). *Changing the odds: Factors increasing access to college*. New York: College Board.

St. John, E. P. (1994). *Prices, productivity and investment: Assessing financial strategies in higher education*. ASHE/ERIC Higher Education Report, No. 3. Washington, DC: George Washington University, School of Education and Human Development.

St. John, E. P. (2006). Education and the public interest: School reform, public finance, and access to higher education. Dordrecht, The Netherlands: Springer.

St. John, E. P. (2008). Financial inequality and academic success: Rethinking the foundations of research on college students. In W. T. Trent, & E. P. St. John (Eds.), *Readings on equal education: Resources, assets, and strengths among successful diverse students: Understanding the contributions of the Gates Millennium Scholars Program, Readings on Equal Education* (Vol. 23, pp. 201–228). New York: AMS Press, Inc.

St. John, E. P., Gross, J. P. K., Musoba, G. D., & Chung, A. S. (2006). Postsecondary encouragement and academic success: Degree attainment by Indiana's Twenty-first Century Scholars. In St. John, E. P. (Ed.), *Readings on equal education: Public policy and equal educational opportunity: School reforms, postsecondary encouragement, and state policies on postsecondary education* (Vol. 21, pp. 257–291). New York: AMS Press, Inc.

St. John, E. P., & Mirón, L. F. (2003). A critical-empirical perspective on urban school reform. In L. F. Mirón & E. P. St. John (Eds.), *Reinterpreting urban school reform: Have urban schools failed, or has the reform movement failed urban schools?* (pp. 279–298). Albany, NY: SUNY Press.

St. John, E. P. & Wilkerson, M. (Eds.), (2006). Reframing persistence research to support academic success: New Directions for Institutional Research, No. 130. San Francisco: Jossey-Bass.

Sedlacek, W. E., & Sheu, H. B. (2004). Academic success of Gates Millennium Scholars. In E. P. St. John (Ed.), Readings on equal education: Improving access and college success for diverse students: Studies of the Gates Millennium Scholars Program (Vol. 20, pp. 181–198). New York: AMS Press, Inc.

Tierney, W. G., & Venegas, K. (2007), The Cultural Ecology of Financial Aid Decision Making. In E. P. St. John (Ed.), *Readings on equal education:*

Confronting educational inequality: Reframing, building understanding, and making change (Vol. 22, pp. 1–36). New York: AMS Press, Inc.

U.S. Department of Education (2006) A test of leadership: Changing the future of U.S. higher education, Washington, DC: Authors.

Wooden, O. (2007). High School Guidance Counselors as Reproductive Forces in the Lives of African American Students: A Study of a Georgia High School. In E. P. St. John (Ed.), *Readings on equal education: Confronting educational inequality: Reframing, building under-standing, and making change* (Vol. 22, pp. 245–282). New York: AMS Press, Inc.

INDEX